"Like no planner experience you've ever had. Enjoy the wild ride."
-AB

Let's get into IT.

"...It's good to have a personal agenda."

If found, there is a reward.
Name:
Email:

Copyright 2022 by Angel Brynner

All Rights Reserved

Printed in the United States

Kokopellima Press.
www.kokopellimapress.com

Catologing-in-Publication Data

Brynner, Angel

Globalboho Revisionist 3 month Agenda

Paperback ISBN: 978-1-950077-92-2

Hardcover ISBN: 978-1-950077-94-6

This is a work of non-fiction. No part of This publication may be reproduced or transmitted in any form or by an means, electronic or mechanical, including photocopying, recording, NFT or any other information storage and retrieval system, without written permission of the Publisher.

Cover artwork and book design:

AOLAB/AngelBrynner.

Website: http://www.angelbrynner.com

Globalboho

Revisionist Agenda.

3 month Daily Freewrite edition

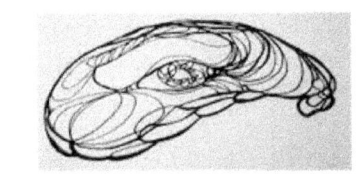

angel brynner.

KokoPelliMa Press

OTHER KOKOPELLIMA PRESS BOOKS BY ANGEL BRYNNER

Eutaxis   Ecclesia   Exodus

Erebus   Exist   Esthesis   Epicharis

Elision   Elysum   Empyrean

AOLAB Active Art (therapy) decks BY ANGEL BRYNNER

ZION   HALCYON   DELUGE   BLOOD OF MY BLOOD

FLESH OF MY FLESH   BONE OF MY BONE

BLACKWATER OVERFLOW   EDEN   ZENITH

AOLAB Travelogues BY ANGEL BRYNNER

BOTTOM OF THE NINTH WARD BULLETINS   BLACKWATER RISING

Anthologies BY ANGEL BRYNNER

FIRESTARTER   FIREWALKER

AOLAB Active Art Revisionist books BY ANGEL BRYNNER

(The road to) ZION grievechonic

(The road to) HALCYON grievechronic

(The road to) DELUGE grievechronic

(The road to) BLOOD grievechronic

Globalboho Revisionist

3 month Daily Freewrite edition

agenda.

Globalboho Geist

An explanation of the Globalboho revisionist agenda protocol to help you get your sea legs.

A perfect place to begin.

INSTRUCTIONS:
IT'S SIMPLE.

SECTION ONE: the gear up.
IMAGINE YOUR IDEAL SEASON, MONTH, WEEK & DAY.
EXPLORE, DEFINE & WRITE OUT THE COMPONENTS.

SECTION TWO:
AIM AT WALKING THEM OUT. DOCUMENT AS YOU GO.

Give yourself the GOLD STAR from jump
& just do what you think it'd take to deserve it.

Yep. Simply do that sh*t. On repeat.

Instead of the sh*t you keep doing that ain't working.

You do not have to use all of the prompts but
the more you know as you go, the better
you'll flow. &When it comes to figuring out
the baseline structure of <u>Your intended life</u>
Have fun with it.

GO HAM [hard as a m*therf*cka]

or~ Aim at laid-back discipline & automation.

Every Day Is An '"In-Process" Shot'
At Living Your Best Life.

Oh. & <u>USE it.</u> Write in the margins.
Scrawl all over it lovingly or
beat the f*ck outta this agenda.
Sacrifice it to the pursuit of truly
knowing **you** & Manifesting
your penultimate life, well lived.

Said the Globalboho way?

ENJOY THE RIDE.

IN THIS three month
GLOBALBOHO REVISIONIST AGENDA
YOU'LL HAVE THE:

GB GEAR UP SEASONAL LAYOUTS
GB GNOSIS SPRINGBOARD SECTION
SAMPLE IDEAL MONTH, WEEK, DAY[FW]/DAY[HC]SPREADS
3 MONTHLY GROUPS (5 SPREADS EACH)
13 WEEKLY SPREADS
90 FREE WRITE DAILY SPREADS
+ bonus-bonus 7 HARDCORE DAILIES to test drive

WHY SO MANY? BECAUSE MISTAKES ARE BEAUTIFUL, HILARIOUS &

ACTUALLY PAR FOR THE **REAL** COURSE... & BECAUSE WE ALL

COURSE-CORRECT AS WE GO & AS WHAT WE LEARN ABOUT

OURSELVES EXPANDS.

A LOT OF **to do's** EXPAND FROM ONE DAY INTO THE NEXT...
SO THAT 21ST CENTURY amplified glitch IS DESIGNED into
THE **GB REVISIONIST** HARDCORE DAILIES.
Expand, carry over, " sorta same day, different verse" if you need to...

THIS IS KINDA HARDCORE. If you work it.
PACE YOURSELF.

Peace,
-Angel Brynner.

Globalboho

Gear Up.

A few seasonal spreads that can be used to plan your months or as indexes, habit trackers & logs.

A perfect place to begin.

date	month	month	month
1			
2			
3			
4			
5			
6			
7			
8			
9			
10			
11			
12			
13			
14			
15			
16			
17			
18			
19			
20			
21			
22			
23			
24			
25			
26			
27			
28			
29			
30			
31			

Seasonal calendar

date	month	month	month
1			
2			
3			
4			
5			
6			
7			
8			
9			
10			
11			
12			
13			
14			
15			
16			
17			
18			
19			
20			
21			
22			
23			
24			
25			
26			
27			
28			
29			
30			
31			

Seasonal calendar

Seasonal Grooming grid
BINGO [what & when?]:

FOCUS:

Color:

Scent:

Products/supplies:

Go.	See.
Do.	Serve.

seasonal Travel

Away **Stay-cation** Dream trek

Locale
dates
Url/link
T2dt [things to do there]
T2gb4 [things to get b4]

Locale
dates
Url/link
T2dt [things to do there]
T2gb4 [things to get b4]

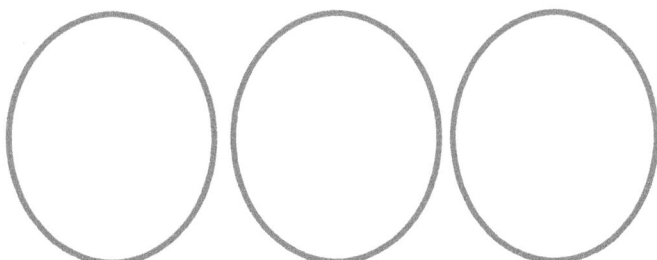

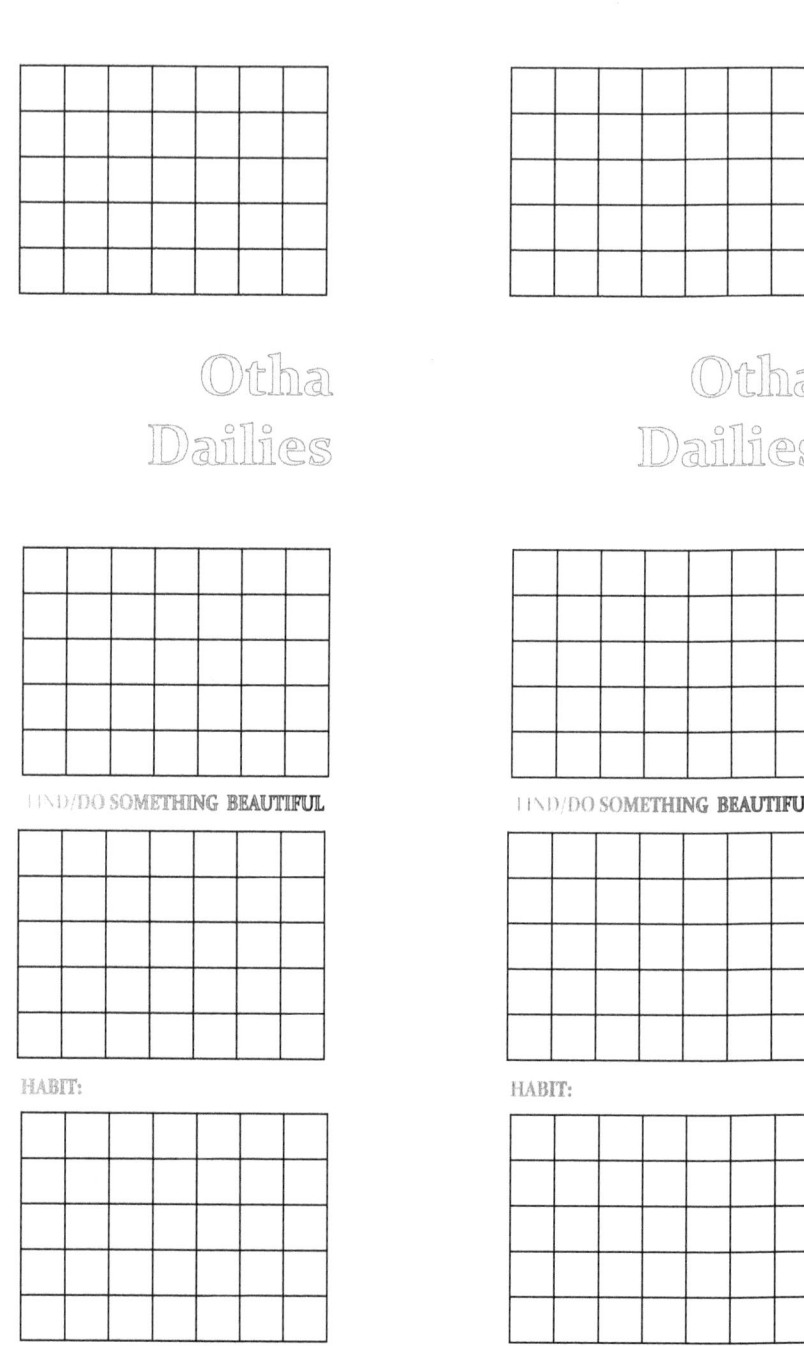

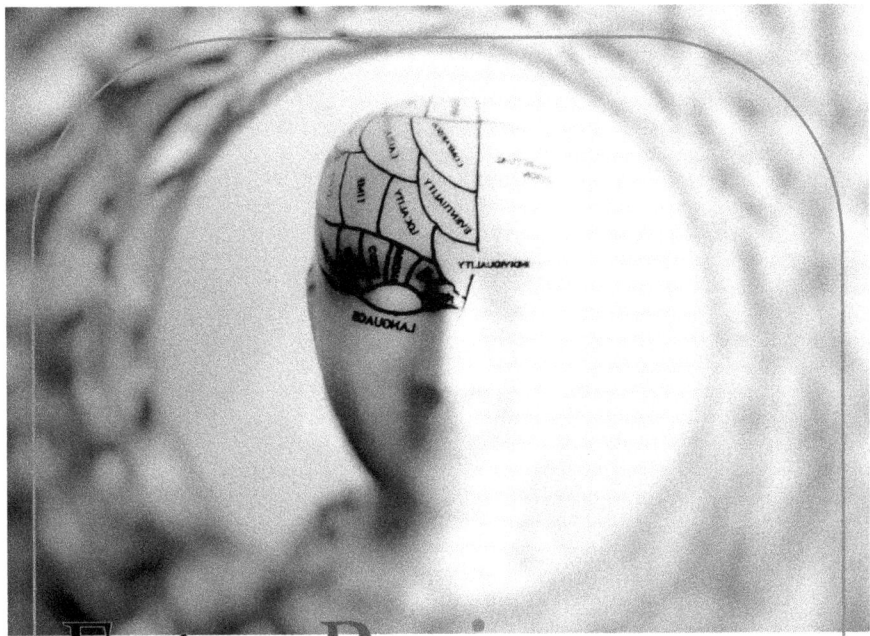

Extra Brain maps

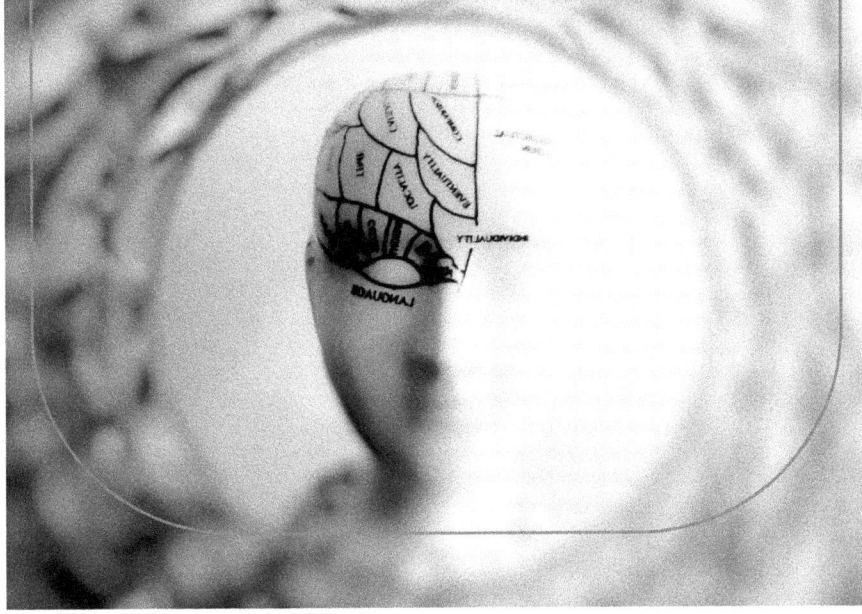

NOTES

Globalboho Gnosis

A few info sheets on different holistic roads that may pique your interest on the road to deep diving YOU.

The "good news" is
the world ain't what it used to be.
It's a wilder kind of war out there
Than before...& a little extra
weaponry rocked on the way to
your whathaveyous couldn't hurt.
So...gear up & get out there & win!

Helmet of Salvation/Ephesians 6:17

Breastplate of Righteousness /Ephesians 6:

Belt of Truth /Ephesians 6:14

Sword of the Spirit /Ephesians 6:17

Shield of Faith/Ephesians 6:16

Feet of Peace/Ephesians 6:15

"& when you've done all
you can think
To do, stand."
- Ephesians 6:13

[Dive deeper on your own]

ARMOR of GOD

solfeggio frequencies

174 hz/ removes pain
285 hz/ influences energy field
369 hz/ liberation from guilt & fear
417 hz/ facilitates change
528 hz/ repairs DNA (love frequency)
639 hz/ heals relationships
741 hz/ awaken intuition
852 hz/ attracts soul tribe
963 hz/ connect with light & spirit

Vibe Tribe [Hertz]:

174   285
369   417
528   639
741   852
963

extras:
432 hz/ miracle tone of nature

Brain waves:

THETA   4 to 8 hz/ meditation & creativity
BETA   13 to 35 hz/ problem solving
ALPHA   8 to 13 hz/ relaxed reflection
DELTA   0.5 to 4 hz/ deep sleep
GAMMA   35+ hz/ heightened awareness

[Dive deeper on your own]

Hertz Vibe Tribe

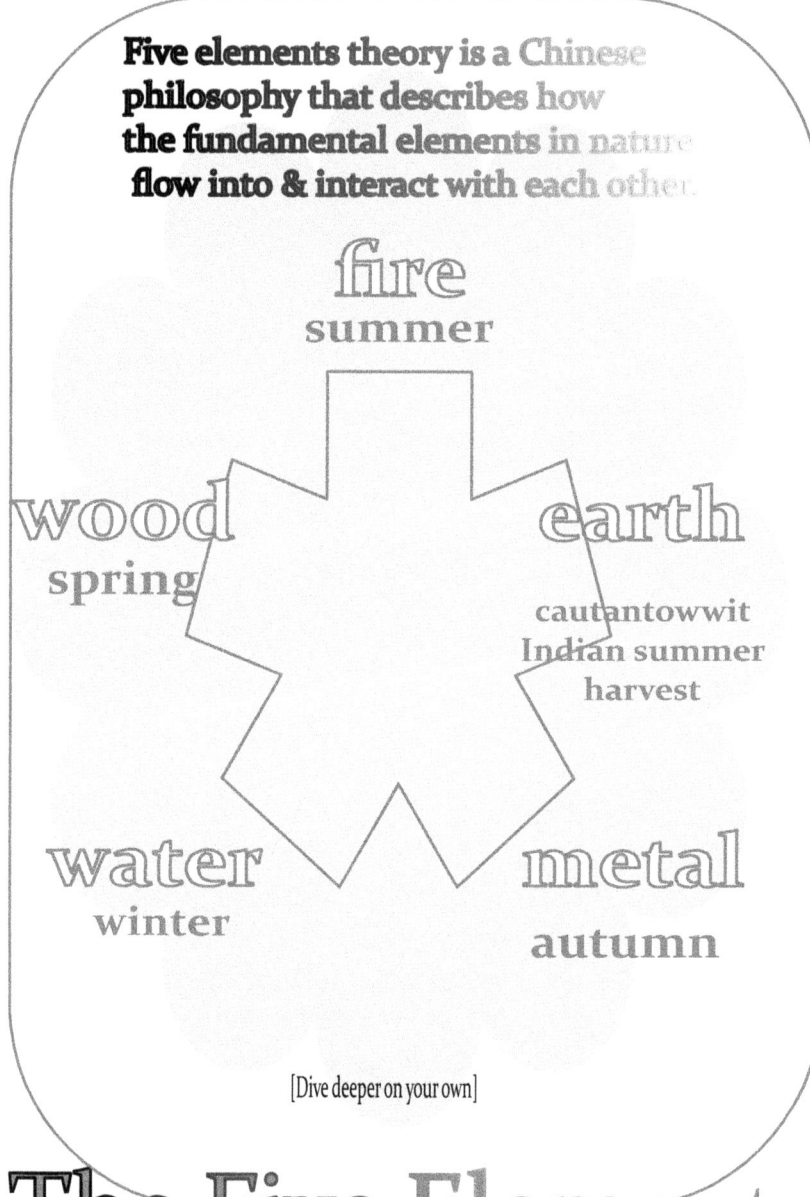

The Five Elements

Short & Sweet:

A "Loka"
Is a state of
consciousness
One is interacting
With the world
from, whether
One is aware of
It or not. They sync
With spiritual realms
Above & below ours
In Hinduism.

[Dive deeper on your own]

A "Chakra"
is usually
seen as an
Energy center
That needs to
"be in balance."

The Upper Lokas [Level of Awareness]	location	Deals with / Awareness of:
Satyaloka		illumination
Tapoloka		Divine sight
Janaloka		Divine love
Maharloka		Direct recognition/ Universal unity
Svargaloka		Willpower/Mind over matter
Bhuvarloka		Reason/ Seat of the soul
Bhuloka	earth	Memory/ Time transcendence
The 7 chakras taught in the west:	**Location:**	**Deals with / Awareness of:**
Sahasrara	crown	Inspiration & oneness
Vishuddhi	throat	communication
Anahata	heart	Pure love & compassion
Manipura	Solar plexus	Empowerment free will
Svadhisthana	sacral	Sex, power, creativity, desire, intimacy
Muladhara	root	Grounding & survival
The Lower Lokas [animal instincts/ states of darkness/ Levels of fixation]	**location**	**Deals with/ fixated on**
Atala	hips	Fear & lust
Vitala	thighs	Anger & resentment
Sutala	knees	Jealousy & envy
Talatala	calves	Confusion & doubt
Rasatala	ankles	Selfishness & pride
Mahatala	feet	consciencelessness
Patala	soles	Hatred & malice

The 21 (actual) chakras

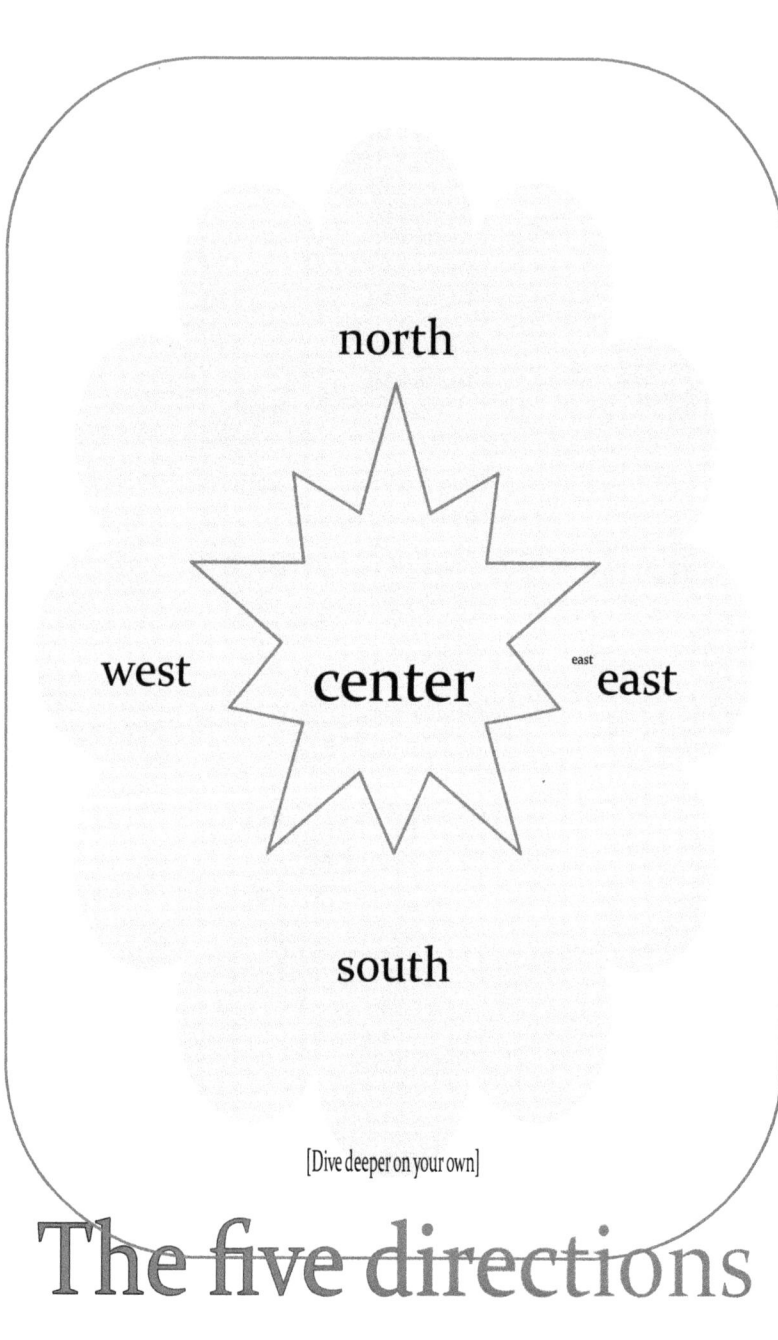

[Dive deeper on your own]

The five directions

According to Trungpa, we don't Wait until we die to enter the BARDO realm that Tibetan Buddhists See as waiting for us Upon death. We dance in & out of the 6 states as we live Our lives. Our Experience of the Present is always Colored by one Of six psychological States.

Freedom From this Madness is Possible.

Dive deeper on your own.

The god realm
[bliss]

The jealous god realm
[jealousy & lust for entertainment]

The human realm
[passion & desire]

The animal realm
[ignorance]

The hungry ghost realm
[poverty & possessiveness]

The hell realm
[aggression & hatred]

Chogyam Trungpa's Bardos

NOTES

The Ideals...

JUST4FUN

resusciate
reflect
reframe
relax
&r
restore
repair
relate
rally

Recalibrate.
Rebrand.
Revamp.
Redo.
Recast.

Revise your reality.

174		285
369	Vibe	417
528	Tribe	639
	[Hertz]:	
741		852
	963	

START
CYCLE
STOP

START
CYCLE
STOP

SEASON:
HARVEST   AUTUMN
WINTER   SPRING
     SUMMER
Seasonal focus:

NEW MOON:
FULL MOON:

HOLIDAYS:
This month's " I & i" DAY:
This month's "I & i" HOUR:

ideal MONTH:
JAN FEB MAR
APR MAY JUN
JUL AUG SEP
OCT NOV DEC

This month's HIGHEST TIMELINE log-line:

This month's affirmation:

This month's workout focus:

This month's physical challenge:

This month's shower & bathing meditation:

Movie of your life

bigGOAL:
Aim to do's

bigTASK:
Gotta do's

PICK4 Impossible   PICK4 SANCTUARY   PICK4 SELF-CARE
Things 2 try: GETERDONES: GETERDONES:

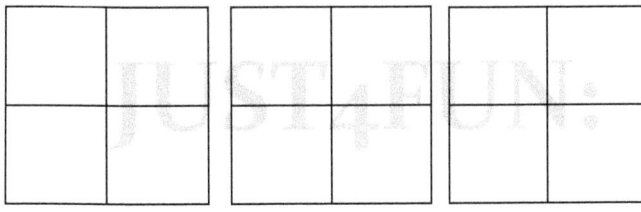
JUST4FUN:

New Moon Resonance

1. Imagine what you aim to Bring into your zone..
2. Set new intentions.
3. Journal & Meditate.
4. Scrub &/or soak your body.
5. Get out in some moonlight.

New/Things 2do.

1. Cleanse your space [Mental & physical].
2. Crystals! Charge 'em if ya got'em.
3. Celebrate any wins.
4. Release what no longer serves you.
5. Get out in some moonlight.

Things 2do/Full.

Full Moon Resonance

ideal POINT OF THE MONTH:

[NECESSARY] COUNTERPOINT OF THE MONTH:

(EVERY POINT HAS A COUNTERPOINT)

WHO ARE YOU?	PICK 4 MOVIES 2 WATCH:		PICK 4 BOOKS 2 READ:	
HOW DO YOU EXPRESS IT?				

		THEME SONG		POET	FLOWER
		COLOR		CRYSTAL	HERB

M	T	W	T	F	S	S

BUILD YOU UP BETTER HABIT TO IMPROVE:

GIVE IT UP OR REPLACE ?

WITH WHAT ?   HOW ?:

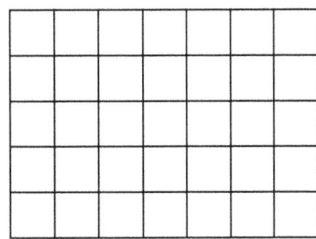

TREAT YOURSELF
Curious about it? LEARN IT

Wish you were able 2 do it? TRY IT

Place you want 2go? GO 2IT

Love to have it outside? TRY IT @HOME

JUST4FUN FOCUS:

THING 2LOVE ABOUT YOU

SPIRIT SUBJECT 2 FOCUS: ON

ODD INTEREST 2DEEP DIVE:

BEAUTY FEATURE/FOCUS:

CLEAN UP NICE FOCUS:

STYLE FOCUS:

SMELL 2 LOVE:

SHAKE THAT ASS!/NOW MOovVE!!

FIND/DO SOMETHING BEAUTIFUL

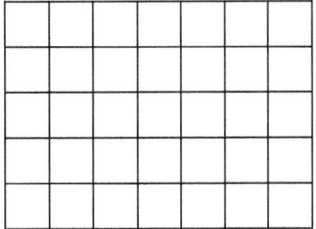

TRAVEL:
SCHEDULED   STAY-CATION

THINGS2DOTHERE

DREAM TREK:

VISUALS

HABIT:

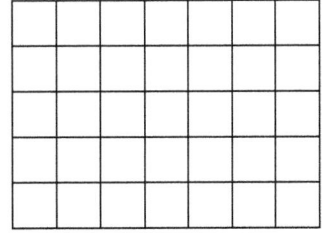

Project codename: Dawn: D-Day: Modus Operandi [M.O.]:	Magii Specialists Masterminds ("Who CAN shoot the dayum dawg?"): 1. 2. 3. 4.	KNOWN [Accessible] INTEL Gnosis needed [people, books, TEDx talks, documentaries, examples]:	Project codename: Dawn: D-Day: Modus Operandi [M.O.]:	Magii Specialists Masterminds ("Who CAN shoot the dayum dawg?"): 1. 2. 3. 4.	KNOWN [Accessible] INTEL Gnosis needed [people, books, TEDx talks, documentaries, examples]:
How2Skin it Steps: E.g., Make a detailed supplies needed list	Dawn/M/D Day 8/22/23/ 9/13 / 10/1/23	New INTEL: issues & fixes as they arise: e.g., Delivery delays,	How2Skin it Steps: E.g., Make a detailed supplies needed list	Dawn/M/D Day 8/22/23/ 9/13 / 10/1/23	New INTEL: issues & fixes as they arise: e.g., Delivery delays,

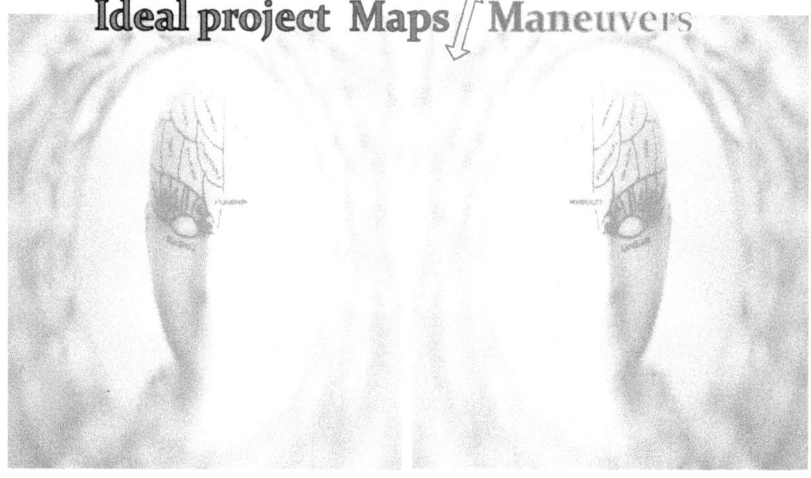

Ideal project Maps / Maneuvers

Ideal project Maps \ Maneuvers

Project codename:	Magii Specialists Masterminds ("Who CAN shoot the dayum dawg?"):	KNOWN [Accessible] INTEL Gnosis needed [people, books, TEDx talks, documentaries, examples]:	Project codename:	Magii Specialists Masterminds ("Who CAN shoot the dayum dawg?"):	KNOWN [Accessible] INTEL Gnosis needed [people, books, TEDx talks, documentaries, examples]:
Dawn: D-Day:	1.		Dawn: D-Day:	1.	
	2.			2.	
Modus Operandi [M.O.]:	3.		Modus Operandi [M.O.]:	3.	
	4.			4.	

How2Skin it Steps:	Dawn/M/D Day	New INTEL: issues & fixes as they arise:	How2Skin it Steps:	Dawn/M/D Day	New INTEL: issues & fixes as they arise:
E.g., Make a detailed supplies needed list	8/22/23/ 9/13 / 10/1/23	e.g., Delivery delays,	E.g., Make a detailed supplies needed list	8/22/23/ 9/13 / 10/1/23	e.g., Delivery delays,

THE Ideal WEEK:

NOTES:

WEEK OF 26

WEEKLY GREEN DRINK LOG

THE vibe AIMED 4:

THE PLAYLIST:
1.
2.
3.

THE DREAM:

THE MAIN GOAL:

THIS WEEK:

SELF CARE FOCUS

STYLE INSPO:

BEAUTY/GROOMING ZONE:

WORKOUT CHALLENGE FOCUS

MEDITATION/ FOCUS

PRAYER REQUEST

DECOMPRESSION TREAT

THIS WEEK'S WHATHAVEYOUS:

1.
2.
3.
4.
5.
6.
7.

7 THINGS YOU LOVE ABOUT YOU: (SELF PEP TALK)

1.
2.
3.
4.
5.
6.
7.

APPOINTMENTS	TIME & DATE	TYPE

WEEKLY DAY UP AFFIRMATION

THIS WEEK'S NIGHTLY AFFIRMATION

"I AM"...
(OF THE WEEK)

SPIRITUAL SHOTGUN:

What aspect of God, icon, archetype, angel, energy or spirit animal is riding out into the world *with* you this week?

LOVE ON OTHER'S LIST [L.O.O.L]

Who can you quietly do a cool thing for?

Aww~! Brain dump:

Sweethearts,
Did cool things,
Who are you FN with this week?

(FILL AS NEEDED)

How can you bless them for for blessing you?

Target Weekly meal plan:

Whole 30? Keto? Vegan? "All Thai, all week"? Paleo? Vegetarian? Carnivore?
Healthy Decadence?

Fast/ cleanse/ omad/ IF/ Juicing/ FODMAP

Argh! brain dump:

The jerks, the K*rens,
The nonsense,
Who are you so not FN with this week?

Grocery items 2 get 2 hit it:

How did you forgive them to fully let their energy go?

...the WEEKend RIT[UAL]S:

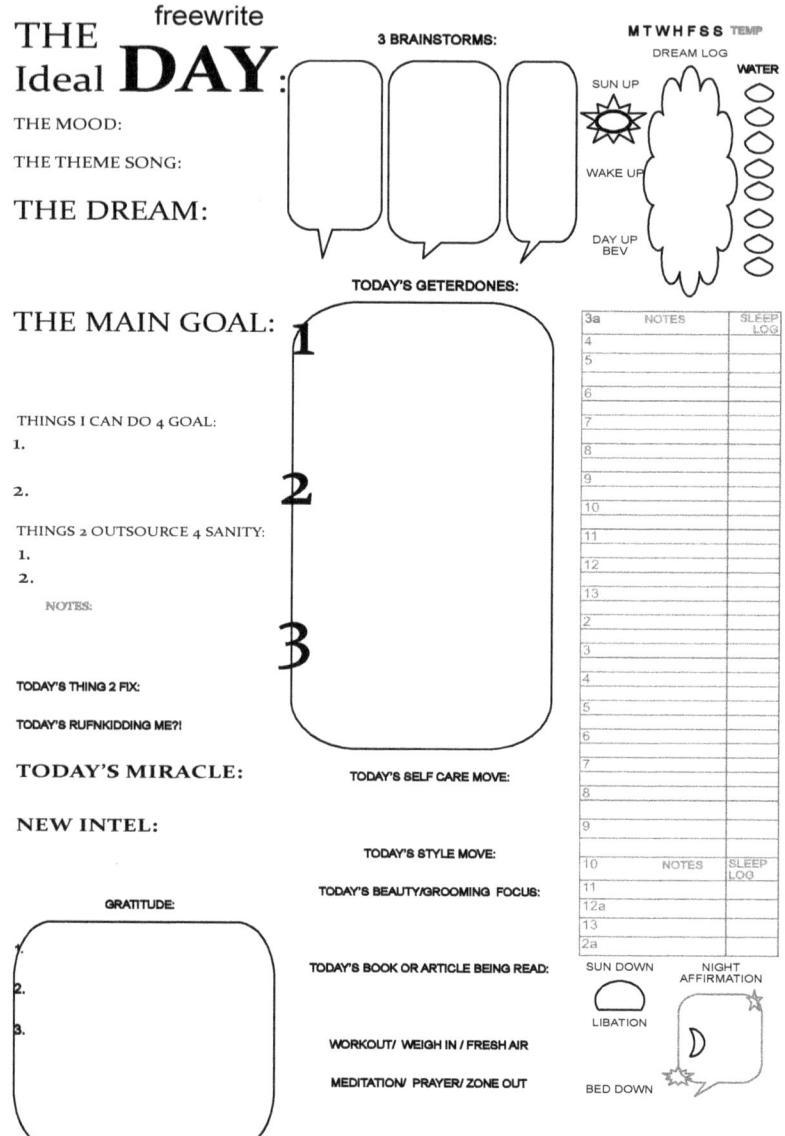

THE
pregaming:

THE recap:

PLAN YOUR MONTH

SECTION.
3 monthlies[5 spreads each].

JUST₄FUN

resuscitate
reflect
reframe
relax
8r
restore
repair
relate
rally

Recalibrate.
Rebrand.
Revamp.
Redo.
Recast.

Revise your reality.

174		285
369	Vibe	417
528	Tribe	639
741	[Hertz]:	852
	963	

START   START
CYCLE   CYCLE
STOP   STOP

SEASON:

HARVEST   AUTUMN
WINTER   SPRING
      SUMMER
Seasonal focus:

NEW MOON:

FULL MOON:

HOLIDAYS:
This month's " I & i" DAY:
This month's "I & i" HOUR:

This month's HIGHEST TIMELINE log-line:

This month's affirmation:

This month's workout focus:

This month's physical challenge:

This month's shower & bathing meditation:

MONTH:
JAN FEB MAR
APR MAY JUN
JUL AUG SEP
OCT NOV DEC

Movie of your life

bigGOAL:
Aim to do's

bigTASK:
Gotta do's

PICK4 Impossible   PICK4 SANCTUARY   PICK4 SELF-CARE
Things 2 try: GETERDONES: GETERDONES:

---	---		---	---		---	---

JUST4FUN:

New Moon Resonance

1. Imagine what you aim to Bring into your zone..
2. Set new intentions.
3. Journal & Meditate.
4. Scrub &/or soak your body.
5. Get out in some moonlight.

New/Things 2do.

1. Cleanse your space [Mental & physical].
2. Crystals! Charge 'em If ya got'em.
3. Celebrate any wins.
4. Release what no longer Serves you.
5. Get out in some moonlight.

Things 2do/Full.

Full Moon Resonance

POINT OF THE MONTH:

[NECESSARY] COUNTERPOINT OF THE MONTH:

(EVERY POINT HAS A COUNTERPOINT)

WHO ARE YOU?

HOW DO YOU EXPRESS IT?

PICK 4 MOVIES 2 WATCH:

PICK 4 BOOKS 2 READ:

THEME SONG

COLOR

POET

CRYSTAL

FLOWER

HERB

M	T	W	T	F	S	S

BUILD YOU UP BETTER HABIT TO IMPROVE:

GIVE IT UP OR REPLACE ?

WITH WHAT ?   HOW ?:

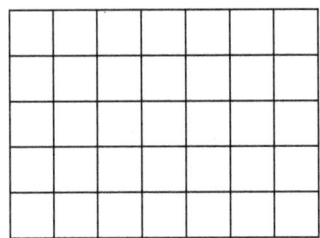

TREAT YOURSELF
Curious about it? LEARN IT

Wish you were able 2 do it? TRY IT

Place you want 2go? GO 2IT

Love to have it outside? TRY IT @HOME

JUST4FUN FOCUS:

THING 2LOVE ABOUT YOU

SPIRIT SUBJECT 2 FOCUS: ON

ODD INTEREST 2DEEP DIVE:

BEAUTY FEATURE/FOCUS:

CLEAN UP NICE FOCUS:

STYLE FOCUS:

SMELL 2 LOVE:

TRAVEL:
SCHEDULED   STAY-CATION

THINGS2DOTHERE

DREAM TREK:

VISUALS

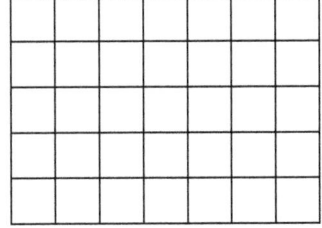

SHAKE THAT ASS!/NOW MOovVE!!

FIND/DO SOMETHING BEAUTIFUL

HABIT:

Project codename:	Magii Specialists Masterminds ("Who CAN shoot the dayum dawg?"):	KNOWN [Accessible] INTEL Gnosis needed [people, books, TEDx talks, documentaries, examples]:	Project codename:	Magii Specialists Masterminds ("Who CAN shoot the dayum dawg?"):	KNOWN [Accessible] INTEL Gnosis needed [people, books, TEDx talks, documentaries, examples]:
Dawn: D-Day: Modus Operandi [M.O.]:	1. 2. 3. 4.		Dawn: D-Day: Modus Operandi [M.O.]:	1. 2. 3. 4.	
How2Skin it Steps: E.g., Make a detailed supplies needed list	Dawn/M/D Day 8/22/23/ 9/13 / 10/1/23	New INTEL: issues & fixes as they arise: e.g., Delivery delays,	How2Skin it Steps: E.g., Make a detailed supplies needed list	Dawn/M/D Day 8/22/23/ 9/13 / 10/1/23	New INTEL: issues & fixes as they arise: e.g., Delivery delays,

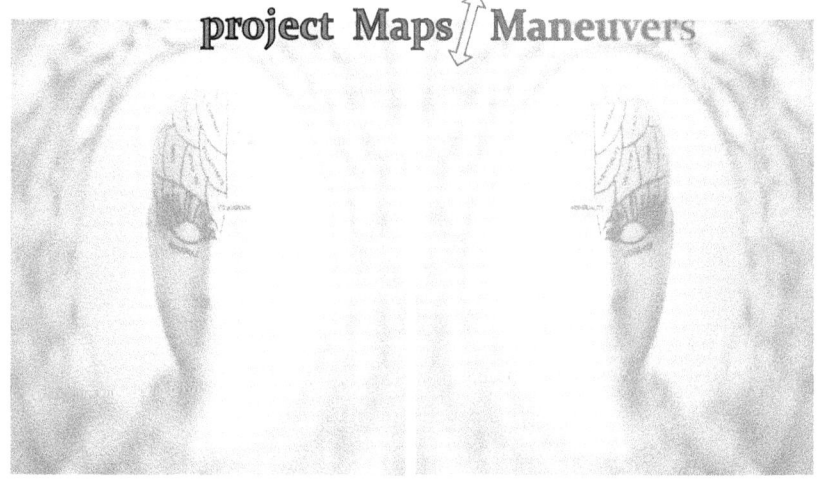

project Maps / Maneuvers

project Maps \ Maneuvers

Project codename:	Magii Specialists Masterminds ("Who CAN shoot the dayum dawg?"):	KNOWN [Accessible] INTEL Gnosis needed [people, books, TEDx talks, documentaries, examples]:	Project codename:	Magii Specialists Masterminds ("Who CAN shoot the dayum dawg?"):	KNOWN [Accessible] INTEL Gnosis needed [people, books, TEDx talks, documentaries, examples]:
Dawn: D-Day: **Modus Operandi [M.O.]:**	1. 2. 3. 4.		**Dawn: D-Day:** **Modus Operandi [M.O.]:**	1. 2. 3. 4.	
How2Skin it Steps: E.g., Make a detailed supplies needed list	**Dawn/M/D Day** 8/22/23/ 9/13 / 10/1/23	**New INTEL:** issues & fixes as they arise: e.g., Delivery delays,	**How2Skin it Steps:** E.g., Make a detailed supplies needed list	**Dawn/M/D Day** 8/22/23/ 9/13 / 10/1/23	**New INTEL:** issues & fixes as they arise: e.g., Delivery delays,

NOTES

JUST4FUN

resusciate · reflect · reframe · relax · 8r · restore · repair · relate · rally

Recalibrate.
Rebrand.
Revamp.
Redo.
Recast.
Revise your reality.

174		285
369	Vibe	417
528	Tribe	639
	[Hertz]:	
741		852
	963	

START
CYCLE
STOP

START
CYCLE
STOP

SEASON:
HARVEST   AUTUMN
WINTER   SPRING
    SUMMER
Seasonal focus:

NEW MOON:
FULL MOON:

HOLIDAYS:
This month's " I & i" DAY:
This month's "I & i" HOUR:

This month's HIGHEST TIMELINE log-line:

This month's affirmation:

This month's workout focus:

This month's physical challenge:

This month's shower & bathing meditation:

MONTH:
JAN FEB MAR
APR MAY JUN
JUL AUG SEP
OCT NOV DEC

Movie of your life

bigGOAL:
Aim to do's

bigTASK:
Gotta do's

PICK4 Impossible   PICK4 SANCTUARY   PICK4 SELF-CARE
Things 2 try: GETERDONES: GETERDONES:

JUST4FUN:

New Moon Resonance

1. Imagine what you aim to Bring into your zone..
2. Set new intentions.
3. Journal & Meditate.
4. Scrub &/or soak your body.
5. Get out in some moonlight.

New/Things 2do.

1. Cleanse your space [Mental & physical].
2. Crystals! Charge 'em If ya got'em.
3. Celebrate any wins.
4. Release what no longer Serves you.
5. Get out in some moonlight.

Things 2do/Full.

Full Moon Resonance

POINT OF THE MONTH:

[NECESSARY] COUNTERPOINT OF THE MONTH:

(EVERY POINT HAS A COUNTERPOINT)

WHO ARE YOU?

HOW DO YOU EXPRESS IT?

PICK 4 MOVIES 2WATCH:

PICK 4 BOOKS 2READ:

THEME SONG

COLOR

POET

CRYSTAL

FLOWER

HERB

M	T	W	T	F	S	S

BUILD YOU UP BETTER HABIT TO IMPROVE:

GIVE IT UP OR REPLACE ?

WITH WHAT ?   HOW ?:

TREAT YOURSELF
Curious about it? LEARN IT

Wish you were able 2 do it? TRY IT

Place you want 2go? GO 2IT

Love to have it outside? TRY IT @HOME

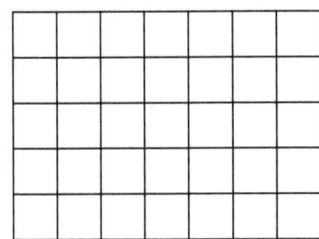

JUST4FUN FOCUS:

THING 2LOVE ABOUT YOU

SPIRIT SUBJECT 2 FOCUS: ON

ODD INTEREST 2DEEP DIVE:

BEAUTY FEATURE/FOCUS:

CLEAN UP NICE FOCUS:

STYLE FOCUS:

SMELL 2 LOVE:

TRAVEL:
SCHEDULED   STAY-CATION

THINGS2DOTHERE

DREAM TREK:

VISUALS

SHAKE THAT ASS!/NOW MOovVE!!

FIND/DO SOMETHING BEAUTIFUL

HABIT:

Project codename:	Magii Specialists Masterminds ("Who CAN shoot the dayum dawg?"):	KNOWN [Accessible] INTEL Gnosis needed [people, books, TEDx talks, documentaries, examples]:	Project codename:	Magii Specialists Masterminds ("Who CAN shoot the dayum dawg?"):	KNOWN [Accessible] INTEL Gnosis needed [people, books, TEDx talks, documentaries, examples]:
Dawn: D-Day: Modus Operandi [M.O.]:	1. 2. 3. 4.		Dawn: D-Day: Modus Operandi [M.O.]:	1. 2. 3. 4.	
How2Skin it Steps: E.g., Make a detailed supplies needed list	Dawn/M/D Day 8/22/23/ 9/13 / 10/1/23	New INTEL: issues & fixes as they arise: e.g., Delivery delays.	How2Skin it Steps: E.g., Make a detailed supplies needed list	Dawn/M/D Day 8/22/23/ 9/13 / 10/1/23	New INTEL: issues & fixes as they arise: e.g., Delivery delays.

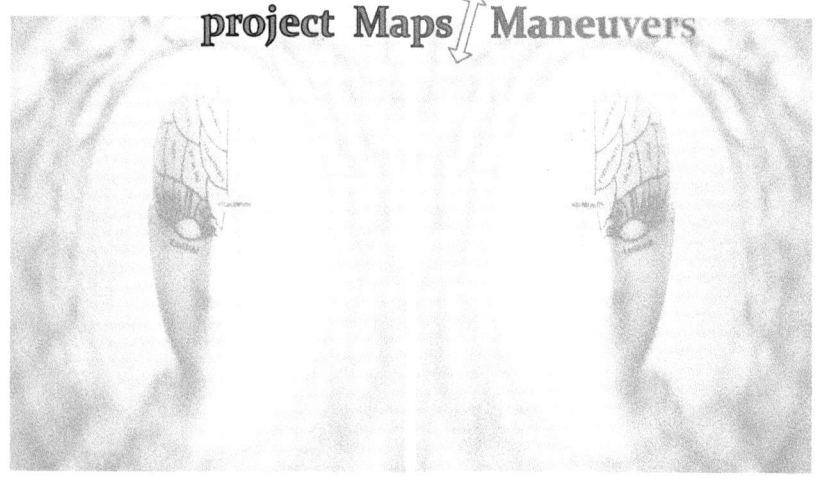

project Maps / Maneuvers

project Maps\Maneuvers

Project codename:	Magii Specialists Masterminds ("Who CAN shoot the dayum dawg?"):	KNOWN [Accessible] INTEL Gnosis needed [people, books, TEDx talks, documentaries, examples]:	Project codename:	Magii Specialists Masterminds ("Who CAN shoot the dayum dawg?"):	KNOWN [Accessible] INTEL Gnosis needed [people, books, TEDx talks, documentaries, examples]:
Dawn: D-Day:	1.		Dawn: D-Day:	1.	
	2.			2.	
Modus Operandi [M.O.]:	3.		Modus Operandi [M.O.]:	3.	
	4.			4.	

How2Skin it Steps: E.g., Make a detailed supplies needed list	Dawn/M/D Day 8/22/23/ 9/13 / 10/1/23	New INTEL: issues & fixes as they arise: e.g., Delivery delays.	How2Skin it Steps: E.g., Make a detailed supplies needed list	Dawn/M/D Day 8/22/23/ 9/13 / 10/1/23	New INTEL: issues & fixes as they arise: e.g., Delivery delays,

JUST4FUN

resuscitate · reflect · reframe · relax · 8r · restore · repair · relate · rally

Recalibrate.

Rebrand.

Revamp.

Redo.

Recast.

Revise your reality.

	174		285	
START	369	Vibe	417	START
CYCLE	528	Tribe [Hertz]:	639	CYCLE
STOP	741		852	STOP
		963		

SEASON:
HARVEST AUTUMN
WINTER SPRING
     SUMMER
Seasonal focus:

NEW MOON:
FULL MOON:

HOLIDAYS:
This month's " I & i" DAY:
This month's "I & i" HOUR:

This month's HIGHEST TIMELINE log-line:

This month's affirmation:

This month's workout focus:

This month's physical challenge:

This month's shower & bathing meditation:

MONTH:
JAN FEB MAR
APR MAY JUN
JUL AUG SEP
OCT NOV DEC

Movie of your life

bigGOAL:
Aim to do's

bigTASK:
Gotta do's

PICK4 Impossible   PICK4 SANCTUARY   PICK4 SELF-CARE
    Things 2 try: GETERDONES: GETERDONES:

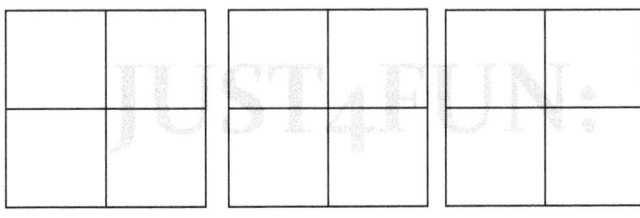
JUST4FUN:

New Moon Resonance

1. Imagine what you aim to Bring into your zone..
2. Set new intentions.
3. Journal & Meditate.
4. Scrub &/or soak your body.
5. Get out in some moonlight.

New/Things 2do.

1. Cleanse your space [Mental & physical].
2. Crystals! Charge 'em If ya got'em.
3. Celebrate any wins.
4. Release what no longer Serves you.
5. Get out in some moonlight.

Things 2do/Full.

Full Moon Resonance

POINT OF THE MONTH:

[NECESSARY] COUNTERPOINT OF THE MONTH:

(EVERY POINT HAS A COUNTERPOINT)

WHO ARE YOU?

HOW DO YOU EXPRESS IT?

PICK 4 MOVIES 2 WATCH:

PICK 4 BOOKS 2 READ:

THEME SONG

COLOR

POET

CRYSTAL

FLOWER

HERB

M	T	W	T	F	S	S

BUILD YOU UP BETTER HABIT TO IMPROVE:

GIVE IT UP OR REPLACE?

WITH WHAT?   HOW?:

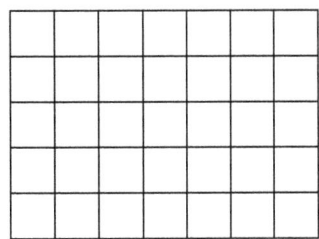

TREAT YOURSELF

Curious about it? LEARN IT

Wish you were able 2 do it? TRY IT

Place you want 2go? GO 2IT

Love to have it outside? TRY IT @HOME

JUST4FUN FOCUS:

THING 2LOVE ABOUT YOU

SPIRIT SUBJECT 2 FOCUS: ON

ODD INTEREST 2DEEP DIVE:

BEAUTY FEATURE/FOCUS:

CLEAN UP NICE FOCUS:

STYLE FOCUS:

SMELL 2 LOVE:

SHAKE THAT ASS!/NOW MOovVE!!

FIND/DO SOMETHING BEAUTIFUL

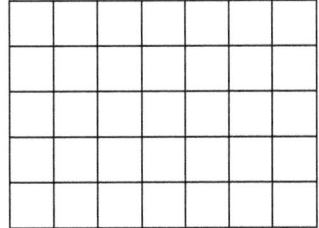

TRAVEL:

SCHEDULED   STAY-CATION

THINGS2DOTHERE

DREAM TREK:

VISUALS

HABIT:

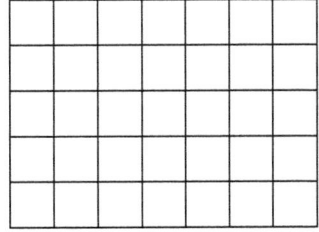

Project codename:	Magii Specialists Masterminds ("Who CAN shoot the dayum dawg?"):	KNOWN [Accessible] INTEL Gnosis needed [people, books, TEDx talks, documentaries, examples]:	Project codename:	Magii Specialists Masterminds ("Who CAN shoot the dayum dawg?"):	KNOWN [Accessible] INTEL Gnosis needed [people, books, TEDx talks, documentaries, examples]:
Dawn: D-Day:	1.		Dawn: D-Day:	1.	
	2.			2.	
Modus Operandi [M.O.]:	3.		Modus Operandi [M.O.]:	3.	
	4.			4.	
How2Skin it Steps: *E.g., Make a detailed supplies needed list*	Dawn/M/D Day 8/22/23/ 9/13 / 10/1/23	New INTEL: issues & fixes as they arise: e.g., Delivery delays,	How2Skin it Steps: *E.g., Make a detailed supplies needed list*	Dawn/M/D Day 8/22/23/ 9/13 / 10/1/23	New INTEL: issues & fixes as they arise: e.g., Delivery delays,

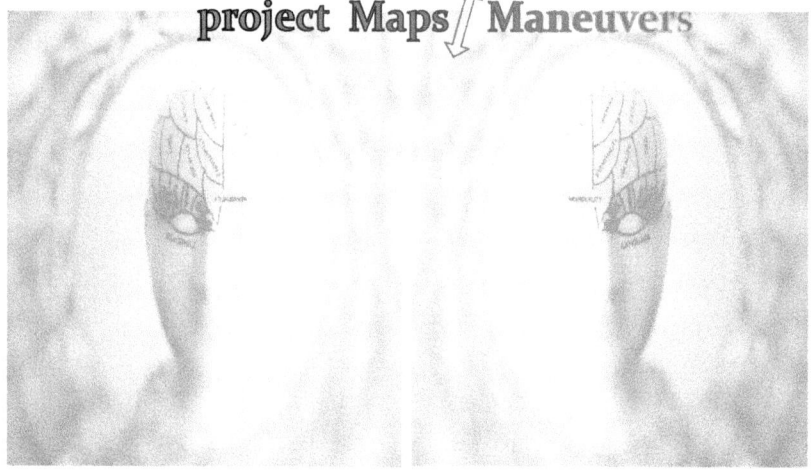

project Maps / Maneuvers

project Maps \ Maneuvers

Project codename:	Magii Specialists Masterminds ("Who CAN shoot the dayum dawg?"):	KNOWN [Accessible] INTEL Gnosis needed [people, books, TEDx talks, documentaries, examples]:	Project codename:	Magii Specialists Masterminds ("Who CAN shoot the dayum dawg?"):	KNOWN [Accessible] INTEL Gnosis needed [people, books, TEDx talks, documentaries, examples]:
	1.			1.	
Dawn: D-Day:	2.		Dawn: D-Day:	2.	
Modus Operandi [M.O.]:	3.		Modus Operandi [M.O.]:	3.	
	4.			4.	
How2Skin it Steps: E.g., Make a detailed supplies needed list	Dawn/M/D Day 8/22/23/ 9/13 / 10/1/23	New INTEL: issues & fixes as they arise: e.g., Delivery delays.	How2Skin it Steps: E.g., Make a detailed supplies needed list	Dawn/M/D Day 8/22/23/ 9/13 / 10/1/23	New INTEL: issues & fixes as they arise: e.g., Delivery delays.

PLAN YOUR WEEK

SECTION.
13 weeklies.

# THE WEEK:

NOTES:

WEEK OF 26

WEEKLY GREEN DRINK LOG

THE vibe AIMED 4:

THE PLAYLIST:
1.
2.
3.

THE DREAM:

THE MAIN GOAL:

THIS WEEK:

SELF CARE FOCUS

STYLE INSPO:

BEAUTY/GROOMING ZONE:

WORKOUT CHALLENGE FOCUS

MEDITATION/ FOCUS

PRAYER REQUEST

DECOMPRESSION TREAT

THIS WEEK'S WHATHAVEYOUS:

1.
2.
3.
4.
5.
6.
7.

7 THINGS YOU LOVE ABOUT YOU: (SELF PEP TALK)

1.
2.
3.
4.
5.
6.
7.

APPOINTMENTS	TIME & DATE	TYPE

WEEKLY DAY UP AFFIRMATION

THIS WEEK'S NIGHTLY AFFIRMATION

"I AM"...
(OF THE WEEK)

SPIRITUAL SHOTGUN:

What aspect of God, icon, archetype, angel, energy or spirit animal is riding out into the world *with* you this week?

LOVE ON OTHER'S LIST [L.O.O.L]

Who can you quietly do a cool thing for?

Aww~! Brain dump:

Sweethearts,
Did cool things,
Who are you FN with this week?

(FILL AS NEEDED)

How can you bless them for for blessing you?

Target Weekly meal plan:

Whole 30? Keto? Vegan? "All Thai, all week"? Paleo? Vegetarian? Carnivore? Healthy Decadence?

Fast/ cleanse/ omad/ IF/ Juicing/ FODMAP

Grocery items 2 get 2 hit it:

...the WEEKend RIT[UAL]S:

Argh! brain dump:

The jerks, the K*rens,
The nonsense,
Who are you so not FN with this week?

How did you forgive them **to** fully let their energy go?

THE WEEK:

THE vibe AIMED 4:

THE PLAYLIST:
1.
2.
3.

THE DREAM:

THE MAIN GOAL:

NOTES:

WEEK OF 26

WEEKLY GREEN DRINK LOG

THIS WEEK:

SELF CARE FOCUS

STYLE INSPO:

BEAUTY/GROOMING ZONE:

WORKOUT CHALLENGE FOCUS

MEDITATION/ FOCUS

PRAYER REQUEST

DECOMPRESSION TREAT

THIS WEEK'S WHATHAVEYOUS:

1.
2.
3.
4.
5.
6.
7.

APPOINTMENTS	TIME & DATE	TYPE

7 THINGS YOU LOVE ABOUT YOU: (SELF PEP TALK)

1.
2.
3.
4.
5.
6.
7.

WEEKLY DAY UP AFFIRMATION

THIS WEEK'S NIGHTLY AFFIRMATION

"I AM"...
(OF THE WEEK)

SPIRITUAL SHOTGUN:

What aspect of God, icon, archetype, angel, energy or spirit animal is riding out into the world *with* you this week?

LOVE ON OTHER'S LIST [L.O.O.L]

Who can you quietly do a cool thing for?

Aww~! Brain dump:

Sweethearts,
Did cool things,
Who are you FN with this week?

(FILL AS NEEDED)

How can you bless them for for blessing you?

Target Weekly meal plan:

Whole 30? Keto? Vegan? "All Thai, all week"? Paleo? Vegetarian? Carnivore?
Healthy Decadence?

Fast/ cleanse/ omad/ IF/ Juicing/ FODMAP

Argh! brain dump:

The jerks, the K*rens,
The nonsense,
Who are you so not FN with this week?

Grocery items 2 get 2 hit it:

How did you forgive them to fully let their energy go?

...the WEEKend RIT[UAL]S:

THE WEEK:

THE vibe AIMED 4:

THE PLAYLIST:
1.
2.
3.

THE DREAM:

THE MAIN GOAL:

NOTES:

WEEK ___ OF 26

WEEKLY GREEN DRINK LOG ◇ ◇ ◇ ◇ ◇ ◇

THIS WEEK:

SELF CARE FOCUS

STYLE INSPO:

BEAUTY/GROOMING ZONE:

WORKOUT CHALLENGE FOCUS

MEDITATION/ FOCUS

PRAYER REQUEST

DECOMPRESSION TREAT

THIS WEEK'S WHATHAVEYOUS:

1.
2.
3.
4.
5.
6.
7.

APPOINTMENTS	TIME & DATE	TYPE

7 THINGS YOU LOVE ABOUT YOU: (SELF PEP TALK)

1.
2.
3.
4.
5.
6.
7.

WEEKLY DAY UP AFFIRMATION

THIS WEEK'S NIGHTLY AFFIRMATION

"I AM..."
(OF THE WEEK)

SPIRITUAL SHOTGUN:
What aspect of God, icon, archetype, angel, energy or spirit animal is riding out into the world *with* you this week?

LOVE ON OTHER'S LIST [L.O.O.L]
Who can you quietly do a cool thing for?

Aww~! Brain dump:
Sweethearts,
Did cool things,
Who are you FN with this week?

(FILL AS NEEDED)

How can you bless them for for blessing you?

Target Weekly meal plan:
Whole 30? Keto? Vegan? "All Thai, all week"? Paleo? Vegetarian? Carnivore? Healthy Decadence?

Fast/ cleanse/ omad/ IF/ Juicing/ FODMAP

Argh! brain dump:
The jerks, the K*rens,
The nonsense,
Who are you so not FN with this week?

Grocery items 2 get 2 hit it:

How did you forgive them to fully let their energy go?

...the WEEKend RIT[UAL]S:

THE WEEK:

NOTES:

WEEK OF 26

WEEKLY GREEN DRINK LOG

THE vibe AIMED 4:

THE PLAYLIST:
1.
2.
3.

THE DREAM:

THE MAIN GOAL:

THIS WEEK:

SELF CARE FOCUS

STYLE INSPO:

BEAUTY/GROOMING ZONE:

WORKOUT CHALLENGE FOCUS

MEDITATION/ FOCUS

PRAYER REQUEST

DECOMPRESSION TREAT

THIS WEEK'S WHATHAVEYOUS:

1.
2.
3.
4.
5.
6.
7.

APPOINTMENTS	TIME & DATE	TYPE

7 THINGS YOU LOVE ABOUT YOU: (SELF PEP TALK)

1.
2.
3.
4.
5.
6.
7.

WEEKLY DAY UP AFFIRMATION

THIS WEEK'S NIGHTLY AFFIRMATION

"I AM..."
(OF THE WEEK)

SPIRITUAL SHOTGUN:

What aspect of God, icon, archetype, angel, energy or spirit animal is riding out into the world *with* you this week?

LOVE ON OTHER'S LIST [L.O.O.L]

Who can you quietly do a cool thing for?

Aww~! Brain dump:

Sweethearts,
Did cool things,
Who are you FN with this week?

(FILL AS NEEDED)

How can you bless them for for blessing you?

Target Weekly meal plan:

Whole 30? Keto? Vegan? "All Thai, all week"? Paleo? Vegetarian? Carnivore?
Healthy Decadence?

Fast/ cleanse/ omad/ IF/ Juicing/ FODMAP

Argh! brain dump:

The jerks, the K*rens,
The nonsense,
Who are you so not FN with this week?

Grocery items 2 get 2 hit it:

How did you forgive them **to** fully let their energy go?

...the WEEKend RIT[UAL]S:

THE WEEK:

THE vibe AIMED 4:

THE PLAYLIST:
1.
2.
3.

THE DREAM:

THE MAIN GOAL:

NOTES:

WEEK OF 26

WEEKLY GREEN DRINK LOG

THIS WEEK:

SELF CARE FOCUS

STYLE INSPO:

BEAUTY/GROOMING ZONE:

WORKOUT CHALLENGE FOCUS

MEDITATION/ FOCUS

PRAYER REQUEST

DECOMPRESSION TREAT

THIS WEEK'S WHATHAVEYOUS:

1.
2.
3.
4.
5.
6.
7.

7 THINGS YOU LOVE ABOUT YOU: (SELF PEP TALK)

1.
2.
3.
4.
5.
6.
7.

APPOINTMENTS	TIME & DATE	TYPE

WEEKLY DAY UP AFFIRMATION

THIS WEEK'S NIGHTLY AFFIRMATION

"I AM"...
(OF THE WEEK)

SPIRITUAL SHOTGUN:

What aspect of God, icon, archetype, angel, energy or spirit animal is riding out into the world *with* you this week?

LOVE ON OTHER'S LIST [L.O.O.L]

Who can you quietly do a cool thing for?

Aww~! Brain dump:

Sweethearts,
Did cool things,
Who are you FN with this week?

(FILL AS NEEDED)

How can you bless them for for blessing you?

Target Weekly meal plan:

Whole 30? Keto? Vegan? "All Thai, all week"? Paleo? Vegetarian? Carnivore?
Healthy Decadence?

Fast/ cleanse/ omad/ IF/ Juicing/ FODMAP

Argh! brain dump:

The jerks, the K*rens,
The nonsense,
Who are you so not FN with this week?

Grocery items 2 get 2 hit it:

How did you forgive them **to** fully let their energy go?

...the WEEKend RIT[UAL]S:

THE WEEK:

THE vibe AIMED 4:

THE PLAYLIST:
1.
2.
3.

THE DREAM:

THE MAIN GOAL:

NOTES:

WEEK   OF 26

WEEKLY GREEN DRINK LOG

THIS WEEK:

SELF CARE FOCUS

STYLE INSPO:

BEAUTY/GROOMING ZONE:

WORKOUT CHALLENGE FOCUS

MEDITATION/ FOCUS

PRAYER REQUEST

DECOMPRESSION TREAT

THIS WEEK'S WHATHAVEYOUS:

1.
2.
3.
4.
5.
6.
7.

APPOINTMENTS	TIME & DATE	TYPE

7 THINGS YOU LOVE ABOUT YOU: (SELF PEP TALK)

1.
2.
3.
4.
5.
6.
7.

WEEKLY DAY UP AFFIRMATION

THIS WEEK'S NIGHTLY AFFIRMATION

"I AM..."
(OF THE WEEK)

SPIRITUAL SHOTGUN:

What aspect of God, icon, archetype, angel, energy or spirit animal is riding out into the world *with* you this week?

LOVE ON OTHER'S LIST [L.O.O.L]

Who can you quietly do a cool thing for?

Aww~! Brain dump:

Sweethearts,
Did cool things,
Who are you FN with this week?

(FILL AS NEEDED)

How can you bless them for for blessing you?

Target Weekly meal plan:

Whole 30? Keto? Vegan? "All Thai, all week"? Paleo? Vegetarian? Carnivore?
Healthy Decadence?

Fast/ cleanse/ omad/ IF/ Juicing/ FODMAP

Argh! brain dump:

The jerks, the K*rens,
The nonsense,
Who are you so not FN with this week?

Grocery items 2 get 2 hit it:

How did you forgive them **to** fully let their energy go?

...the WEEKend RIT[UAL]S:

THE WEEK:

THE vibe AIMED 4:

THE PLAYLIST:
1.
2.
3.

THE DREAM:

THE MAIN GOAL:

NOTES:

WEEK OF 26

WEEKLY GREEN DRINK LOG

THIS WEEK:

SELF CARE FOCUS

STYLE INSPO:

BEAUTY/GROOMING ZONE:

WORKOUT CHALLENGE FOCUS

MEDITATION/ FOCUS

PRAYER REQUEST

DECOMPRESSION TREAT

THIS WEEK'S WHATHAVEYOUS:

1.
2.
3.
4.
5.
6.
7.

APPOINTMENTS	TIME & DATE	TYPE

7 THINGS YOU LOVE ABOUT YOU: (SELF PEP TALK)

1.
2.
3.
4.
5.
6.
7.

WEEKLY DAY UP AFFIRMATION

THIS WEEK'S NIGHTLY AFFIRMATION

"I AM..."
(OF THE WEEK)

SPIRITUAL SHOTGUN:

What aspect of God, icon, archetype, angel, energy or spirit animal is riding out into the world *with* you this week?

LOVE ON OTHER'S LIST [L.O.O.L]

Who can you quietly do a cool thing for?

Aww~! Brain dump:

Sweethearts,
Did cool things,
Who are you FN with this week?

(FILL AS NEEDED)

How can you bless them for for blessing you?

Target Weekly meal plan:

Whole 30? Keto? Vegan? "All Thai, all week"? Paleo? Vegetarian? Carnivore? Healthy Decadence?

Fast/ cleanse/ omad/ IF/ Juicing/ FODMAP

Argh! brain dump:

The jerks, the K*rens,
The nonsense,
Who are you so not FN with this week?

Grocery items 2 get 2 hit it:

How did you forgive them **to** fully let their energy go?

...the WEEKend RIT[UAL]S:

THE WEEK:

THE vibe AIMED 4:

THE PLAYLIST:
1.
2.
3.

THE DREAM:

THE MAIN GOAL:

NOTES:

WEEK OF 26

WEEKLY GREEN DRINK LOG ◯ ◯ ◯ ◯ ◯ ◯

THIS WEEK:

SELF CARE FOCUS

STYLE INSPO:

BEAUTY/GROOMING ZONE:

WORKOUT CHALLENGE FOCUS

MEDITATION/ FOCUS

PRAYER REQUEST

DECOMPRESSION TREAT

THIS WEEK'S WHATHAVEYOUS:

1.
2.
3.
4.
5.
6.
7.

APPOINTMENTS	TIME & DATE	TYPE

7 THINGS YOU LOVE ABOUT YOU: (SELF PEP TALK)

1.
2.
3.
4.
5.
6.
7.

WEEKLY DAY UP AFFIRMATION

THIS WEEK'S NIGHTLY AFFIRMATION

"I AM..."
(OF THE WEEK)

SPIRITUAL SHOTGUN:
What aspect of God, icon, archetype, angel, energy or spirit animal is riding out into the world *with* you this week?

LOVE ON OTHER'S LIST [L.O.O.L]
Who can you quietly do a cool thing for?

Aww~! Brain dump:
Sweethearts,
Did cool things,
Who are you FN with this week?

(FILL AS NEEDED)

How can you bless them for for blessing you?

Target Weekly meal plan:
Whole 30? Keto? Vegan? "All Thai, all week"? Paleo? Vegetarian? Carnivore? Healthy Decadence?

Fast/ cleanse/ omad/ IF/ Juicing/ FODMAP

Argh! brain dump:
The jerks, the K*rens,
The nonsense,
Who are you so not FN with this week?

Grocery items 2 get 2 hit it:

How did you forgive them **to** fully let their energy go?

...the WEEKend RIT[UAL]S:

THE WEEK:

THE vibe AIMED 4:

THE PLAYLIST:
1.
2.
3.

THE DREAM:

THE MAIN GOAL:

NOTES:

WEEK OF 26

WEEKLY GREEN DRINK LOG

THIS WEEK:

SELF CARE FOCUS

STYLE INSPO:

BEAUTY/GROOMING ZONE:

WORKOUT CHALLENGE FOCUS

MEDITATION/ FOCUS

PRAYER REQUEST

DECOMPRESSION TREAT

THIS WEEK'S WHATHAVEYOUS:

1.
2.
3.
4.
5.
6.
7.

APPOINTMENTS	TIME & DATE	TYPE

7 THINGS YOU LOVE ABOUT YOU: (SELF PEP TALK)

1.
2.
3.
4.
5.
6.
7.

WEEKLY DAY UP AFFIRMATION

THIS WEEK'S NIGHTLY AFFIRMATION

"I AM..."
(OF THE WEEK)

SPIRITUAL SHOTGUN:

What aspect of God, icon, archetype, angel, energy or spirit animal is riding out into the world *with* you this week?

LOVE ON OTHER'S LIST [L.O.O.L]

Who can you quietly do a cool thing for?

Aww~! Brain dump:

Sweethearts,
Did cool things,
Who are you FN with this week?

(FILL AS NEEDED)

Target Weekly meal plan:

Whole 30? Keto? Vegan? "All Thai, all week"? Paleo? Vegetarian? Carnivore? Healthy Decadence?

Fast/ cleanse/ omad/ IF/ Juicing/ FODMAP

Grocery items 2 get 2 hit it:

...the WEEKend RIT[UAL]S:

How can you bless them for for blessing you?

Argh! brain dump:

The jerks, the K*rens,
The nonsense,
Who are you so not FN with this week?

How did you forgive them **to** fully let their energy go?

THE WEEK:

THE vibe AIMED 4:

THE PLAYLIST:
1.
2.
3.

THE DREAM:

THE MAIN GOAL:

NOTES:

WEEK   OF 26

WEEKLY GREEN DRINK LOG

THIS WEEK:

SELF CARE FOCUS

STYLE INSPO:

BEAUTY/GROOMING ZONE:

WORKOUT CHALLENGE FOCUS

MEDITATION/ FOCUS

PRAYER REQUEST

DECOMPRESSION TREAT

THIS WEEK'S WHATHAVEYOUS:

1.
2.
3.
4.
5.
6.
7.

APPOINTMENTS	TIME & DATE	TYPE

7 THINGS YOU LOVE ABOUT YOU: (SELF PEP TALK)

1.
2.
3.
4.
5.
6.
7.

WEEKLY DAY UP AFFIRMATION

THIS WEEK'S NIGHTLY AFFIRMATION

"I AM…"
(OF THE WEEK)

SPIRITUAL SHOTGUN:

What aspect of God, icon, archetype, angel, energy or spirit animal is riding out into the world *with* you this week?

LOVE ON OTHER'S LIST [L.O.O.L]

Who can you quietly do a cool thing for?

Aww~! Brain dump:

Sweethearts,
Did cool things,
Who are you FN with this week?

(FILL AS NEEDED)

How can you bless them for for blessing you?

Target Weekly meal plan:

Whole 30? Keto? Vegan? "All Thai, all week"? Paleo? Vegetarian? Carnivore? Healthy Decadence?

Fast/ cleanse/ omad/ IF/ Juicing/ FODMAP

Argh! brain dump:

The jerks, the K*rens,
The nonsense,
Who are you so not FN with this week?

Grocery items 2 get 2 hit it:

How did you forgive them **to** fully let their energy go?

…the WEEKend RIT[UAL]S:

THE WEEK:

THE vibe AIMED 4:

THE PLAYLIST:
1.
2.
3.

THE DREAM:

THE MAIN GOAL:

NOTES:

WEEK OF 26

WEEKLY GREEN DRINK LOG

THIS WEEK:

SELF CARE FOCUS

STYLE INSPO:

BEAUTY/GROOMING ZONE:

WORKOUT CHALLENGE FOCUS

MEDITATION/ FOCUS

PRAYER REQUEST

DECOMPRESSION TREAT

THIS WEEK'S WHATHAVEYOUS:

1.
2.
3.
4.
5.
6.
7.

APPOINTMENTS	TIME & DATE	TYPE

7 THINGS YOU LOVE ABOUT YOU: (SELF PEP TALK)

1.
2.
3.
4.
5.
6.
7.

WEEKLY DAY UP AFFIRMATION

THIS WEEK'S NIGHTLY AFFIRMATION

"I AM..."
(OF THE WEEK)

SPIRITUAL SHOTGUN:

What aspect of God, icon, archetype, angel, energy or spirit animal is riding out into the world *with* you this week?

LOVE ON OTHER'S LIST [L.O.O.L]

Who can you quietly do a cool thing for?

Aww~! Brain dump:

Sweethearts,
Did cool things,
Who are you FN with this week?

(FILL AS NEEDED)

How can you bless them for for blessing you?

Target Weekly meal plan:

Whole 30? Keto? Vegan? "All Thai, all week"? Paleo? Vegetarian? Carnivore?
Healthy Decadence?

Fast/ cleanse/ omad/ IF/ Juicing/ FODMAP

Argh! brain dump:

The jerks, the K*rens,
The nonsense,
Who are you so not FN with this week?

Grocery items 2 get 2 hit it:

How did you forgive them **to** fully let their energy go?

...the WEEKend RIT[UAL]S:

THE WEEK:

NOTES:

WEEK OF 26

WEEKLY GREEN DRINK LOG

THE vibe AIMED 4:

THE PLAYLIST:
1.
2.
3.

THE DREAM:

THE MAIN GOAL:

THIS WEEK:
- SELF CARE FOCUS
- STYLE INSPO:
- BEAUTY/GROOMING ZONE:
- WORKOUT CHALLENGE FOCUS
- MEDITATION/ FOCUS
- PRAYER REQUEST
- DECOMPRESSION TREAT

THIS WEEK'S WHATHAVEYOUS:

1.
2.
3.
4.
5.
6.
7.

7 THINGS YOU LOVE ABOUT YOU: (SELF PEP TALK)
1.
2.
3.
4.
5.
6.
7.

APPOINTMENTS	TIME & DATE	TYPE

WEEKLY DAY UP AFFIRMATION

THIS WEEK'S NIGHTLY AFFIRMATION

"I AM"...
(OF THE WEEK)

SPIRITUAL SHOTGUN:
What aspect of God, icon, archetype, angel, energy or spirit animal is riding out into the world *with* you this week?

LOVE ON OTHER'S LIST [L.O.O.L]
Who can you quietly do a cool thing for?

Aww~! Brain dump:
Sweethearts,
Did cool things,
Who are you FN with this week?

(FILL AS NEEDED)

How can you bless them for for blessing you?

Target Weekly meal plan:
Whole 30? Keto? Vegan? "All Thai, all week"? Paleo? Vegetarian? Carnivore? Healthy Decadence?

Fast/ cleanse/ omad/ IF/ Juicing/ FODMAP

Argh! brain dump:
The jerks, the K*rens,
The nonsense,
Who are you so not FN with this week?

Grocery items 2 get 2 hit it:

How did you forgive them to fully let their energy go?

...the WEEKend RIT[UAL]S:

THE WEEK:

THE vibe AIMED 4:

THE PLAYLIST:
1.
2.
3.

THE DREAM:

THE MAIN GOAL:

NOTES:

WEEK OF 26

WEEKLY GREEN DRINK LOG

THIS WEEK:

SELF CARE FOCUS

STYLE INSPO:

BEAUTY/GROOMING ZONE:

WORKOUT CHALLENGE FOCUS

MEDITATION/ FOCUS

PRAYER REQUEST

DECOMPRESSION TREAT

THIS WEEK'S WHATHAVEYOUS:

1.
2.
3.
4.
5.
6.
7.

APPOINTMENTS	TIME & DATE	TYPE

7 THINGS YOU LOVE ABOUT YOU: (SELF PEP TALK)

1.
2.
3.
4.
5.
6.
7.

WEEKLY DAY UP AFFIRMATION

THIS WEEK'S NIGHTLY AFFIRMATION

(OF THE WEEK)

SPIRITUAL SHOTGUN:

What aspect of God, icon, archetype, angel, energy or spirit animal is riding out into the world *with* you this week?

LOVE ON OTHER'S LIST [L.O.O.L]

Who can you quietly do a cool thing for?

Aww~! Brain dump:

Sweethearts,
Did cool things,
Who are you FN with this week?

(FILL AS NEEDED)

How can you bless them for for blessing you?

Target Weekly meal plan:

Whole 30? Keto? Vegan? "All Thai, all week"? Paleo? Vegetarian? Carnivore?
Healthy Decadence?

Fast/ cleanse/ omad/ IF/ Juicing/ FODMAP

Argh! brain dump:

The jerks, the K*rens,
The nonsense,
Who are you so not FN with this week?

Grocery items 2 get 2 hit it:

How did you forgive them to fully let their energy go?

...the WEEKend RIT[UAL]S:

NOTES

ROCK YOUR DAYS

SECTION.
90 free-write dailies

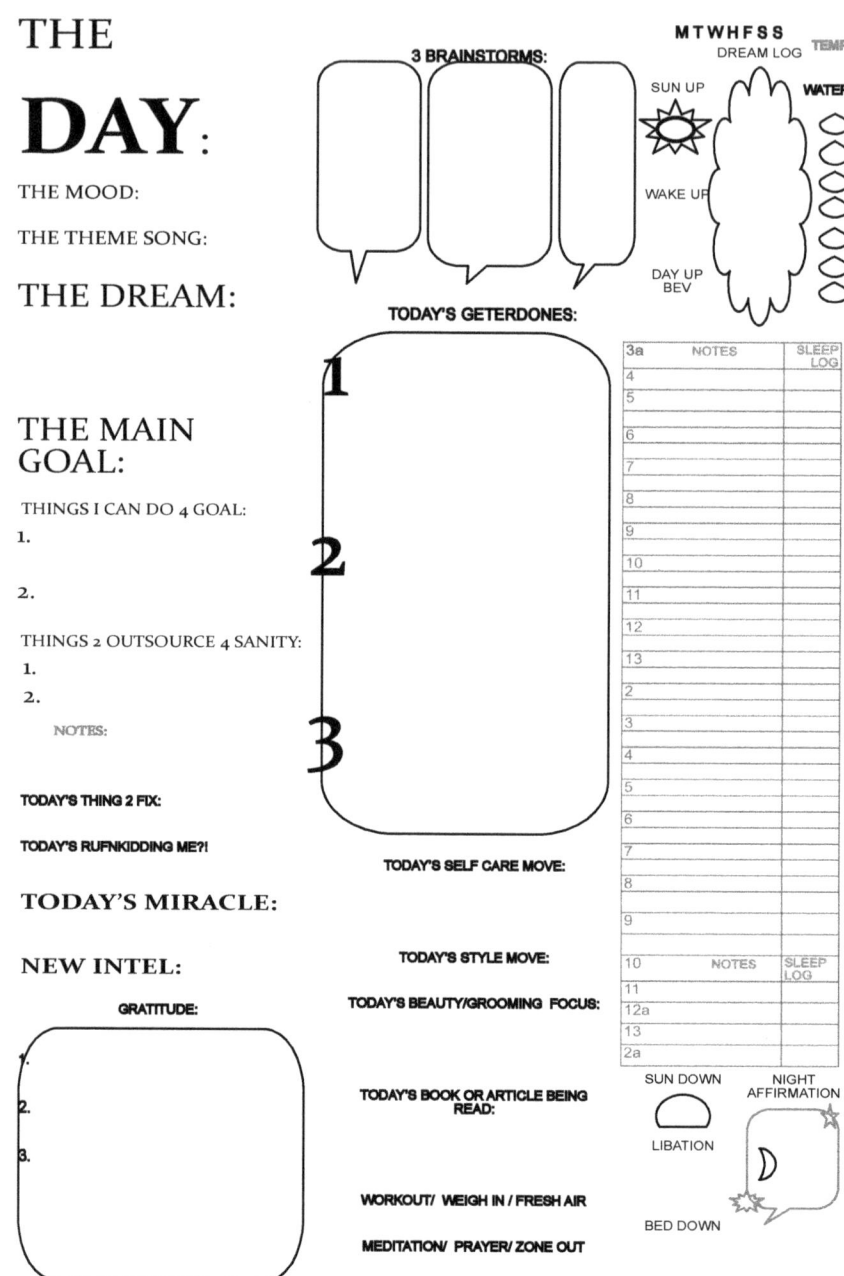

THE
pregaming:

THE recap:

THE DAY:

THE MOOD:

THE THEME SONG:

THE DREAM:

THE MAIN GOAL:

THINGS I CAN DO 4 GOAL:
1.
2.

THINGS 2 OUTSOURCE 4 SANITY:
1.
2.

NOTES:

TODAY'S THING 2 FIX:

TODAY'S RUFNKIDDING ME?!

TODAY'S MIRACLE:

NEW INTEL:

GRATITUDE:
1.
2.
3.

3 BRAINSTORMS:

TODAY'S GETERDONES:
1
2
3

TODAY'S SELF CARE MOVE:

TODAY'S STYLE MOVE:

TODAY'S BEAUTY/GROOMING FOCUS:

TODAY'S BOOK OR ARTICLE BEING READ:

WORKOUT/ WEIGH IN / FRESH AIR

MEDITATION/ PRAYER/ ZONE OUT

M T W H F S S
DREAM LOG   TEMP

SUN UP   WATER

WAKE UP

DAY UP BEV

	NOTES	SLEEP LOG
3a		
4		
5		
6		
7		
8		
9		
10		
11		
12		
13		
2		
3		
4		
5		
6		
7		
8		
9		
10	NOTES	SLEEP LOG
11		
12a		
13		
2a		

SUN DOWN   NIGHT AFFIRMATION

LIBATION

BED DOWN

Introduction

THE pregaming:

THE recap:

THE
DAY:

THE MOOD:

THE THEME SONG:

THE DREAM:

THE MAIN GOAL:

THINGS I CAN DO 4 GOAL:
1.

2.

THINGS 2 OUTSOURCE 4 SANITY:
1.
2.

NOTES:

TODAY'S THING 2 FIX:

TODAY'S RUFNKIDDING ME?!

TODAY'S MIRACLE:

NEW INTEL:

GRATITUDE:
1.
2.
3.

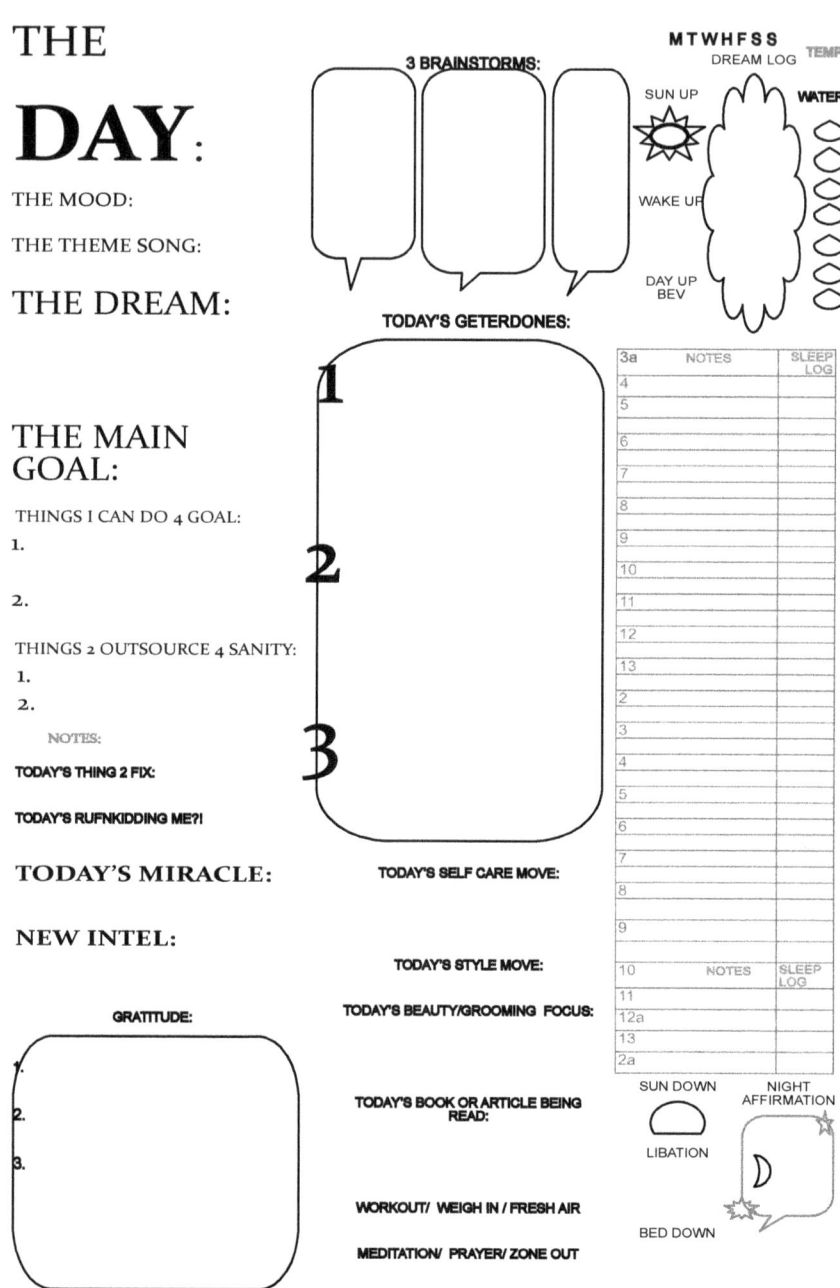

3 BRAINSTORMS:

TODAY'S GETERDONES:
1
2
3

TODAY'S SELF CARE MOVE:

TODAY'S STYLE MOVE:

TODAY'S BEAUTY/GROOMING FOCUS:

TODAY'S BOOK OR ARTICLE BEING READ:

WORKOUT/ WEIGH IN / FRESH AIR

MEDITATION/ PRAYER/ ZONE OUT

M T W H F S S
DREAM LOG — TEMP

SUN UP — WATER

WAKE UP

DAY UP BEV

NOTES — SLEEP LOG
3a
4
5
6
7
8
9
10
11
12
13
2
3
4
5
6
7
8
9
10 — NOTES — SLEEP LOG
11
12a
13
2a

SUN DOWN — NIGHT AFFIRMATION

LIBATION

BED DOWN

THE pregaming:

THE recap:

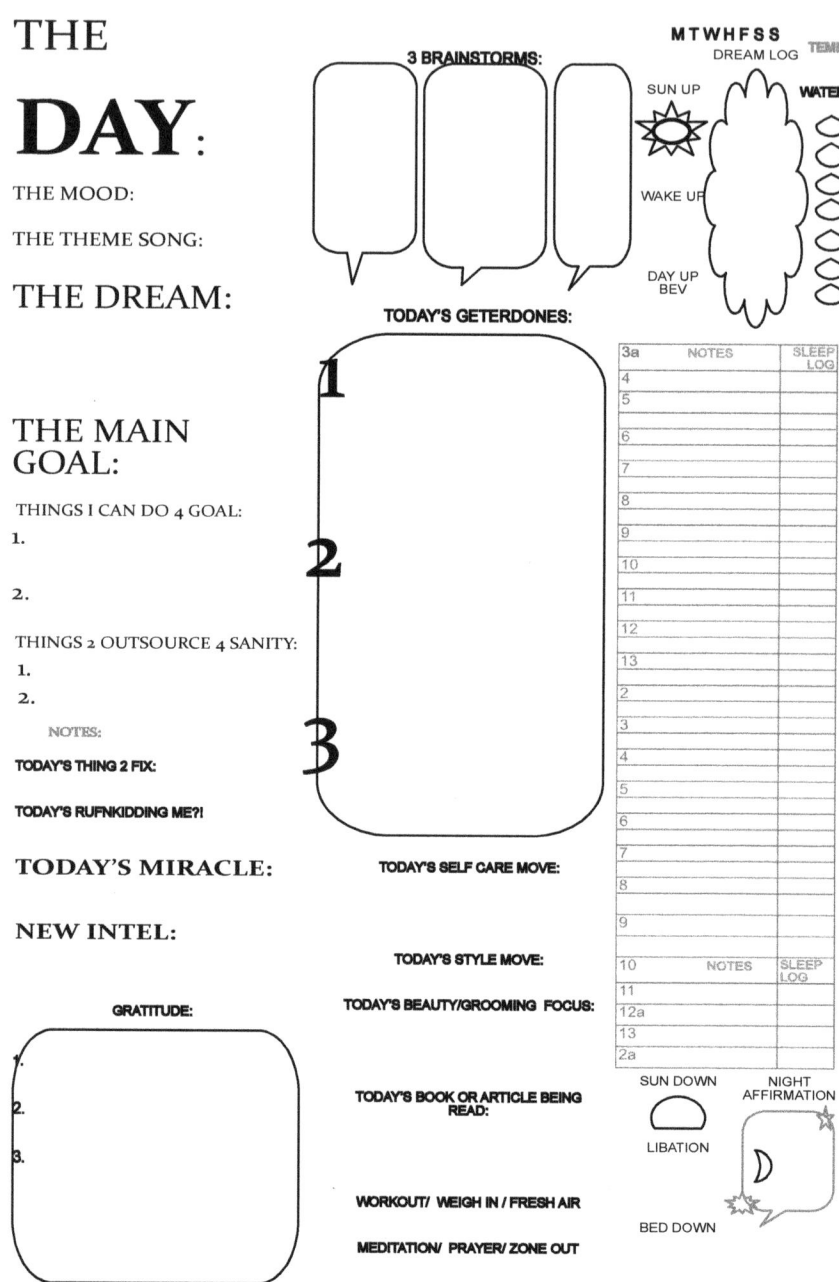

THE
pregaming:

THE recap:

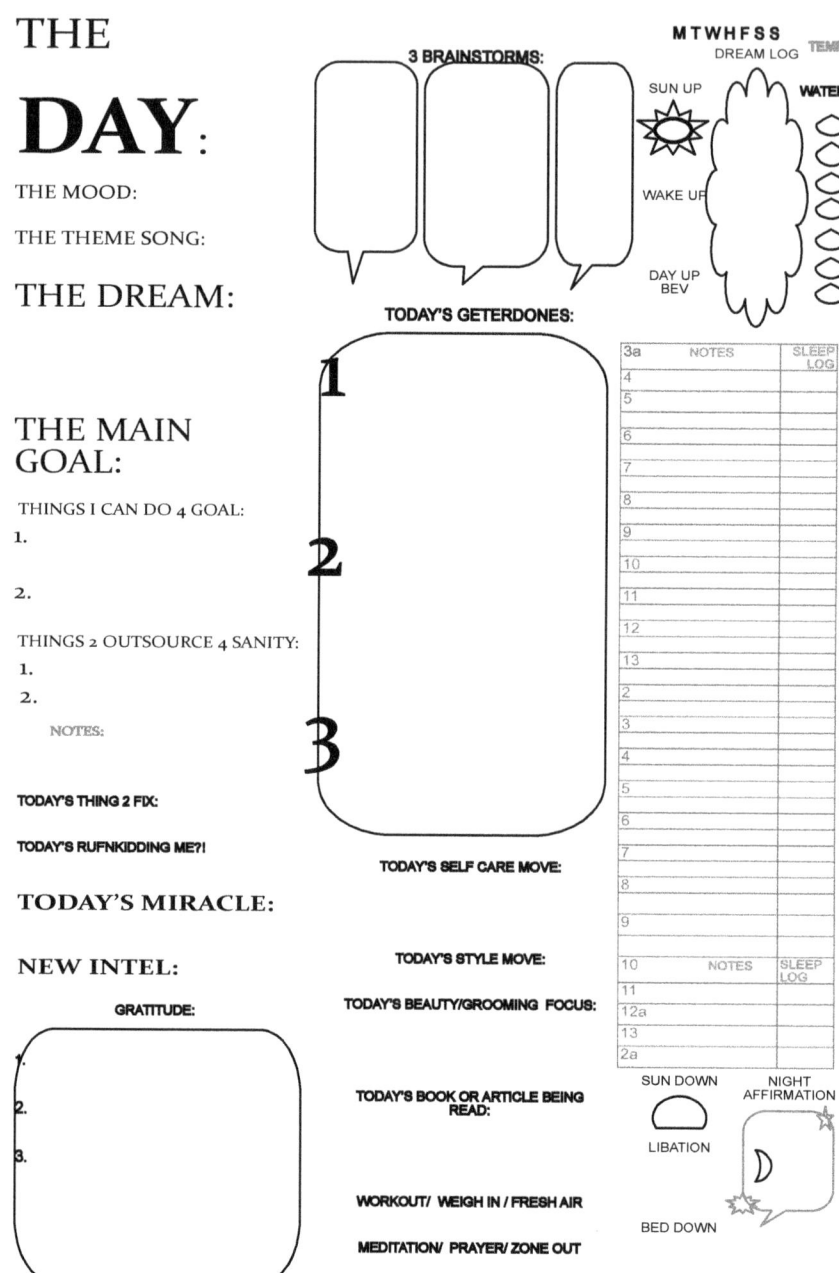

THE
pregaming:

THE recap:

THE
pregaming:

THE recap:

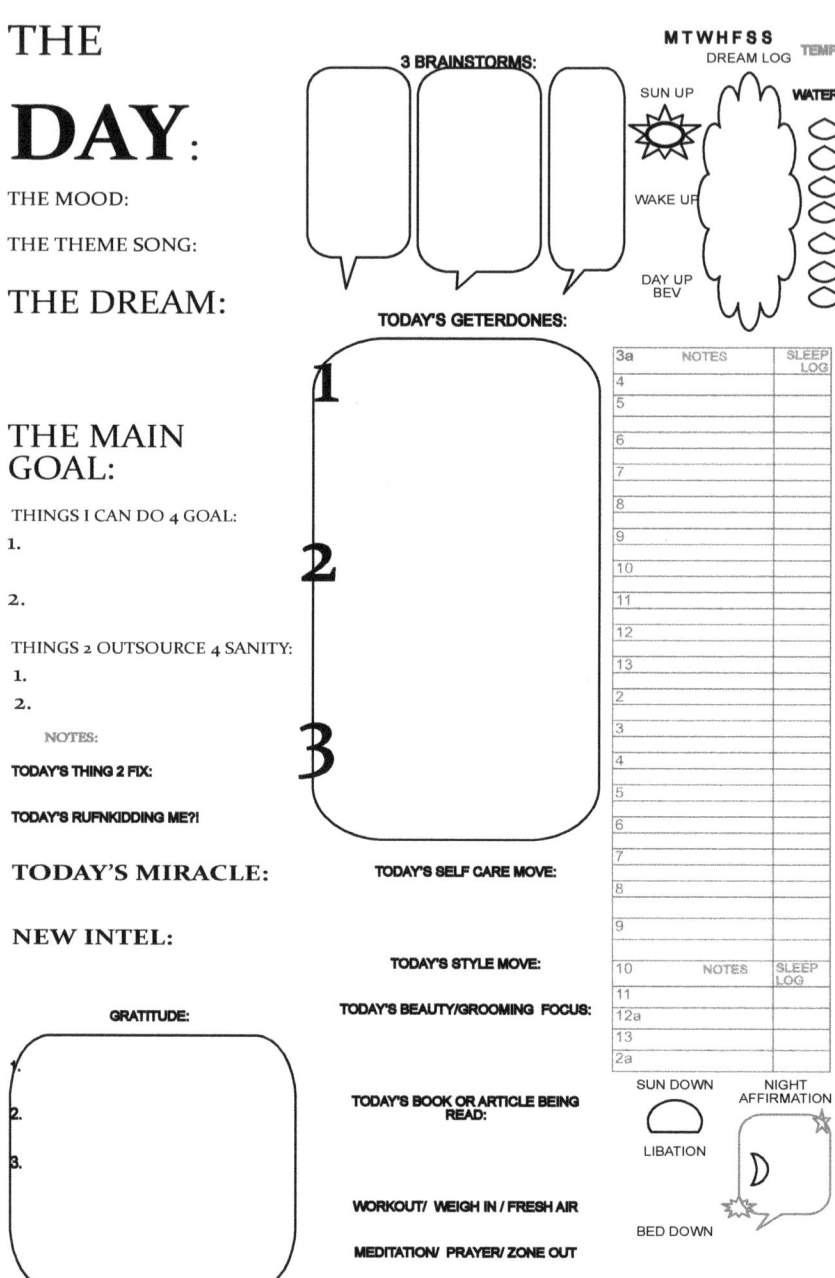

WhataReyouDoing?

THE pregaming:

THE recap:

THE DAY:

THE MOOD:

THE THEME SONG:

THE DREAM:

THE MAIN GOAL:

THINGS I CAN DO 4 GOAL:
1.
2.

THINGS 2 OUTSOURCE 4 SANITY:
1.
2.

NOTES:

TODAY'S THING 2 FIX:

TODAY'S RUFNKIDDING ME?!

TODAY'S MIRACLE:

NEW INTEL:

GRATITUDE:
1.
2.
3.

3 BRAINSTORMS:

TODAY'S GETERDONES:

1.

2.

3.

TODAY'S SELF CARE MOVE:

TODAY'S STYLE MOVE:

TODAY'S BEAUTY/GROOMING FOCUS:

TODAY'S BOOK OR ARTICLE BEING READ:

WORKOUT/ WEIGH IN / FRESH AIR

MEDITATION/ PRAYER/ ZONE OUT

M T W H F S S
DREAM LOG   TEMP

SUN UP
WAKE UP
DAY UP
BEV

WATER

	NOTES	SLEEP LOG
3a		
4		
5		
6		
7		
8		
9		
10		
11		
12		
13		
2		
3		
4		
5		
6		
7		
8		
9		
10	NOTES	SLEEP LOG
11		
12a		
13		
2a		

SUN DOWN

LIBATION

BED DOWN

NIGHT AFFIRMATION

THE
pregaming:

THE recap:

THE DAY:

THE MOOD:

THE THEME SONG:

THE DREAM:

THE MAIN GOAL:

THINGS I CAN DO 4 GOAL:
1.
2.

THINGS 2 OUTSOURCE 4 SANITY:
1.
2.

NOTES:

TODAY'S THING 2 FIX:

TODAY'S RUFNKIDDING ME?!

TODAY'S MIRACLE:

NEW INTEL:

GRATITUDE:
1.
2.
3.

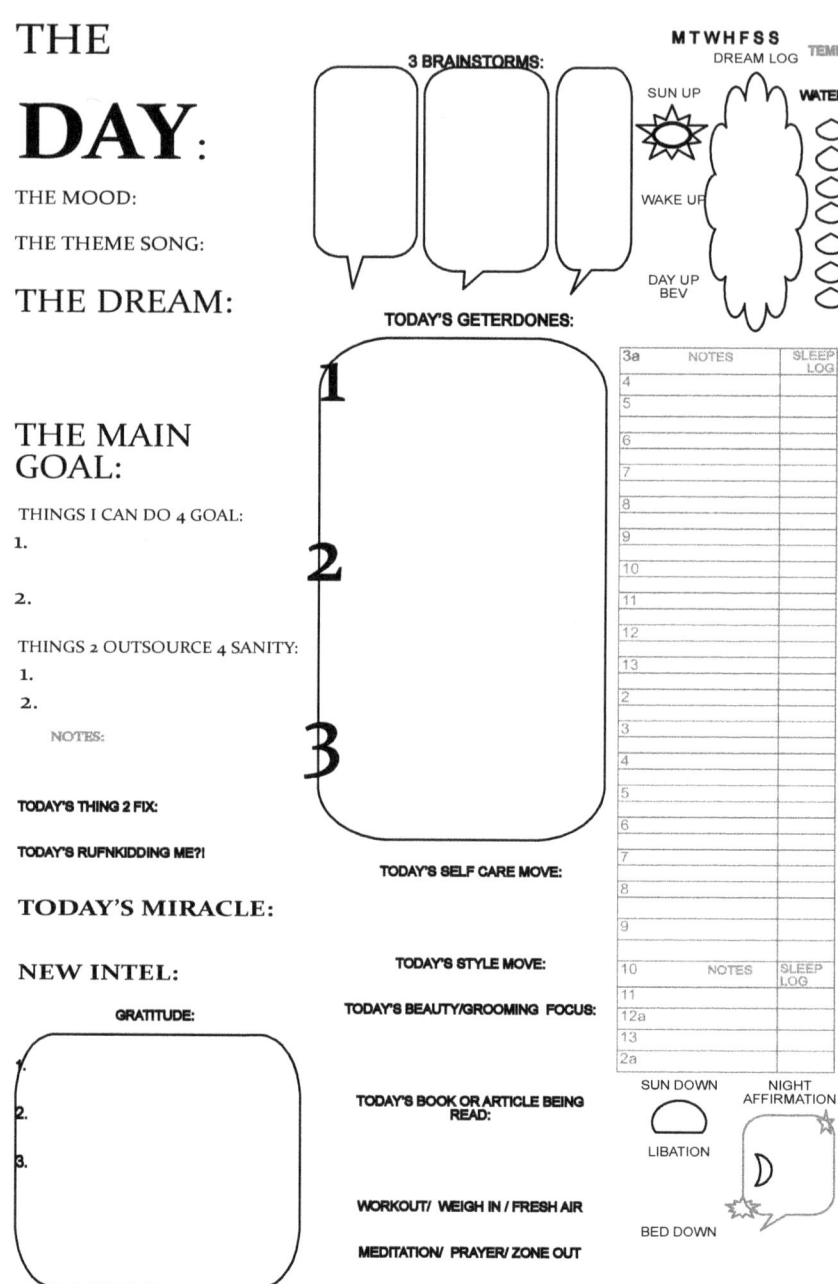

3 BRAINSTORMS:

TODAY'S GETERDONES:
1
2
3

TODAY'S SELF CARE MOVE:

TODAY'S STYLE MOVE:

TODAY'S BEAUTY/GROOMING FOCUS:

TODAY'S BOOK OR ARTICLE BEING READ:

WORKOUT/ WEIGH IN / FRESH AIR

MEDITATION/ PRAYER/ ZONE OUT

M T W H F S S
DREAM LOG   TEMP
SUN UP   WATER
WAKE UP
DAY UP BEV

SUN DOWN   NIGHT AFFIRMATION
LIBATION
BED DOWN

What to Know Beyond Doing?

THE pregaming:

THE recap:

THE DAY:

THE MOOD:

THE THEME SONG:

THE DREAM:

THE MAIN GOAL:

THINGS I CAN DO 4 GOAL:
1.
2.

THINGS 2 OUTSOURCE 4 SANITY:
1.
2.

NOTES:

TODAY'S THING 2 FIX:

TODAY'S RUFNKIDDING ME?!

TODAY'S MIRACLE:

NEW INTEL:

GRATITUDE:
1.
2.
3.

THE
pregaming:

THE recap:

THE
DAY:

THE MOOD:

THE THEME SONG:

THE DREAM:

THE MAIN GOAL:

THINGS I CAN DO 4 GOAL:
1.

2.

THINGS 2 OUTSOURCE 4 SANITY:
1.
2.

NOTES:

TODAY'S THING 2 FIX:

TODAY'S RUFNKIDDING ME?!

TODAY'S MIRACLE:

NEW INTEL:

GRATITUDE:

1.

2.

3.

3 BRAINSTORMS:

TODAY'S GETERDONES:

1

2

3

TODAY'S SELF CARE MOVE:

TODAY'S STYLE MOVE:

TODAY'S BEAUTY/GROOMING FOCUS:

TODAY'S BOOK OR ARTICLE BEING READ:

WORKOUT/ WEIGH IN / FRESH AIR

MEDITATION/ PRAYER/ ZONE OUT

THE
pregaming:

THE recap:

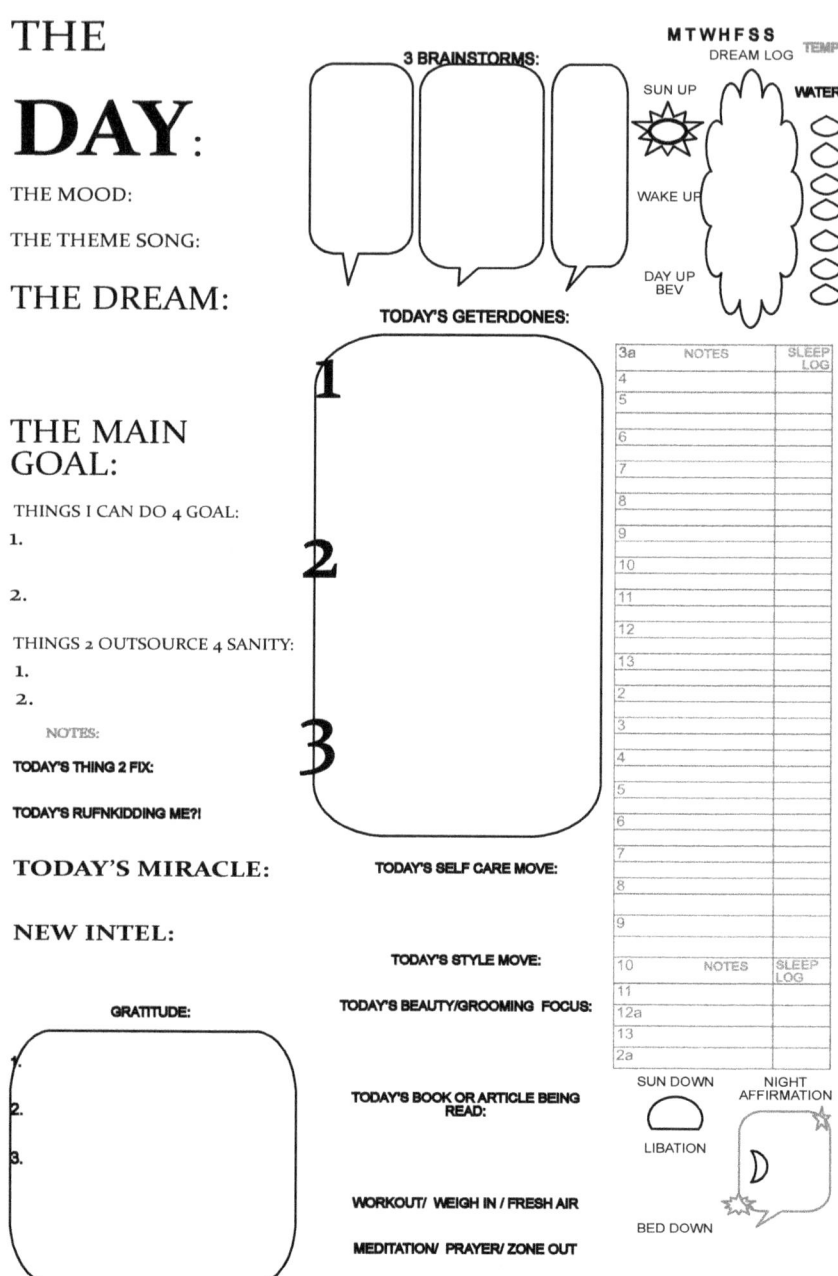

THE pregaming:

THE recap:

THE
DAY:

THE MOOD:

THE THEME SONG:

THE DREAM:

THE MAIN GOAL:

THINGS I CAN DO 4 GOAL:
1.

2.

THINGS 2 OUTSOURCE 4 SANITY:
1.
2.
NOTES:

TODAY'S THING 2 FIX:

TODAY'S RUFNKIDDING ME?!

TODAY'S MIRACLE:

NEW INTEL:

GRATITUDE:

1.

2.

3.

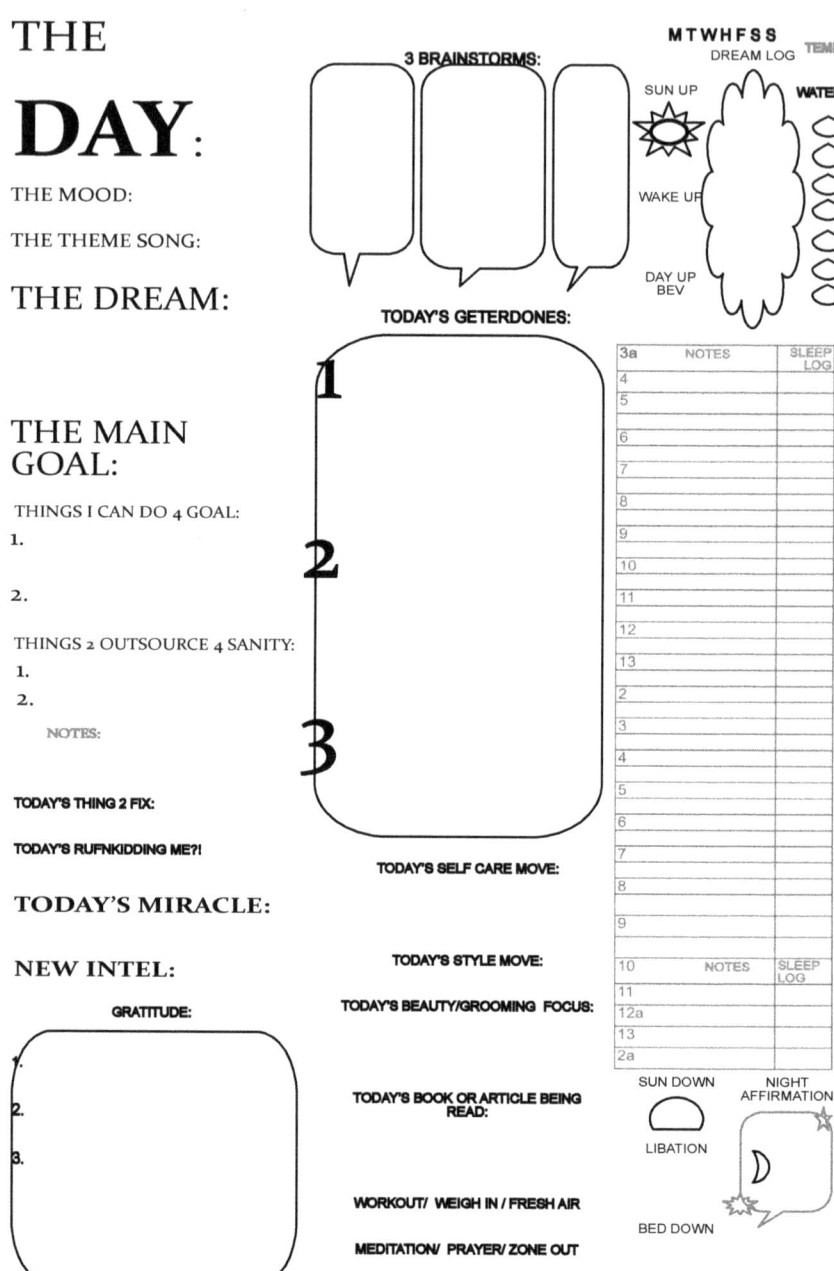

3 BRAINSTORMS:

TODAY'S GETERDONES:

1

2

3

TODAY'S SELF CARE MOVE:

TODAY'S STYLE MOVE:

TODAY'S BEAUTY/GROOMING FOCUS:

TODAY'S BOOK OR ARTICLE BEING READ:

WORKOUT/ WEIGH IN / FRESH AIR

MEDITATION/ PRAYER/ ZONE OUT

M T W H F S S
DREAM LOG   TEMP

SUN UP

WATER

WAKE UP

DAY UP BEV

3a	NOTES	SLEEP LOG
4		
5		
6		
7		
8		
9		
10		
11		
12		
13		
2		
3		
4		
5		
6		
7		
8		
9		
10	NOTES	SLEEP LOG
11		
12a		
13		
2a		

SUN DOWN

LIBATION

NIGHT AFFIRMATION

BED DOWN

THE
pregaming:

THE recap:

THE pregaming:

THE recap:

THE DAY:

THE MOOD:

THE THEME SONG:

THE DREAM:

THE MAIN GOAL:

THINGS I CAN DO 4 GOAL:
1.
2.

THINGS 2 OUTSOURCE 4 SANITY:
1.
2.

NOTES:

TODAY'S THING 2 FIX:

TODAY'S RUFNKIDDING ME?!

TODAY'S MIRACLE:

NEW INTEL:

GRATITUDE:
1.
2.
3.

3 BRAINSTORMS:

TODAY'S GETERDONES:
1
2
3

TODAY'S SELF CARE MOVE:

TODAY'S STYLE MOVE:

TODAY'S BEAUTY/GROOMING FOCUS:

TODAY'S BOOK OR ARTICLE BEING READ:

WORKOUT/ WEIGH IN / FRESH AIR

MEDITATION/ PRAYER/ ZONE OUT

M T W H F S S
DREAM LOG — TEMP

SUN UP
WAKE UP
DAY UP
BEV

WATER

3a	NOTES	SLEEP LOG
4		
5		
6		
7		
8		
9		
10		
11		
12		
13		
2		
3		
4		
5		
6		
7		
8		
9		
10	NOTES	SLEEP LOG
11		
12a		
13		
2a		

SUN DOWN
LIBATION

NIGHT AFFIRMATION

BED DOWN

THE
pregaming:

THE recap:

THE DAY:

THE MOOD:

THE THEME SONG:

THE DREAM:

THE MAIN GOAL:

THINGS I CAN DO 4 GOAL:
1.
2.

THINGS 2 OUTSOURCE 4 SANITY:
1.
2.

NOTES:

TODAY'S THING 2 FIX:

TODAY'S RUFNKIDDING ME?!

TODAY'S MIRACLE:

NEW INTEL:

GRATITUDE:
1.
2.
3.

3 BRAINSTORMS:

TODAY'S GETERDONES:
1
2
3

TODAY'S SELF CARE MOVE:

TODAY'S STYLE MOVE:

TODAY'S BEAUTY/GROOMING FOCUS:

TODAY'S BOOK OR ARTICLE BEING READ:

WORKOUT/ WEIGH IN / FRESH AIR

MEDITATION/ PRAYER/ ZONE OUT

M T W H F S S
DREAM LOG   TEMP
SUN UP   WATER
WAKE UP
DAY UP BEV

	NOTES	SLEEP LOG
3a		
4		
5		
6		
7		
8		
9		
10		
11		
12		
13		
2		
3		
4		
5		
6		
7		
8		
9		
10	NOTES	SLEEP LOG
11		
12a		
13		
2a		

SUN DOWN   NIGHT AFFIRMATION
LIBATION
BED DOWN

THE
pregaming:

THE recap:

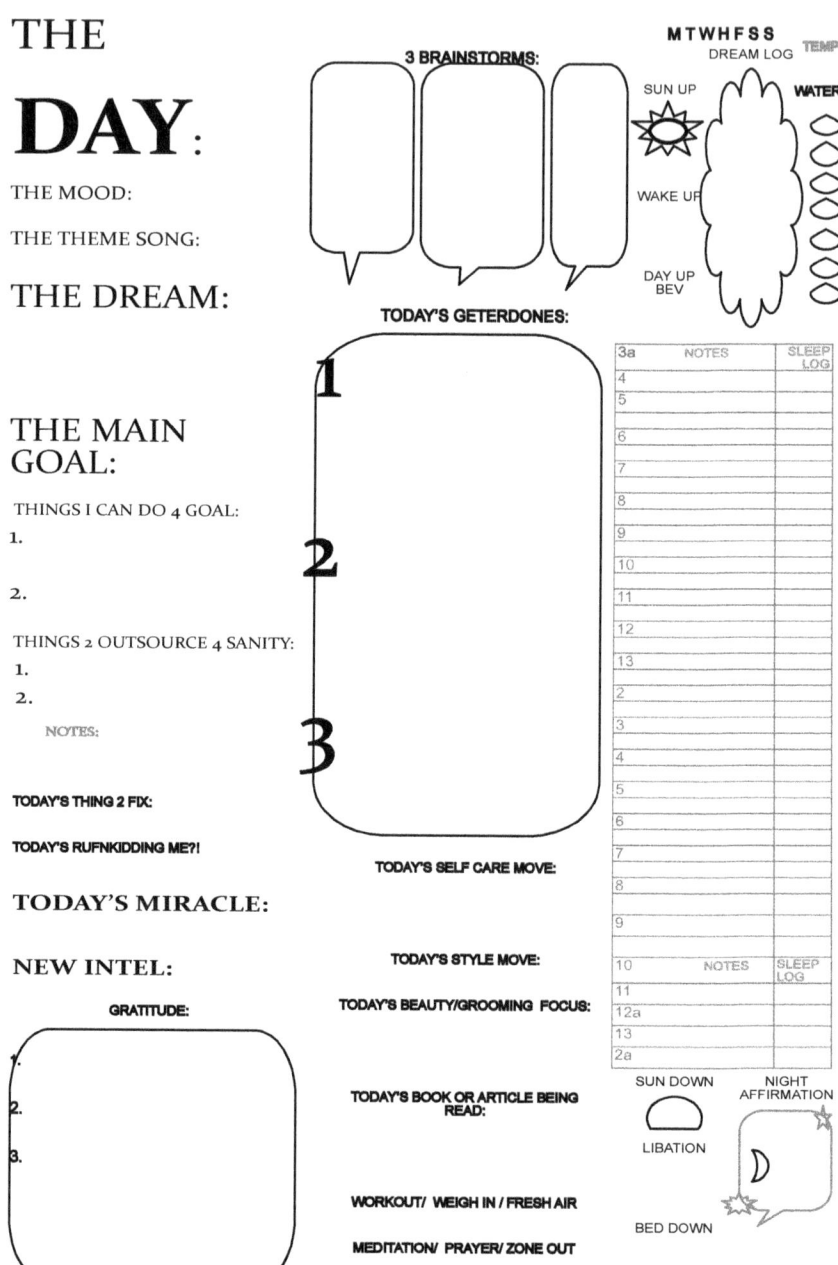

THE
pregaming:

THE recap:

THE
DAY:

THE MOOD:

THE THEME SONG:

THE DREAM:

THE MAIN GOAL:

THINGS I CAN DO 4 GOAL:
1.
2.

THINGS 2 OUTSOURCE 4 SANITY:
1.
2.

NOTES:

TODAY'S THING 2 FIX:

TODAY'S RUFNKIDDING ME?!

TODAY'S MIRACLE:

NEW INTEL:

GRATITUDE:
1.
2.
3.

3 BRAINSTORMS:

TODAY'S GETERDONES:

1
2
3

TODAY'S SELF CARE MOVE:

TODAY'S STYLE MOVE:

TODAY'S BEAUTY/GROOMING FOCUS:

TODAY'S BOOK OR ARTICLE BEING READ:

WORKOUT/ WEIGH IN / FRESH AIR

MEDITATION/ PRAYER/ ZONE OUT

THE pregaming:

THE recap:

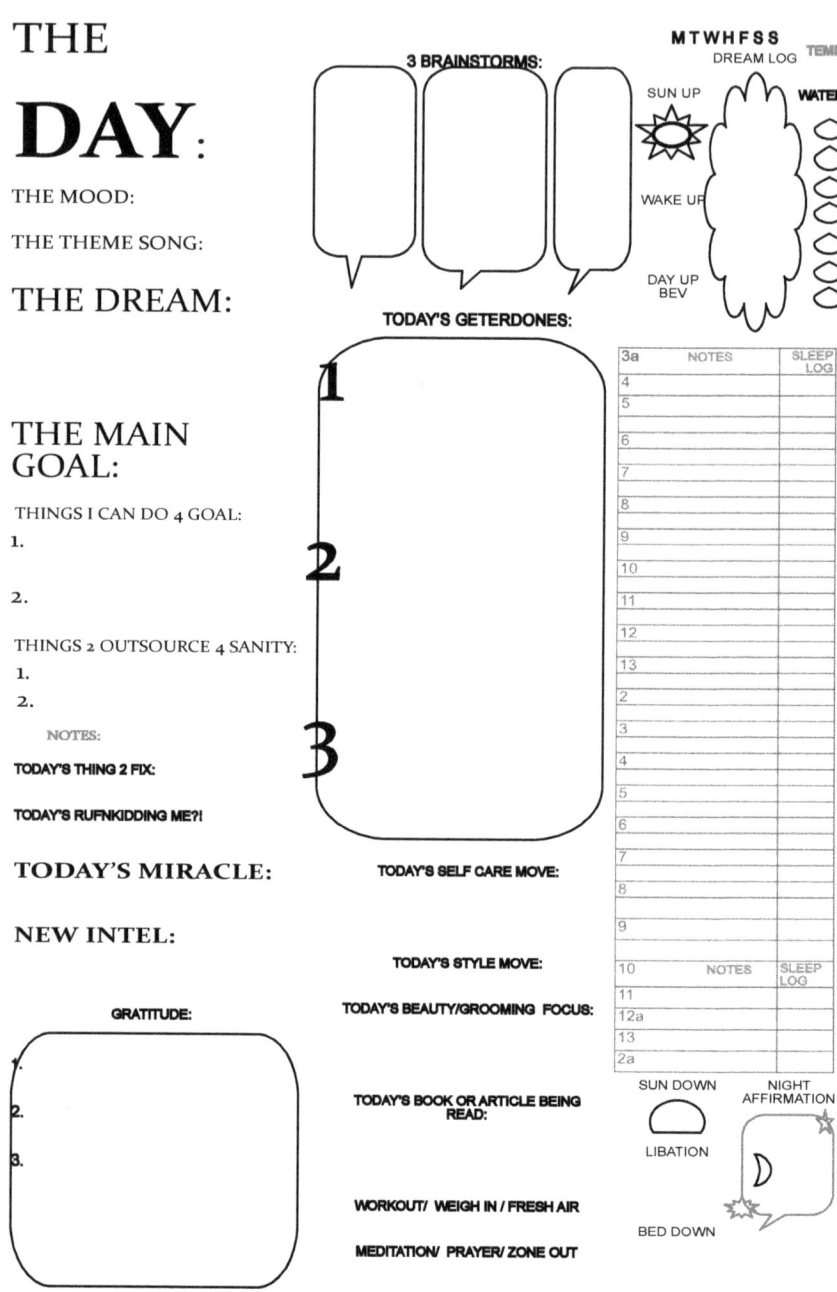

THE pregaming:

THE recap:

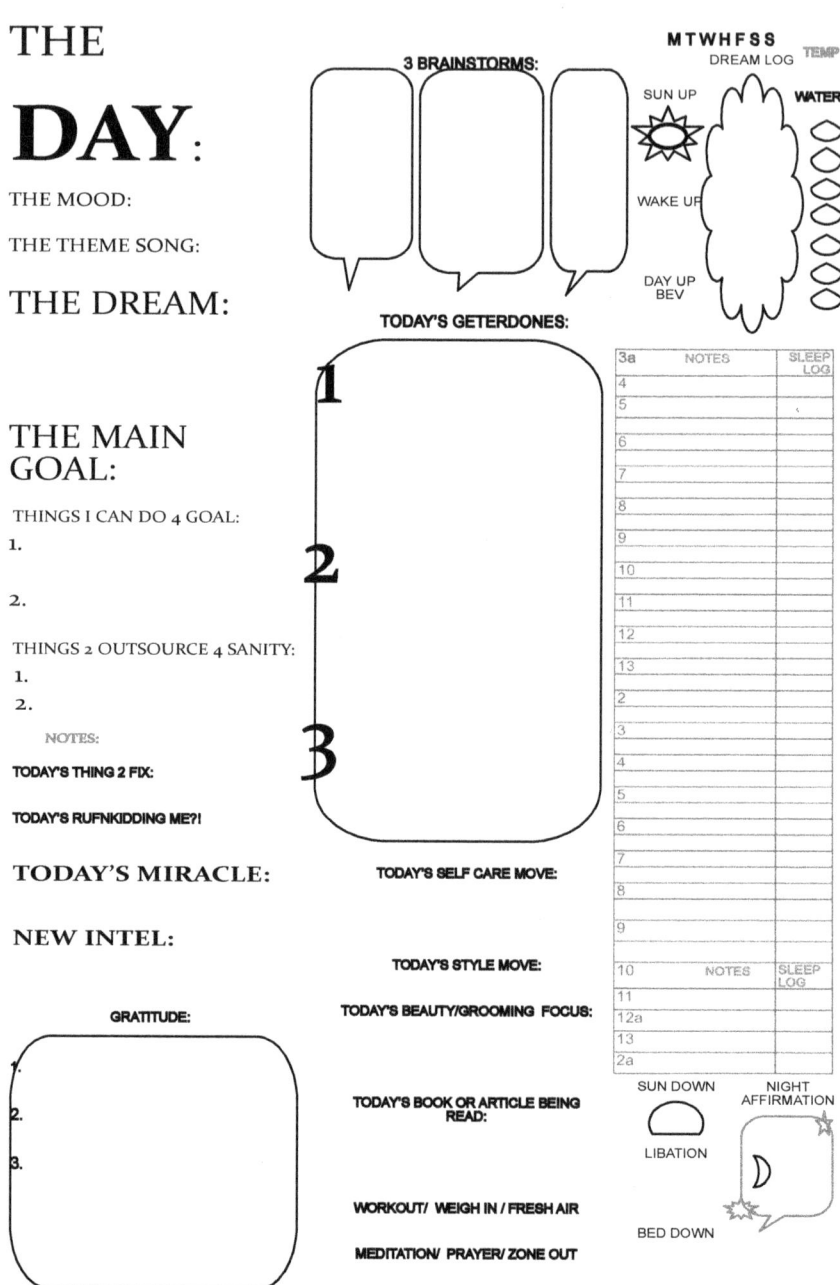

THE pregaming:

THE recap:

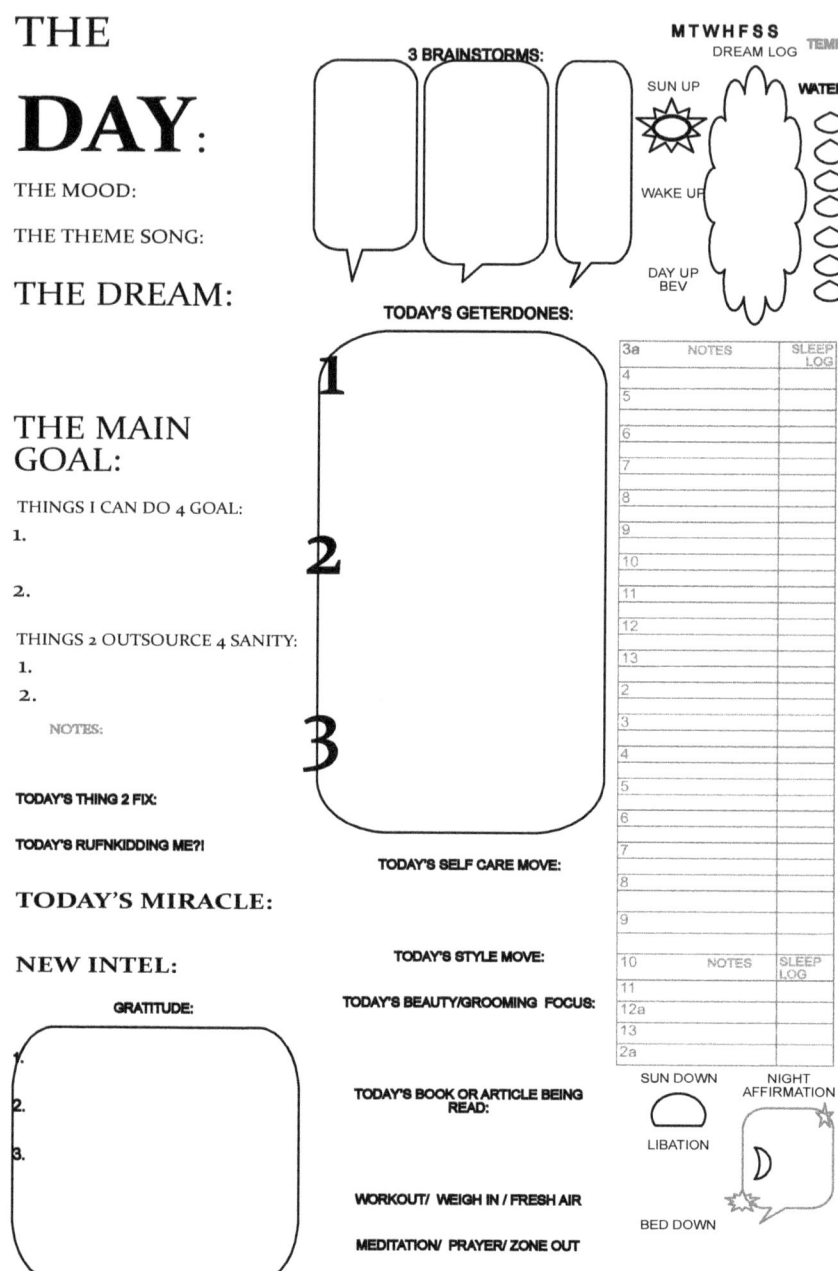

THE pregaming:

THE recap:

THE DAY:

THE MOOD:

THE THEME SONG:

THE DREAM:

THE MAIN GOAL:

THINGS I CAN DO 4 GOAL:
1.
2.

THINGS 2 OUTSOURCE 4 SANITY:
1.
2.

NOTES:

TODAY'S THING 2 FIX:

TODAY'S RUFNKIDDING ME?!

TODAY'S MIRACLE:

NEW INTEL:

GRATITUDE:
1.
2.
3.

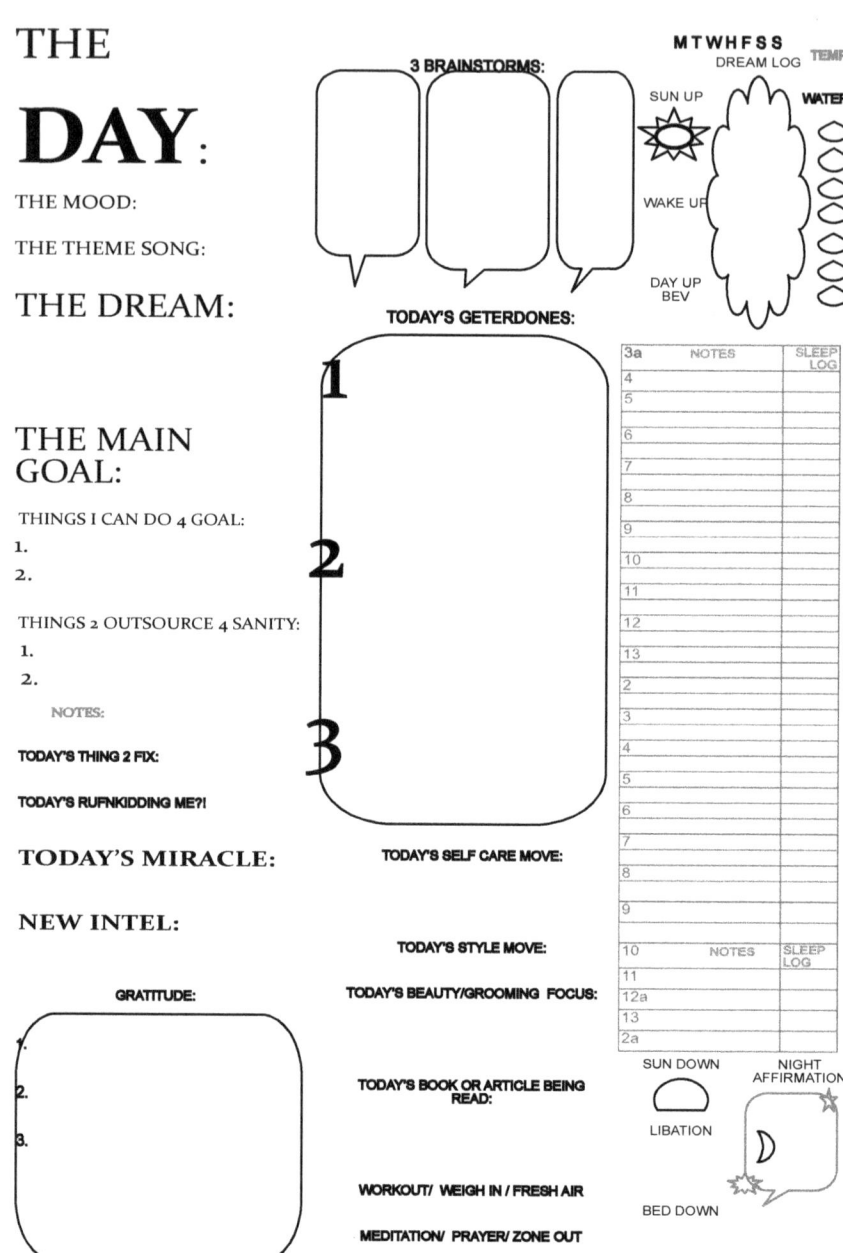

3 BRAINSTORMS:

TODAY'S GETERDONES:
1
2
3

TODAY'S SELF CARE MOVE:

TODAY'S STYLE MOVE:

TODAY'S BEAUTY/GROOMING FOCUS:

TODAY'S BOOK OR ARTICLE BEING READ:

WORKOUT/ WEIGH IN / FRESH AIR

MEDITATION/ PRAYER/ ZONE OUT

M T W H F S S
DREAM LOG   TEMP

SUN UP
WAKE UP
DAY UP BEV

WATER

NOTES | SLEEP LOG
3a
4
5
6
7
8
9
10
11
12
13
2
3
4
5
6
7
8
9
10 NOTES | SLEEP LOG
11
12a
13
2a

SUN DOWN
LIBATION
BED DOWN

NIGHT AFFIRMATION

THE
pregaming:

THE recap:

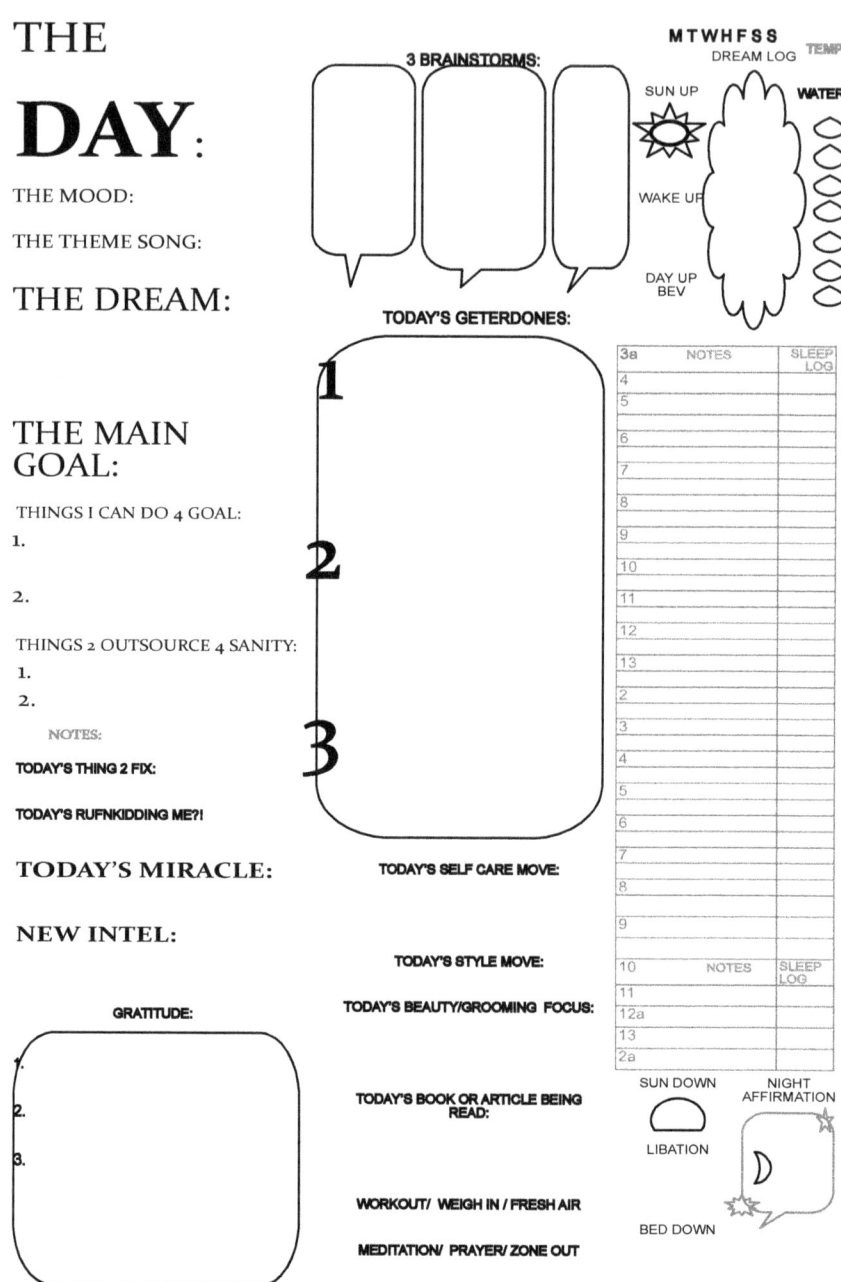

THE
pregaming:

THE recap:

THE DAY:

THE MOOD:

THE THEME SONG:

THE DREAM:

THE MAIN GOAL:

THINGS I CAN DO 4 GOAL:
1.
2.

THINGS 2 OUTSOURCE 4 SANITY:
1.
2.

NOTES:

TODAY'S THING 2 FIX:

TODAY'S RUFNKIDDING ME?!

TODAY'S MIRACLE:

NEW INTEL:

GRATITUDE:
1.
2.
3.

3 BRAINSTORMS:

TODAY'S GETERDONES:
1
2
3

TODAY'S SELF CARE MOVE:

TODAY'S STYLE MOVE:

TODAY'S BEAUTY/GROOMING FOCUS:

TODAY'S BOOK OR ARTICLE BEING READ:

WORKOUT/ WEIGH IN / FRESH AIR

MEDITATION/ PRAYER/ ZONE OUT

M T W H F S S

DREAM LOG   TEMP

SUN UP

WAKE UP

DAY UP BEV

WATER

3a	NOTES	SLEEP LOG
4		
5		
6		
7		
8		
9		
10		
11		
12		
13		
2		
3		
4		
5		
6		
7		
8		
9		
10	NOTES	SLEEP LOG
11		
12a		
13		
2a		

SUN DOWN

LIBATION

BED DOWN

NIGHT AFFIRMATION

THE pregaming:

THE recap:

THE
DAY:

THE MOOD:

THE THEME SONG:

THE DREAM:

THE MAIN GOAL:

THINGS I CAN DO 4 GOAL:
1.
2.

THINGS 2 OUTSOURCE 4 SANITY:
1.
2.

NOTES:

TODAY'S THING 2 FIX:

TODAY'S RUFNKIDDING ME?!

TODAY'S MIRACLE:

NEW INTEL:

GRATITUDE:
1.
2.
3.

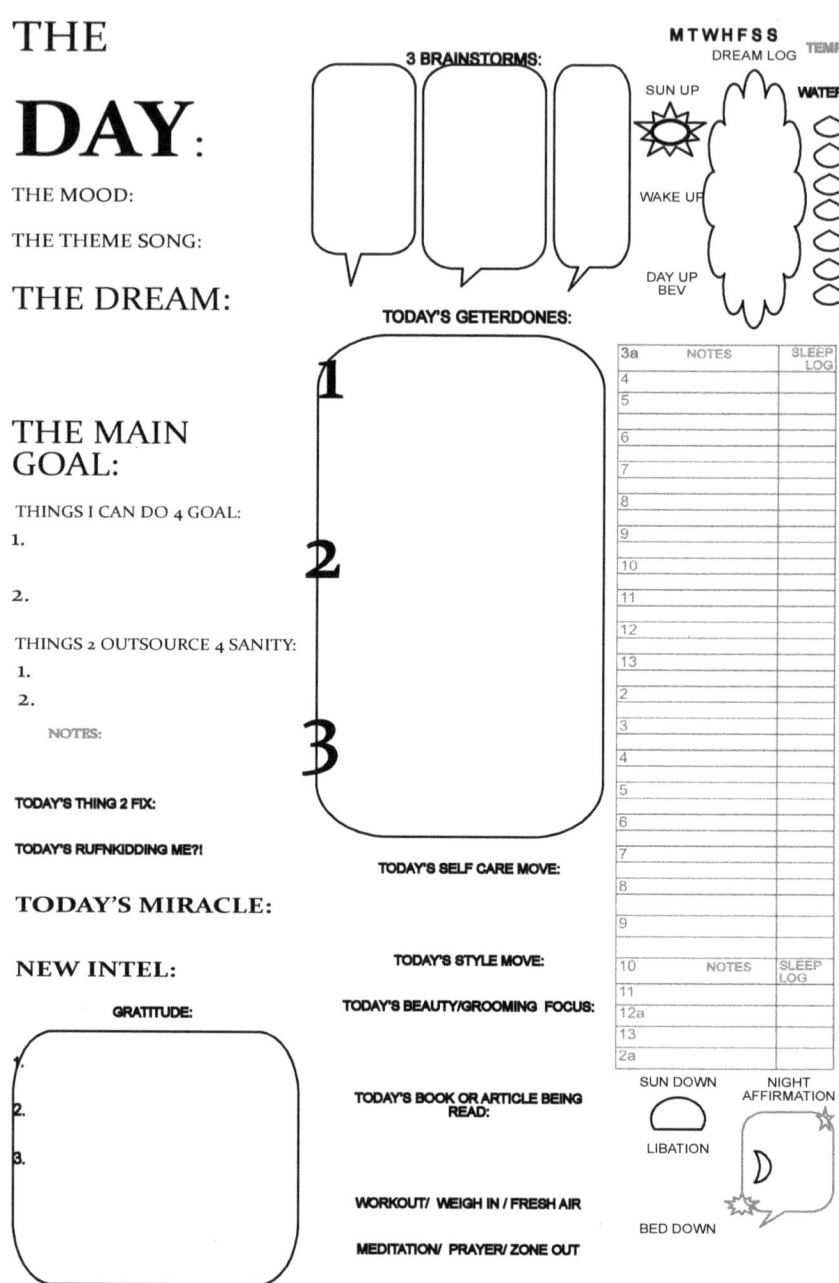

3 BRAINSTORMS:

TODAY'S GETERDONES:
1.
2.
3.

TODAY'S SELF CARE MOVE:

TODAY'S STYLE MOVE:

TODAY'S BEAUTY/GROOMING FOCUS:

TODAY'S BOOK OR ARTICLE BEING READ:

WORKOUT/ WEIGH IN / FRESH AIR

MEDITATION/ PRAYER/ ZONE OUT

M T W H F S S
DREAM LOG TEMP

SUN UP WATER

WAKE UP

DAY UP BEV

3a NOTES SLEEP LOG
4
5
6
7
8
9
10
11
12
13
2
3
4
5
6
7
8
9
10 NOTES SLEEP LOG
11
12a
13
2a

SUN DOWN NIGHT AFFIRMATION

LIBATION

BED DOWN

THE
pregaming:

THE recap:

THE DAY:

THE MOOD:

THE THEME SONG:

THE DREAM:

THE MAIN GOAL:

THINGS I CAN DO 4 GOAL:
1.
2.

THINGS 2 OUTSOURCE 4 SANITY:
1.
2.

NOTES:

TODAY'S THING 2 FIX:

TODAY'S RUFNKIDDING ME?!

TODAY'S MIRACLE:

NEW INTEL:

GRATITUDE:
1.
2.
3.

3 BRAINSTORMS:

TODAY'S GETERDONES:
1
2
3

TODAY'S SELF CARE MOVE:

TODAY'S STYLE MOVE:

TODAY'S BEAUTY/GROOMING FOCUS:

TODAY'S BOOK OR ARTICLE BEING READ:

WORKOUT/ WEIGH IN / FRESH AIR

MEDITATION/ PRAYER/ ZONE OUT

M T W H F S S
DREAM LOG   TEMP

SUN UP   WATER

WAKE UP

DAY UP BEV

	NOTES	SLEEP LOG
3a		
4		
5		
6		
7		
8		
9		
10		
11		
12		
13		
2		
3		
4		
5		
6		
7		
8		
9		
10	NOTES	SLEEP LOG
11		
12a		
13		
2a		

SUN DOWN

LIBATION

BED DOWN

NIGHT AFFIRMATION

THE
pregaming:

THE recap:

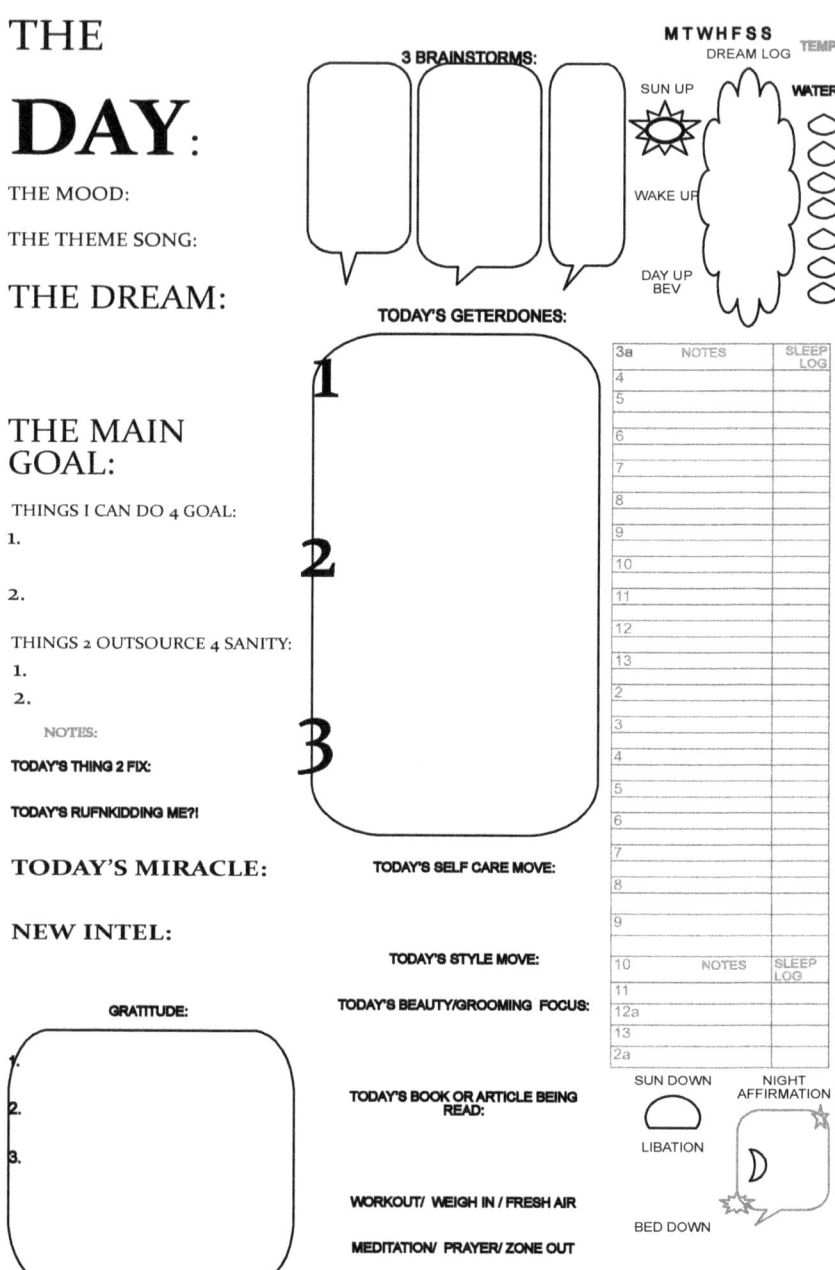

THE
pregaming:

THE recap:

THE
pregaming:

THE recap:

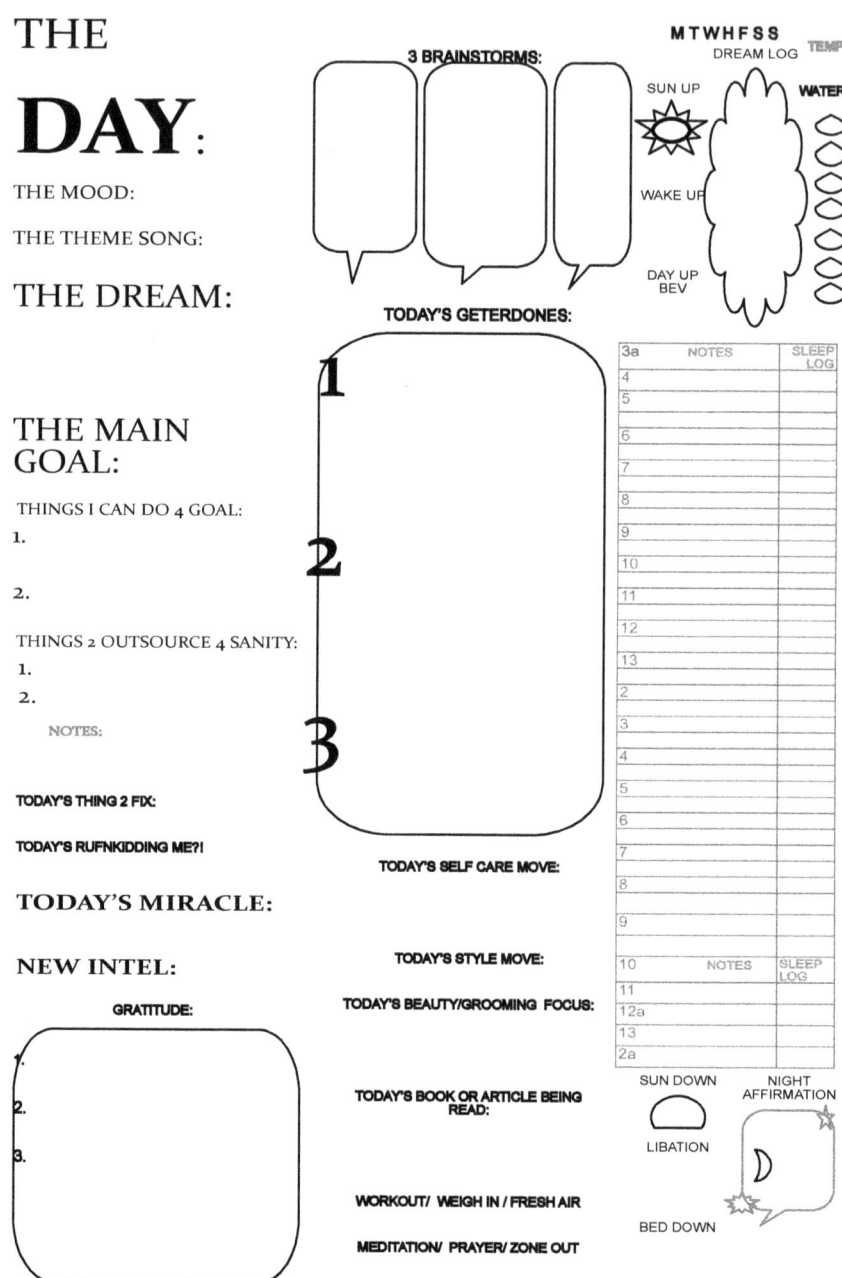

THE
pregaming:

THE recap:

THE DAY:

THE MOOD:

THE THEME SONG:

THE DREAM:

THE MAIN GOAL:

THINGS I CAN DO 4 GOAL:
1.
2.

THINGS 2 OUTSOURCE 4 SANITY:
1.
2.

   NOTES:

TODAY'S THING 2 FIX:

TODAY'S RUFNKIDDING ME?!

TODAY'S MIRACLE:

NEW INTEL:

GRATITUDE:
1.
2.
3.

3 BRAINSTORMS:

TODAY'S GETERDONES:
1
2
3

TODAY'S SELF CARE MOVE:

TODAY'S STYLE MOVE:

TODAY'S BEAUTY/GROOMING FOCUS:

TODAY'S BOOK OR ARTICLE BEING READ:

WORKOUT/ WEIGH IN / FRESH AIR

MEDITATION/ PRAYER/ ZONE OUT

M T W H F S S
DREAM LOG   TEMP

SUN UP   WATER

WAKE UP

DAY UP BEV

3a	NOTES	SLEEP LOG
4		
5		
6		
7		
8		
9		
10		
11		
12		
13		
2		
3		
4		
5		
6		
7		
8		
9		
10	NOTES	SLEEP LOG
11		
12a		
13		
2a		

SUN DOWN   NIGHT AFFIRMATION

LIBATION

BED DOWN

THE pregaming:

THE recap:

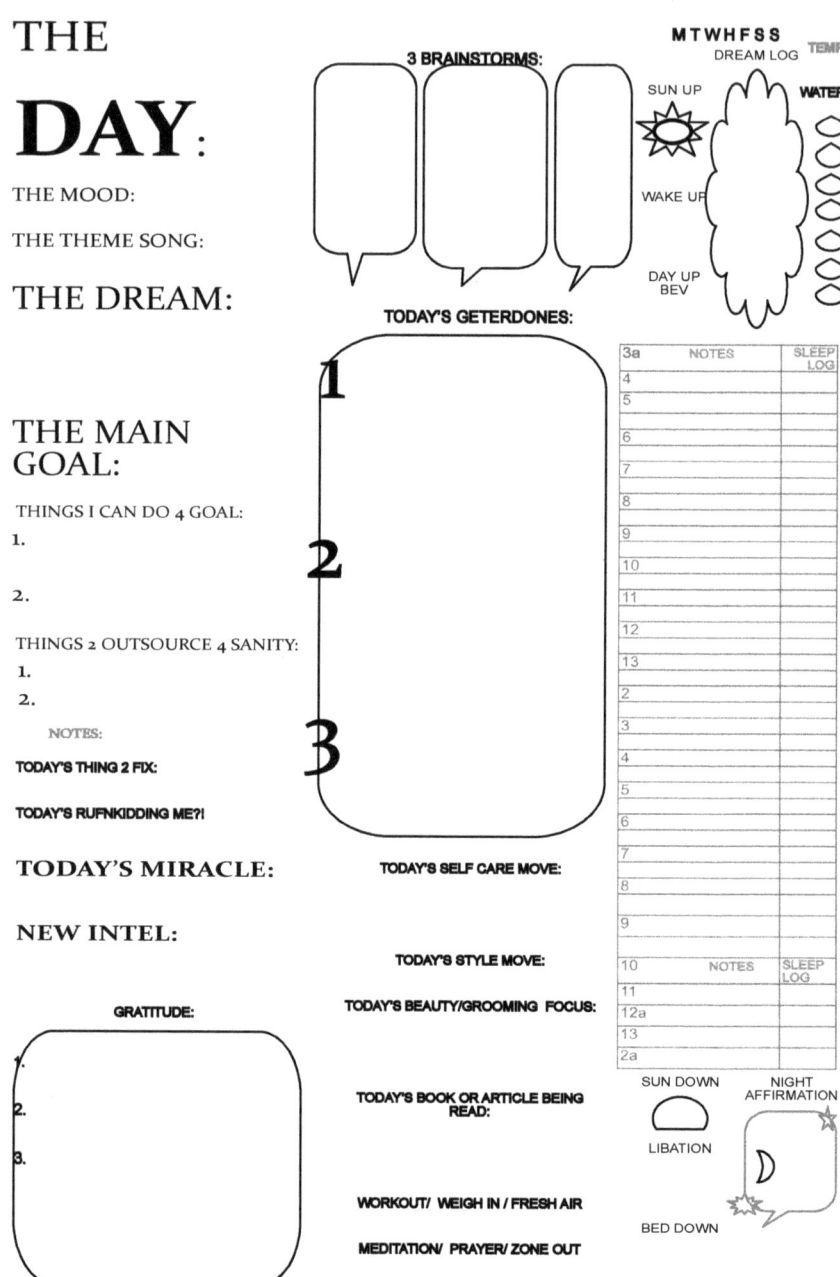

THE
pregaming:

THE recap:

THE
DAY:

THE MOOD:

THE THEME SONG:

THE DREAM:

THE MAIN GOAL:

THINGS I CAN DO 4 GOAL:
1.

2.

THINGS 2 OUTSOURCE 4 SANITY:
1.
2.

NOTES:

TODAY'S THING 2 FIX:

TODAY'S RUFNKIDDING ME?!

TODAY'S MIRACLE:

NEW INTEL:

GRATITUDE:

1.

2.

3.

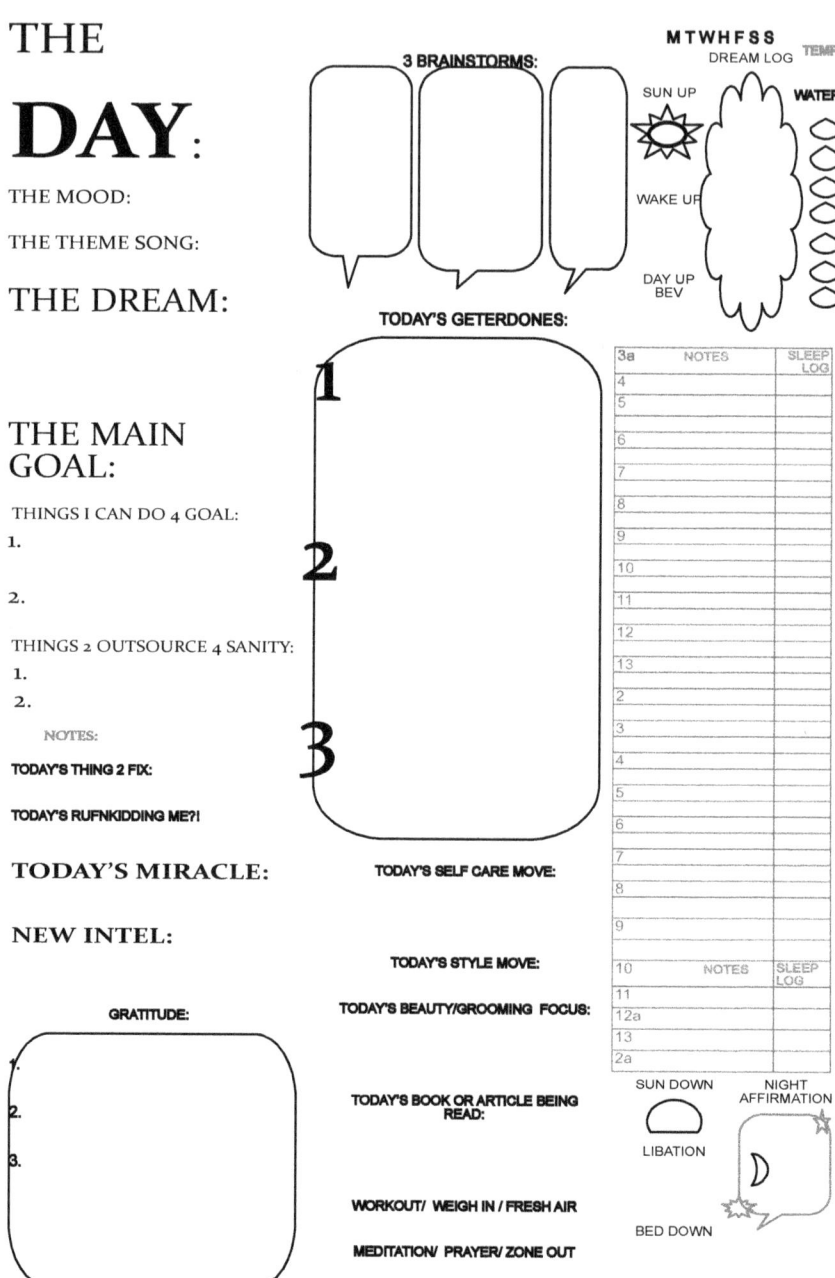

3 BRAINSTORMS:

TODAY'S GETERDONES:

1

2

3

TODAY'S SELF CARE MOVE:

TODAY'S STYLE MOVE:

TODAY'S BEAUTY/GROOMING FOCUS:

TODAY'S BOOK OR ARTICLE BEING READ:

WORKOUT/ WEIGH IN / FRESH AIR

MEDITATION/ PRAYER/ ZONE OUT

M T W H F S S
DREAM LOG   TEMP

SUN UP

WATER

WAKE UP

DAY UP BEV

SUN DOWN

LIBATION

BED DOWN

NIGHT AFFIRMATION

THE
pregaming:

THE recap:

THE
DAY:

THE MOOD:

THE THEME SONG:

THE DREAM:

THE MAIN GOAL:

THINGS I CAN DO 4 GOAL:
1.

2.

THINGS 2 OUTSOURCE 4 SANITY:
1.
2.
   NOTES:

TODAY'S THING 2 FIX:

TODAY'S RUFNKIDDING ME?!

TODAY'S MIRACLE:

NEW INTEL:

GRATITUDE:
1.
2.
3.

3 BRAINSTORMS:

TODAY'S GETERDONES:
1
2
3

TODAY'S SELF CARE MOVE:

TODAY'S STYLE MOVE:

TODAY'S BEAUTY/GROOMING FOCUS:

TODAY'S BOOK OR ARTICLE BEING READ:

WORKOUT/ WEIGH IN / FRESH AIR

MEDITATION/ PRAYER/ ZONE OUT

M T W H F S S
DREAM LOG   TEMP

SUN UP   WATER

WAKE UP

DAY UP BEV

NOTES | SLEEP LOG
3a
4
5
6
7
8
9
10
11
12
13
2
3
4
5
6
7
8
9
10   NOTES | SLEEP LOG
11
12a
13
2a

SUN DOWN   NIGHT AFFIRMATION

LIBATION

BED DOWN

THE
pregaming:

THE recap:

THE
DAY:

THE MOOD:

THE THEME SONG:

THE DREAM:

THE MAIN GOAL:

THINGS I CAN DO 4 GOAL:
1.
2.

THINGS 2 OUTSOURCE 4 SANITY:
1.
2.

NOTES:

TODAY'S THING 2 FIX:

TODAY'S RUFNKIDDING ME?!

TODAY'S MIRACLE:

NEW INTEL:

GRATITUDE:
1.
2.
3.

3 BRAINSTORMS:

TODAY'S GETERDONES:
1.
2.
3.

TODAY'S SELF CARE MOVE:

TODAY'S STYLE MOVE:

TODAY'S BEAUTY/GROOMING FOCUS:

TODAY'S BOOK OR ARTICLE BEING READ:

WORKOUT/ WEIGH IN / FRESH AIR

MEDITATION/ PRAYER/ ZONE OUT

THE
pregaming:

THE recap:

THE DAY:

THE MOOD:

THE THEME SONG:

THE DREAM:

THE MAIN GOAL:

THINGS I CAN DO 4 GOAL:
1.
2.

THINGS 2 OUTSOURCE 4 SANITY:
1.
2.

NOTES:

TODAY'S THING 2 FIX:

TODAY'S RUFNKIDDING ME?!

TODAY'S MIRACLE:

NEW INTEL:

GRATITUDE:
1.
2.
3.

3 BRAINSTORMS:

TODAY'S GETERDONES:
1
2
3

TODAY'S SELF CARE MOVE:

TODAY'S STYLE MOVE:

TODAY'S BEAUTY/GROOMING FOCUS:

TODAY'S BOOK OR ARTICLE BEING READ:

WORKOUT/ WEIGH IN / FRESH AIR

MEDITATION/ PRAYER/ ZONE OUT

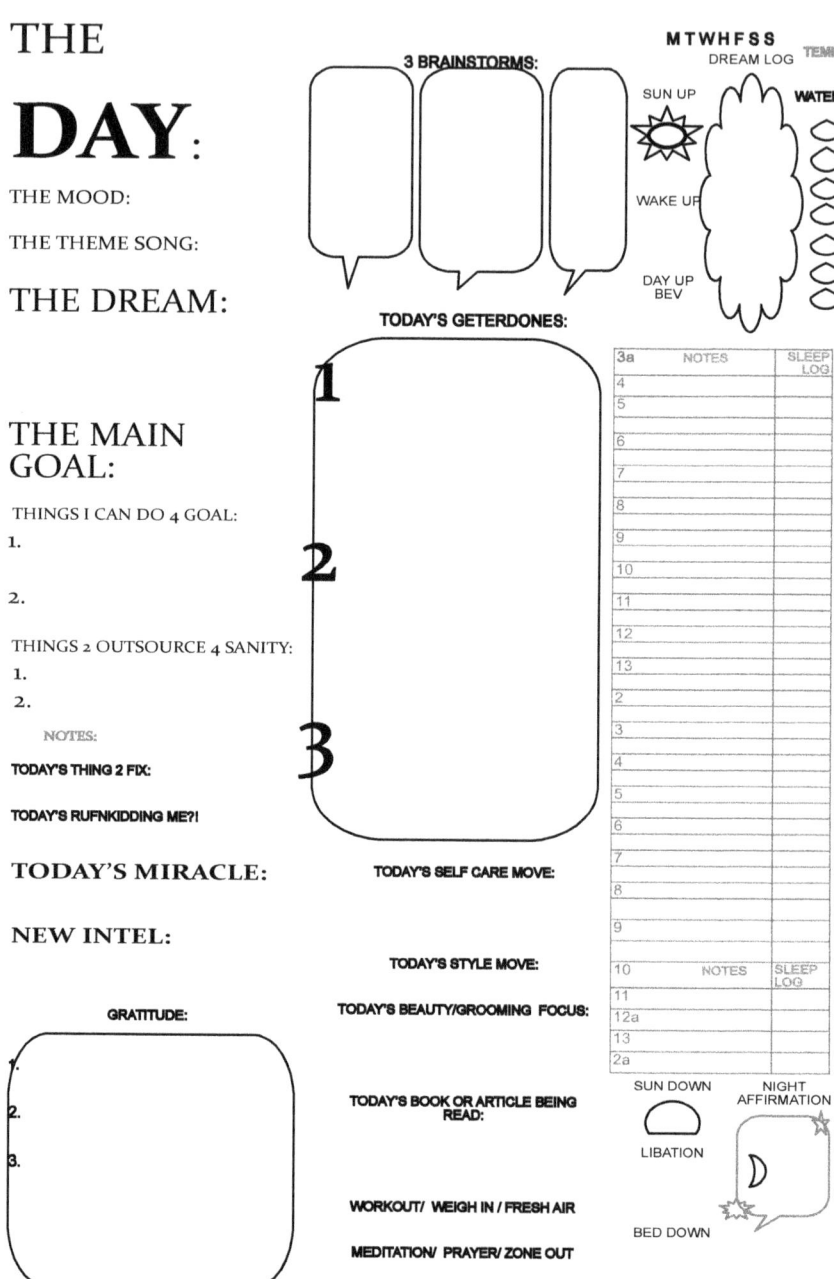

M T W H F S S
DREAM LOG   TEMP
SUN UP   WATER
WAKE UP
DAY UP BEV

3a	NOTES	SLEEP LOG
4		
5		
6		
7		
8		
9		
10		
11		
12		
13		
2		
3		
4		
5		
6		
7		
8		
9		
10	NOTES	SLEEP LOG
11		
12a		
13		
2a		

SUN DOWN
LIBATION

NIGHT AFFIRMATION

BED DOWN

THE pregaming:

THE recap:

THE pregaming:

THE recap:

THE DAY:

THE MOOD:

THE THEME SONG:

THE DREAM:

THE MAIN GOAL:

THINGS I CAN DO 4 GOAL:
1.
2.

THINGS 2 OUTSOURCE 4 SANITY:
1.
2.
   NOTES:

TODAY'S THING 2 FIX:

TODAY'S RUFNKIDDING ME?!

TODAY'S MIRCALE:

NEW INTEL:

GRATITUDE:
1.
2.
3.

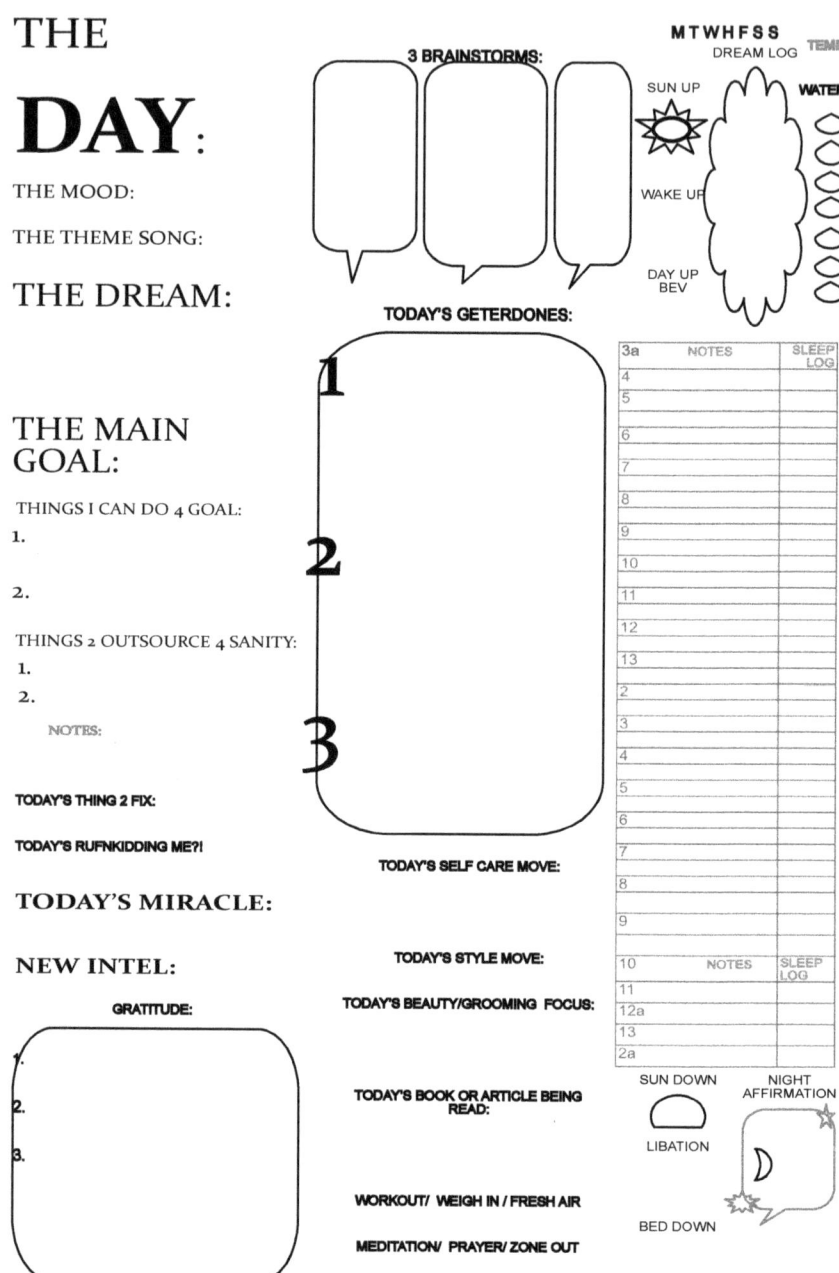

3 BRAINSTORMS:

TODAY'S GETERDONES:
1
2
3

TODAY'S SELF CARE MOVE:

TODAY'S STYLE MOVE:

TODAY'S BEAUTY/GROOMING FOCUS:

TODAY'S BOOK OR ARTICLE BEING READ:

WORKOUT/ WEIGH IN / FRESH AIR

MEDITATION/ PRAYER/ ZONE OUT

M T W H F S S
DREAM LOG TEMP

SUN UP
WAKE UP
DAY UP BEV

WATER

NOTES | SLEEP LOG
3a
4
5
6
7
8
9
10
11
12
13
2
3
4
5
6
7
8
9
10 NOTES SLEEP LOG
11
12a
13
2a

SUN DOWN
LIBATION
BED DOWN

NIGHT AFFIRMATION

THE
pregaming:

THE recap:

THE DAY:

THE MOOD:

THE THEME SONG:

THE DREAM:

THE MAIN GOAL:

THINGS I CAN DO 4 GOAL:
1.
2.

THINGS 2 OUTSOURCE 4 SANITY:
1.
2.

NOTES:

TODAY'S THING 2 FIX:

TODAY'S RUFNKIDDING ME?!

TODAY'S MIRACLE:

NEW INTEL:

GRATITUDE:
1.
2.
3.

THE
pregaming:

THE recap:

THE
pregaming:

THE recap:

THE DAY:

THE MOOD:

THE THEME SONG:

THE DREAM:

THE MAIN GOAL:

THINGS I CAN DO 4 GOAL:
1.
2.

THINGS 2 OUTSOURCE 4 SANITY:
1.
2.

NOTES:

TODAY'S THING 2 FIX:

TODAY'S RUFNKIDDING ME?!

TODAY'S MIRACLE:

NEW INTEL:

GRATITUDE:
1.
2.
3.

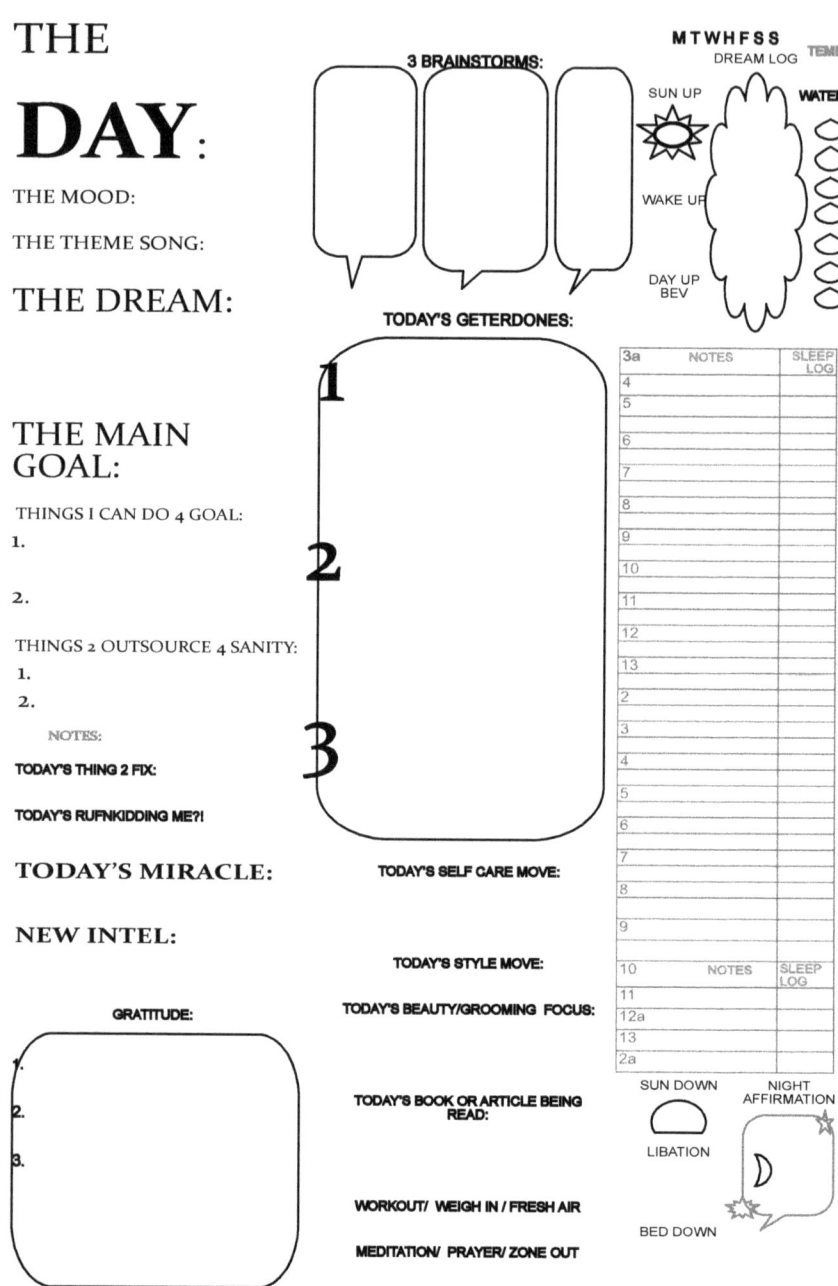

3 BRAINSTORMS:

TODAY'S GETERDONES:
1
2
3

TODAY'S SELF CARE MOVE:

TODAY'S STYLE MOVE:

TODAY'S BEAUTY/GROOMING FOCUS:

TODAY'S BOOK OR ARTICLE BEING READ:

WORKOUT/ WEIGH IN / FRESH AIR

MEDITATION/ PRAYER/ ZONE OUT

M T W H F S S
DREAM LOG   TEMP
SUN UP   WATER
WAKE UP
DAY UP BEV

3a	NOTES	SLEEP LOG
4		
5		
6		
7		
8		
9		
10		
11		
12		
13		
2		
3		
4		
5		
6		
7		
8		
9		
10	NOTES	SLEEP LOG
11		
12a		
13		
2a		

SUN DOWN   NIGHT AFFIRMATION

LIBATION

BED DOWN

THE
pregaming:

THE recap:

THE
DAY:

THE MOOD:

THE THEME SONG:

THE DREAM:

THE MAIN GOAL:

THINGS I CAN DO 4 GOAL:
1.
2.

THINGS 2 OUTSOURCE 4 SANITY:
1.
2.

NOTES:

TODAY'S THING 2 FIX:

TODAY'S RUFNKIDDING ME?!

TODAY'S MIRACLE:

NEW INTEL:

GRATITUDE:
1.
2.
3.

3 BRAINSTORMS:

TODAY'S GETERDONES:
1
2
3

TODAY'S SELF CARE MOVE:

TODAY'S STYLE MOVE:

TODAY'S BEAUTY/GROOMING FOCUS:

TODAY'S BOOK OR ARTICLE BEING READ:

WORKOUT/ WEIGH IN / FRESH AIR

MEDITATION/ PRAYER/ ZONE OUT

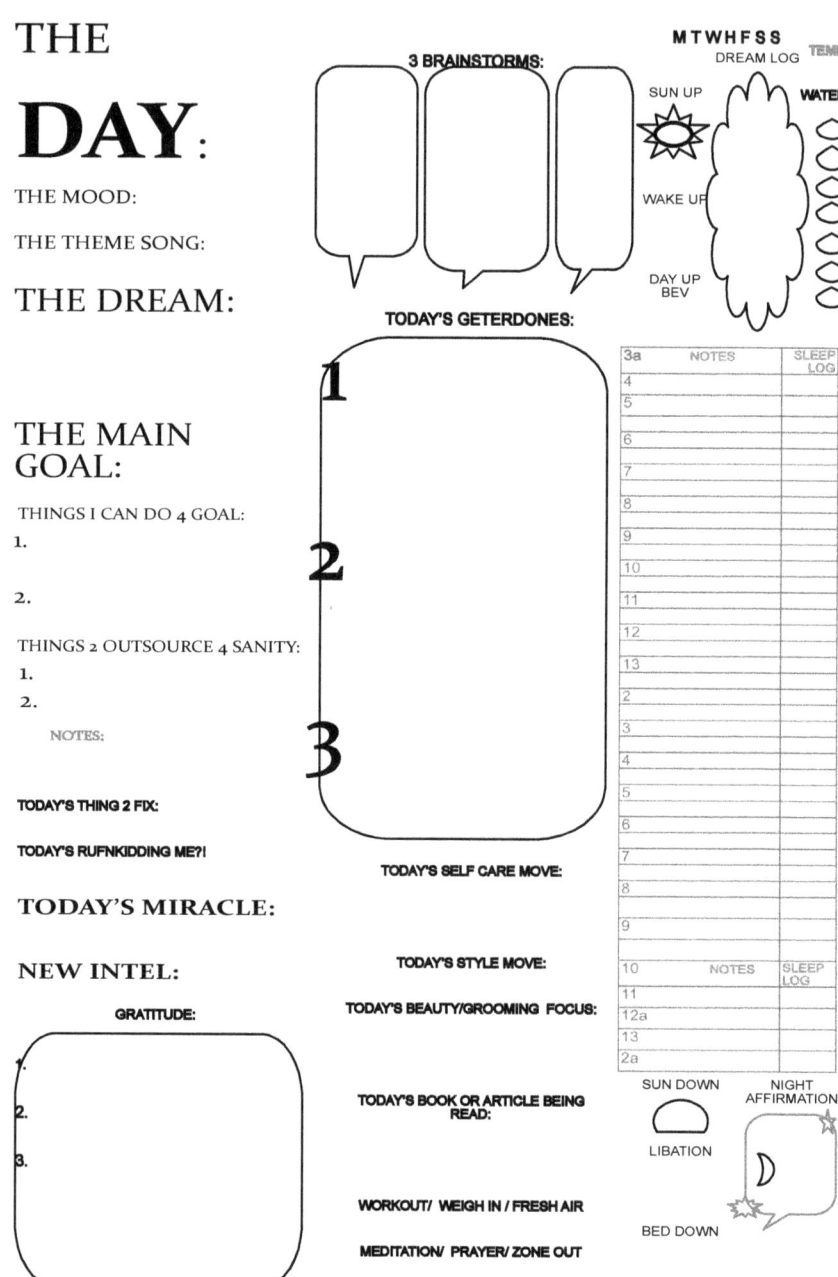

M T W H F S S
DREAM LOG   TEMP
SUN UP
WAKE UP
DAY UP BEV
WATER

	NOTES	SLEEP LOG
3a		
4		
5		
6		
7		
8		
9		
10		
11		
12		
13		
2		
3		
4		
5		
6		
7		
8		
9		
10	NOTES	SLEEP LOG
11		
12a		
13		
2a		

SUN DOWN   NIGHT AFFIRMATION
LIBATION
BED DOWN

THE
pregaming:

THE recap:

THE DAY:

THE MOOD:

THE THEME SONG:

THE DREAM:

THE MAIN GOAL:

THINGS I CAN DO 4 GOAL:
1.
2.

THINGS 2 OUTSOURCE 4 SANITY:
1.
2.

NOTES:

TODAY'S THING 2 FIX:

TODAY'S RUFNKIDDING ME?!

TODAY'S MIRACLE:

NEW INTEL:

GRATITUDE:
1.
2.
3.

3 BRAINSTORMS:

TODAY'S GETERDONES:
1
2
3

TODAY'S SELF CARE MOVE:

TODAY'S STYLE MOVE:

TODAY'S BEAUTY/GROOMING FOCUS:

TODAY'S BOOK OR ARTICLE BEING READ:

WORKOUT/ WEIGH IN / FRESH AIR

MEDITATION/ PRAYER/ ZONE OUT

M T W H F S S
DREAM LOG   TEMP

SUN UP
WAKE UP
DAY UP BEV

WATER

3a	NOTES	SLEEP LOG
4		
5		
6		
7		
8		
9		
10		
11		
12		
13		
2		
3		
4		
5		
6		
7		
8		
9		
10	NOTES	SLEEP LOG
11		
12a		
13		
2a		

SUN DOWN
LIBATION

NIGHT AFFIRMATION

BED DOWN

THE
pregaming:

THE recap:

THE DAY:

THE MOOD:

THE THEME SONG:

THE DREAM:

THE MAIN GOAL:

THINGS I CAN DO 4 GOAL:
1.

2.

THINGS 2 OUTSOURCE 4 SANITY:
1.
2.

NOTES:

TODAY'S THING 2 FIX:

TODAY'S RUFNKIDDING ME?!

TODAY'S MIRACLE:

NEW INTEL:

GRATITUDE:
1.
2.
3.

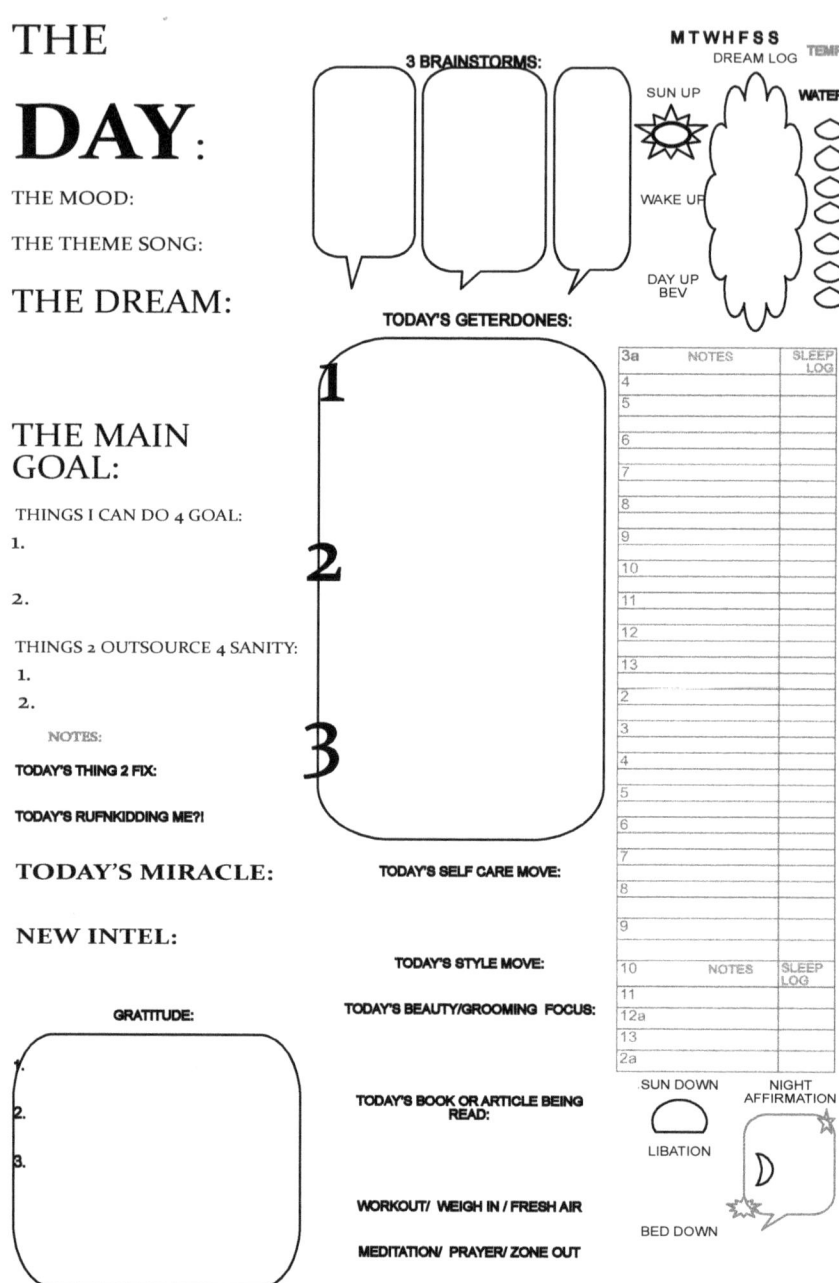

3 BRAINSTORMS:

TODAY'S GETERDONES:
1
2
3

TODAY'S SELF CARE MOVE:

TODAY'S STYLE MOVE:

TODAY'S BEAUTY/GROOMING FOCUS:

TODAY'S BOOK OR ARTICLE BEING READ:

WORKOUT/ WEIGH IN / FRESH AIR

MEDITATION/ PRAYER/ ZONE OUT

M T W H F S S
DREAM LOG   TEMP
SUN UP   WATER
WAKE UP
DAY UP BEV

	NOTES	SLEEP LOG
3a		
4		
5		
6		
7		
8		
9		
10		
11		
12		
13		
2		
3		
4		
5		
6		
7		
8		
9		
10	NOTES	SLEEP LOG
11		
12a		
13		
2a		

SUN DOWN   NIGHT AFFIRMATION
LIBATION
BED DOWN

THE
pregaming:

THE recap:

THE
pregaming:

THE recap:

THE DAY:

THE MOOD:

THE THEME SONG:

THE DREAM:

THE MAIN GOAL:

THINGS I CAN DO 4 GOAL:
1.
2.

THINGS 2 OUTSOURCE 4 SANITY:
1.
2.

NOTES:

TODAY'S THING 2 FIX:

TODAY'S RUFNKIDDING ME?!

TODAY'S MIRACLE:

NEW INTEL:

GRATITUDE:
1.
2.
3.

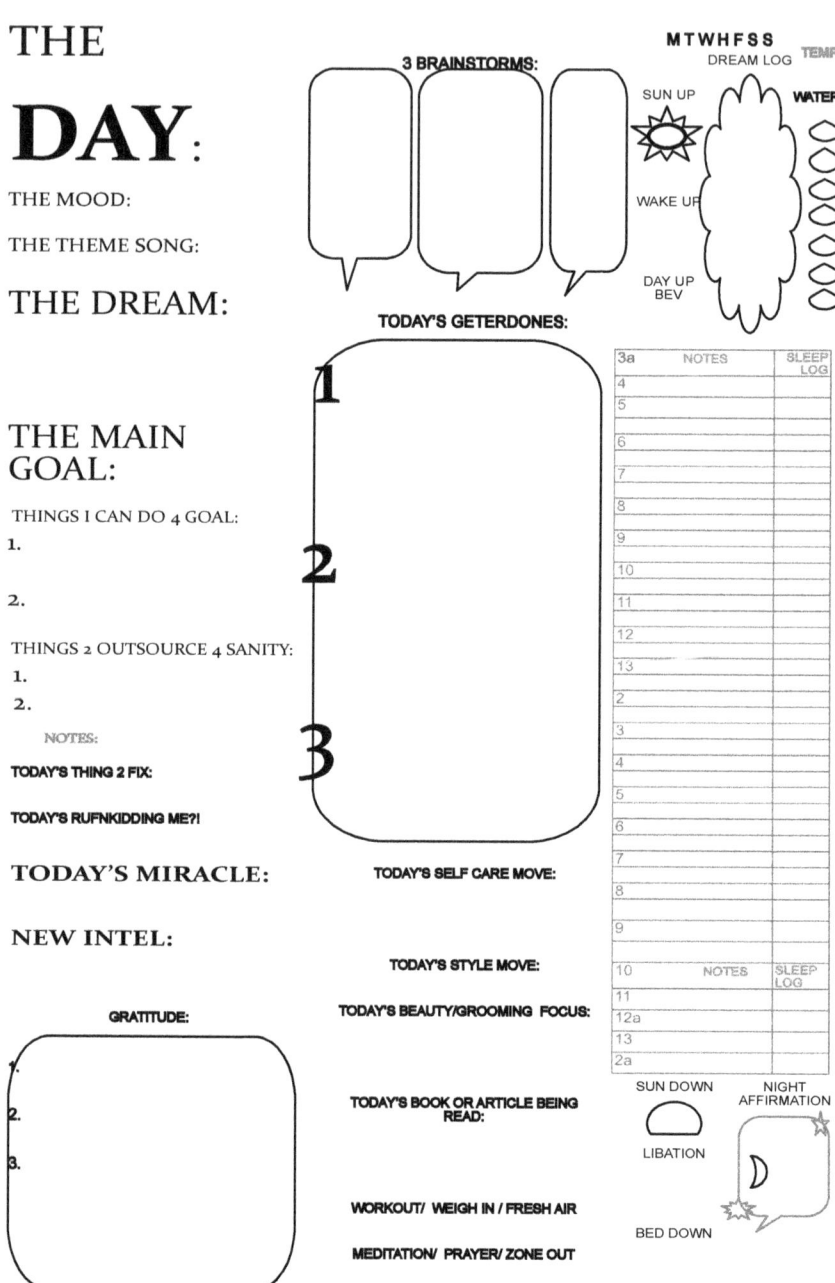

3 BRAINSTORMS:

TODAY'S GETERDONES:
1
2
3

TODAY'S SELF CARE MOVE:

TODAY'S STYLE MOVE:

TODAY'S BEAUTY/GROOMING FOCUS:

TODAY'S BOOK OR ARTICLE BEING READ:

WORKOUT/ WEIGH IN / FRESH AIR

MEDITATION/ PRAYER/ ZONE OUT

M T W H F S S
DREAM LOG   TEMP

SUN UP

WAKE UP

DAY UP BEV

WATER

3a	NOTES	SLEEP LOG
4		
5		
6		
7		
8		
9		
10		
11		
12		
13		
2		
3		
4		
5		
6		
7		
8		
9		
10	NOTES	SLEEP LOG
11		
12a		
13		
2a		

SUN DOWN

LIBATION

BED DOWN

NIGHT AFFIRMATION

THE
pregaming:

THE recap:

THE DAY:

THE MOOD:

THE THEME SONG:

THE DREAM:

THE MAIN GOAL:

THINGS I CAN DO 4 GOAL:
1.

2.

THINGS 2 OUTSOURCE 4 SANITY:
1.
2.

NOTES:

TODAY'S THING 2 FIX:

TODAY'S RUFNKIDDING ME?!

TODAY'S MIRACLE:

NEW INTEL:

GRATITUDE:

1.

2.

3.

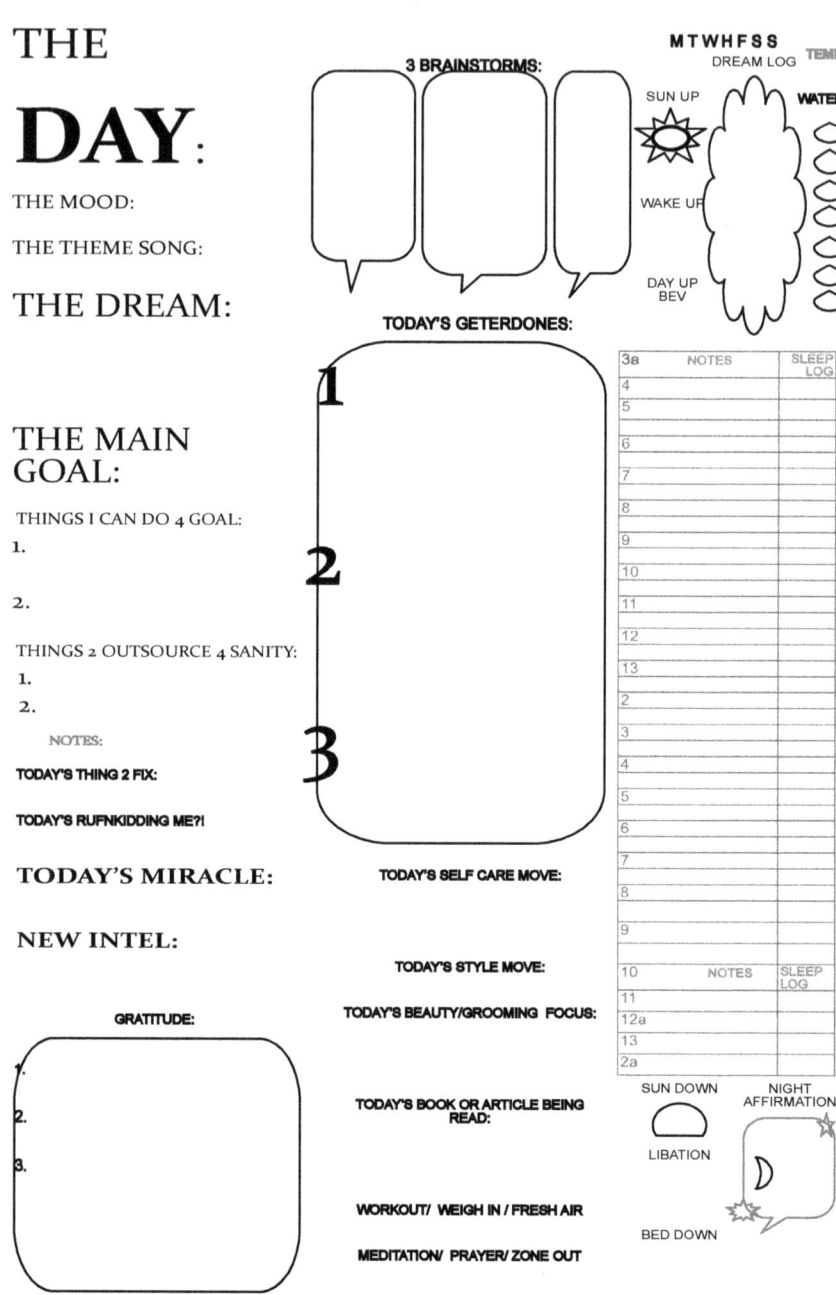

3 BRAINSTORMS:

TODAY'S GETERDONES:

1

2

3

TODAY'S SELF CARE MOVE:

TODAY'S STYLE MOVE:

TODAY'S BEAUTY/GROOMING FOCUS:

TODAY'S BOOK OR ARTICLE BEING READ:

WORKOUT/ WEIGH IN / FRESH AIR

MEDITATION/ PRAYER/ ZONE OUT

M T W H F S S
DREAM LOG TEMP

SUN UP   WATER

WAKE UP

DAY UP BEV

	NOTES	SLEEP LOG
3a		
4		
5		
6		
7		
8		
9		
10		
11		
12		
13		
2		
3		
4		
5		
6		
7		
8		
9		
10	NOTES	SLEEP LOG
11		
12a		
13		
2a		

SUN DOWN   NIGHT AFFIRMATION

LIBATION

BED DOWN

THE
pregaming:

THE recap:

THE
DAY:

THE MOOD:

THE THEME SONG:

THE DREAM:

THE MAIN GOAL:

THINGS I CAN DO 4 GOAL:
1.

2.

THINGS 2 OUTSOURCE 4 SANITY:
1.
2.

NOTES:

TODAY'S THING 2 FIX:

TODAY'S RUFNKIDDING ME?!

TODAY'S MIRACLE:

NEW INTEL:

GRATITUDE:

1.

2.

3.

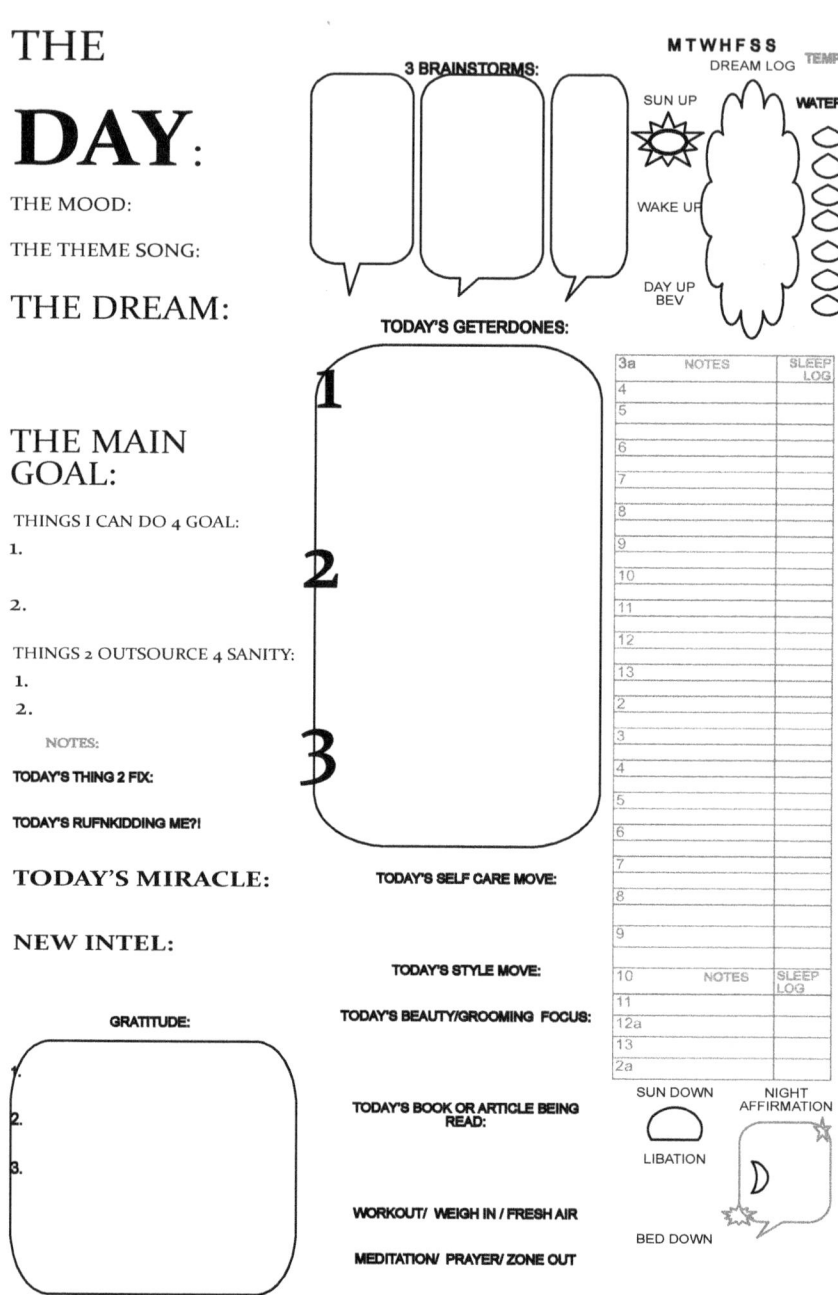

3 BRAINSTORMS:

TODAY'S GETERDONES:

1

2

3

TODAY'S SELF CARE MOVE:

TODAY'S STYLE MOVE:

TODAY'S BEAUTY/GROOMING FOCUS:

TODAY'S BOOK OR ARTICLE BEING READ:

WORKOUT/ WEIGH IN / FRESH AIR

MEDITATION/ PRAYER/ ZONE OUT

M T W H F S S
DREAM LOG   TEMP

SUN UP

WAKE UP

DAY UP BEV

WATER

NOTES | SLEEP LOG
3a
4
5
6
7
8
9
10
11
12
13
2
3
4
5
6
7
8
9
10 | NOTES | SLEEP LOG
11
12a
13
2a

SUN DOWN

LIBATION

BED DOWN

NIGHT AFFIRMATION

THE pregaming:

THE recap:

THE DAY:

THE MOOD:

THE THEME SONG:

THE DREAM:

THE MAIN GOAL:

THINGS I CAN DO 4 GOAL:
1.
2.

THINGS 2 OUTSOURCE 4 SANITY:
1.
2.

NOTES:

TODAY'S THING 2 FIX:

TODAY'S RUFNKIDDING ME?!

TODAY'S MIRACLE:

NEW INTEL:

GRATITUDE:
1.
2.
3.

3 BRAINSTORMS:

TODAY'S GETERDONES:
1
2
3

TODAY'S SELF CARE MOVE:

TODAY'S STYLE MOVE:

TODAY'S BEAUTY/GROOMING FOCUS:

TODAY'S BOOK OR ARTICLE BEING READ:

WORKOUT/ WEIGH IN / FRESH AIR

MEDITATION/ PRAYER/ ZONE OUT

M T W H F S S
DREAM LOG   TEMP

SUN UP

WAKE UP

DAY UP BEV

WATER

3a	NOTES	SLEEP LOG
4		
5		
6		
7		
8		
9		
10		
11		
12		
13		
2		
3		
4		
5		
6		
7		
8		
9		
10	NOTES	SLEEP LOG
11		
12a		
13		
2a		

SUN DOWN

LIBATION

NIGHT AFFIRMATION

BED DOWN

THE
pregaming:

THE recap:

THE DAY:

THE MOOD:

THE THEME SONG:

THE DREAM:

THE MAIN GOAL:

THINGS I CAN DO 4 GOAL:
1.
2.

THINGS 2 OUTSOURCE 4 SANITY:
1.
2.

NOTES:

TODAY'S THING 2 FIX:

TODAY'S RUFNKIDDING ME?!

TODAY'S MIRACLE:

NEW INTEL:

GRATITUDE:
1.
2.
3.

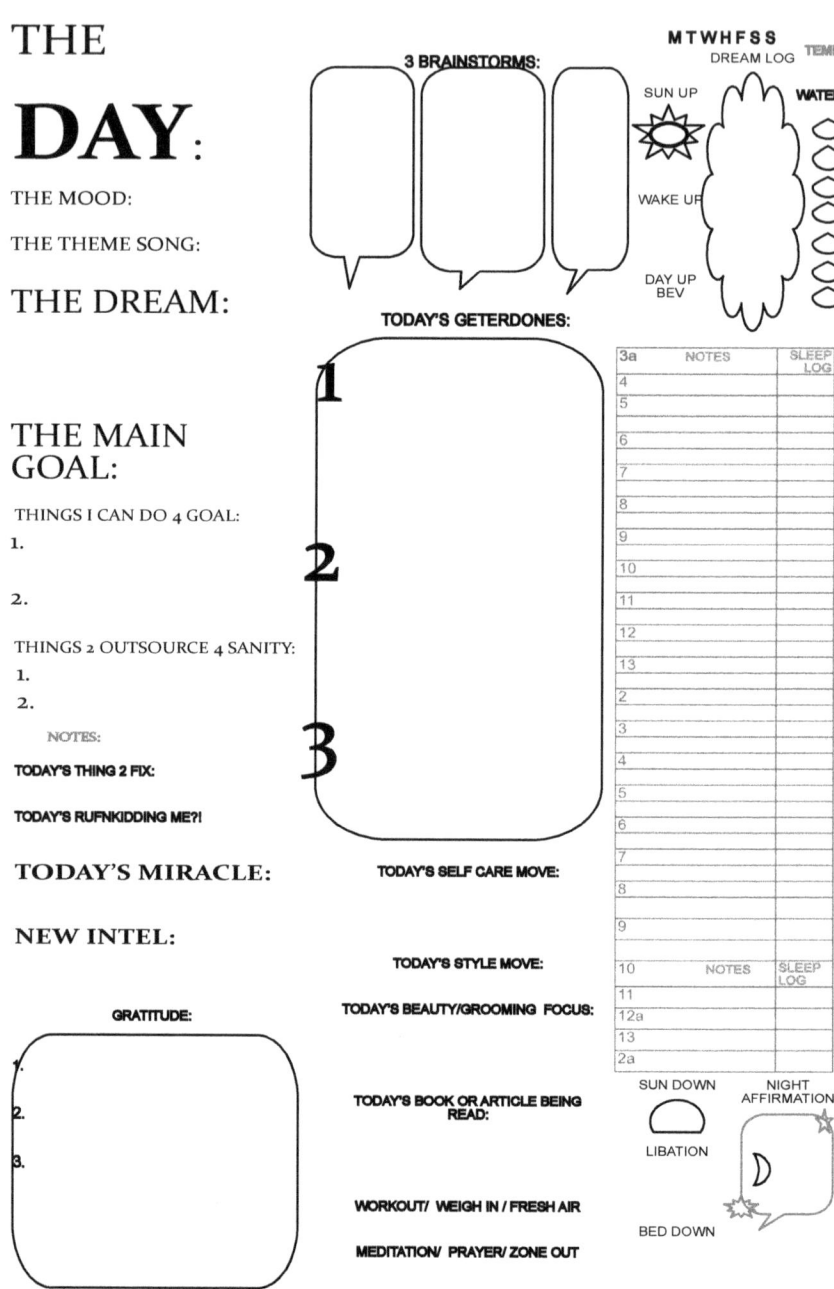

3 BRAINSTORMS:

TODAY'S GETERDONES:
1
2
3

TODAY'S SELF CARE MOVE:

TODAY'S STYLE MOVE:

TODAY'S BEAUTY/GROOMING FOCUS:

TODAY'S BOOK OR ARTICLE BEING READ:

WORKOUT/ WEIGH IN / FRESH AIR

MEDITATION/ PRAYER/ ZONE OUT

M T W H F S S
DREAM LOG   TEMP
SUN UP   WATER
WAKE UP
DAY UP BEV

3a	NOTES	SLEEP LOG
4		
5		
6		
7		
8		
9		
10		
11		
12		
13		
2		
3		
4		
5		
6		
7		
8		
9		
10	NOTES	SLEEP LOG
11		
12a		
13		
2a		

SUN DOWN   NIGHT AFFIRMATION

LIBATION

BED DOWN

THE
pregaming:

THE recap:

THE DAY:

THE MOOD:

THE THEME SONG:

THE DREAM:

THE MAIN GOAL:

THINGS I CAN DO 4 GOAL:
1.
2.

THINGS 2 OUTSOURCE 4 SANITY:
1.
2.

NOTES:

TODAY'S THING 2 FIX:

TODAY'S RUFNKIDDING ME?!

TODAY'S MIRACLE:

NEW INTEL:

GRATITUDE:
1.
2.
3.

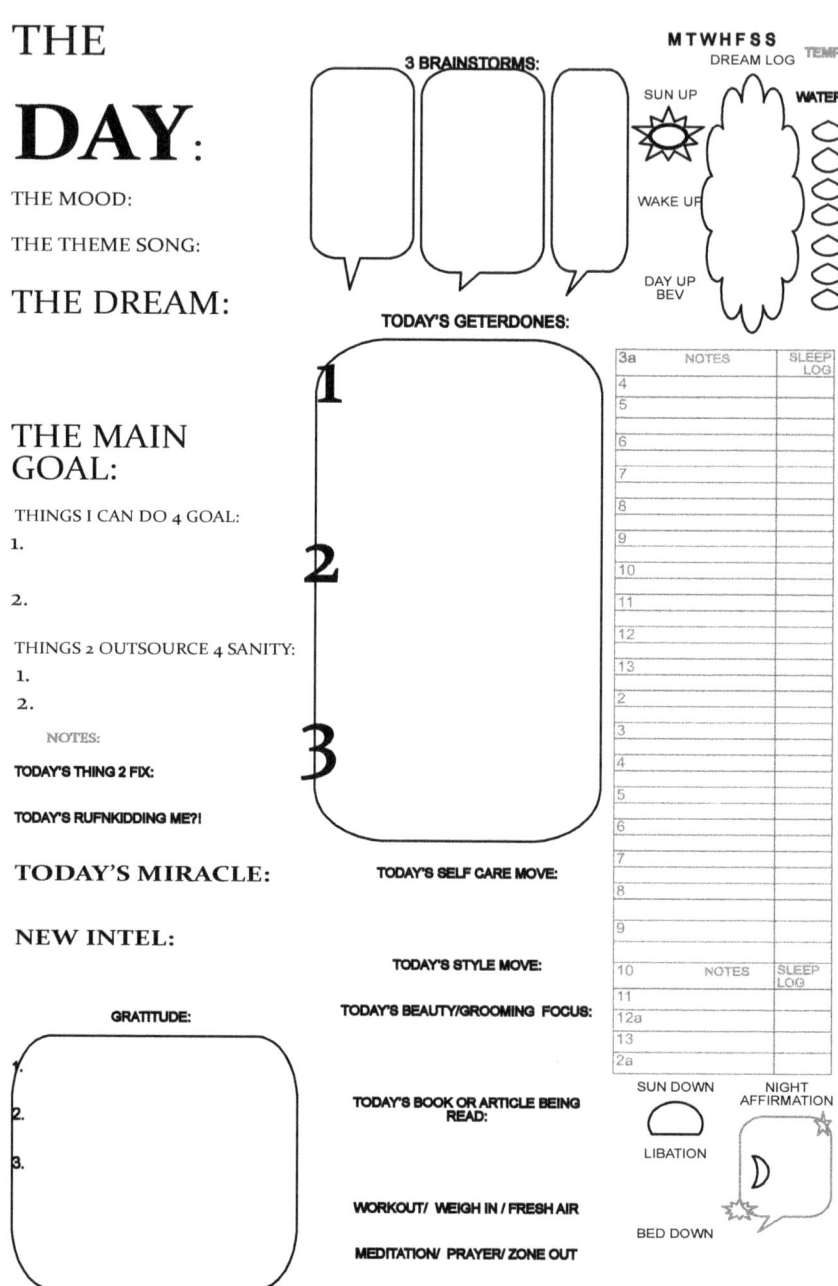

3 BRAINSTORMS:

TODAY'S GETERDONES:
1
2
3

TODAY'S SELF CARE MOVE:

TODAY'S STYLE MOVE:

TODAY'S BEAUTY/GROOMING FOCUS:

TODAY'S BOOK OR ARTICLE BEING READ:

WORKOUT/ WEIGH IN / FRESH AIR

MEDITATION/ PRAYER/ ZONE OUT

M T W H F S S
DREAM LOG   TEMP
SUN UP
WAKE UP
DAY UP BEV
WATER

3a	NOTES	SLEEP LOG
4		
5		
6		
7		
8		
9		
10		
11		
12		
13		
2		
3		
4		
5		
6		
7		
8		
9		
10	NOTES	SLEEP LOG
11		
12a		
13		
2a		

SUN DOWN
LIBATION

NIGHT AFFIRMATION
BED DOWN

THE
pregaming:

THE recap:

THE
DAY:

THE MOOD:

THE THEME SONG:

THE DREAM:

THE MAIN GOAL:

THINGS I CAN DO 4 GOAL:
1.

2.

THINGS 2 OUTSOURCE 4 SANITY:
1.
2.

NOTES:

TODAY'S THING 2 FIX:

TODAY'S RUFNKIDDING ME?!

TODAY'S MIRACLE:

NEW INTEL:

GRATITUDE:
1.
2.
3.

3 BRAINSTORMS:

TODAY'S GETERDONES:

1

2

3

TODAY'S SELF CARE MOVE:

TODAY'S STYLE MOVE:

TODAY'S BEAUTY/GROOMING FOCUS:

TODAY'S BOOK OR ARTICLE BEING READ:

WORKOUT/ WEIGH IN / FRESH AIR

MEDITATION/ PRAYER/ ZONE OUT

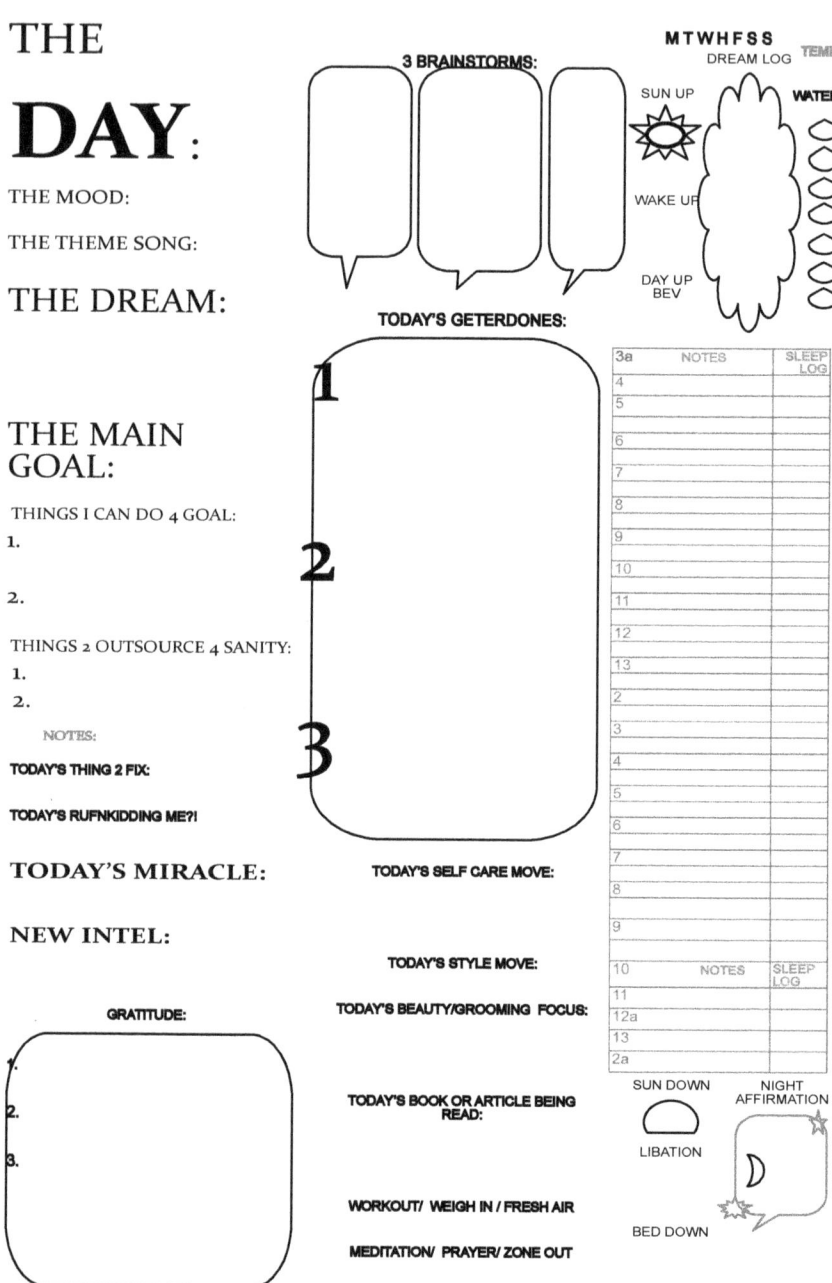

THE pregaming:

THE recap:

THE
DAY:

THE MOOD:

THE THEME SONG:

THE DREAM:

THE MAIN GOAL:

THINGS I CAN DO 4 GOAL:
1.

2.

THINGS 2 OUTSOURCE 4 SANITY:
1.
2.

NOTES:

TODAY'S THING 2 FIX:

TODAY'S RUFNKIDDING ME?!

TODAY'S MIRACLE:

NEW INTEL:

GRATITUDE:

1.

2.

3.

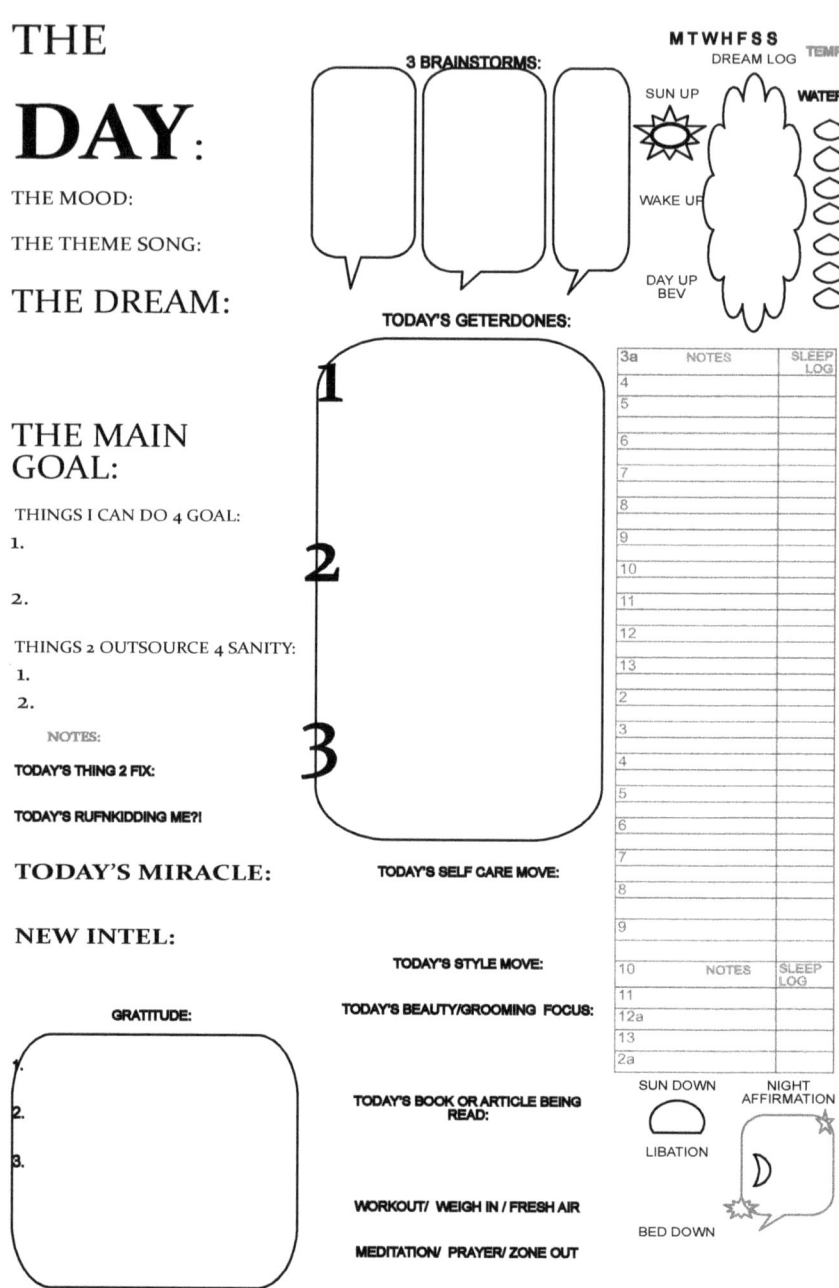

3 BRAINSTORMS:

TODAY'S GETERDONES:

1

2

3

TODAY'S SELF CARE MOVE:

TODAY'S STYLE MOVE:

TODAY'S BEAUTY/GROOMING FOCUS:

TODAY'S BOOK OR ARTICLE BEING READ:

WORKOUT/ WEIGH IN / FRESH AIR

MEDITATION/ PRAYER/ ZONE OUT

MTWHFSS DREAM LOG TEMP

SUN UP   WATER

WAKE UP

DAY UP BEV

NOTES   SLEEP LOG

SUN DOWN   NIGHT AFFIRMATION

LIBATION

BED DOWN

THE
pregaming:

THE recap:

THE DAY:

THE MOOD:

THE THEME SONG:

THE DREAM:

THE MAIN GOAL:

THINGS I CAN DO 4 GOAL:
1.
2.

THINGS 2 OUTSOURCE 4 SANITY:
1.
2.

NOTES:

TODAY'S THING 2 FIX:

TODAY'S RUFNKIDDING ME?!

TODAY'S MIRACLE:

NEW INTEL:

GRATITUDE:
1.
2.
3.

3 BRAINSTORMS:

TODAY'S GETERDONES:
1.
2.
3.

TODAY'S SELF CARE MOVE:

TODAY'S STYLE MOVE:

TODAY'S BEAUTY/GROOMING FOCUS:

TODAY'S BOOK OR ARTICLE BEING READ:

WORKOUT/ WEIGH IN / FRESH AIR

MEDITATION/ PRAYER/ ZONE OUT

M T W H F S S
DREAM LOG   TEMP

SUN UP   WATER

WAKE UP

DAY UP BEV

	NOTES	SLEEP LOG
3a		
4		
5		
6		
7		
8		
9		
10		
11		
12		
13		
2		
3		
4		
5		
6		
7		
8		
9		
10	NOTES	SLEEP LOG
11		
12a		
13		
2a		

SUN DOWN

LIBATION

BED DOWN

NIGHT AFFIRMATION

THE
pregaming:

THE recap:

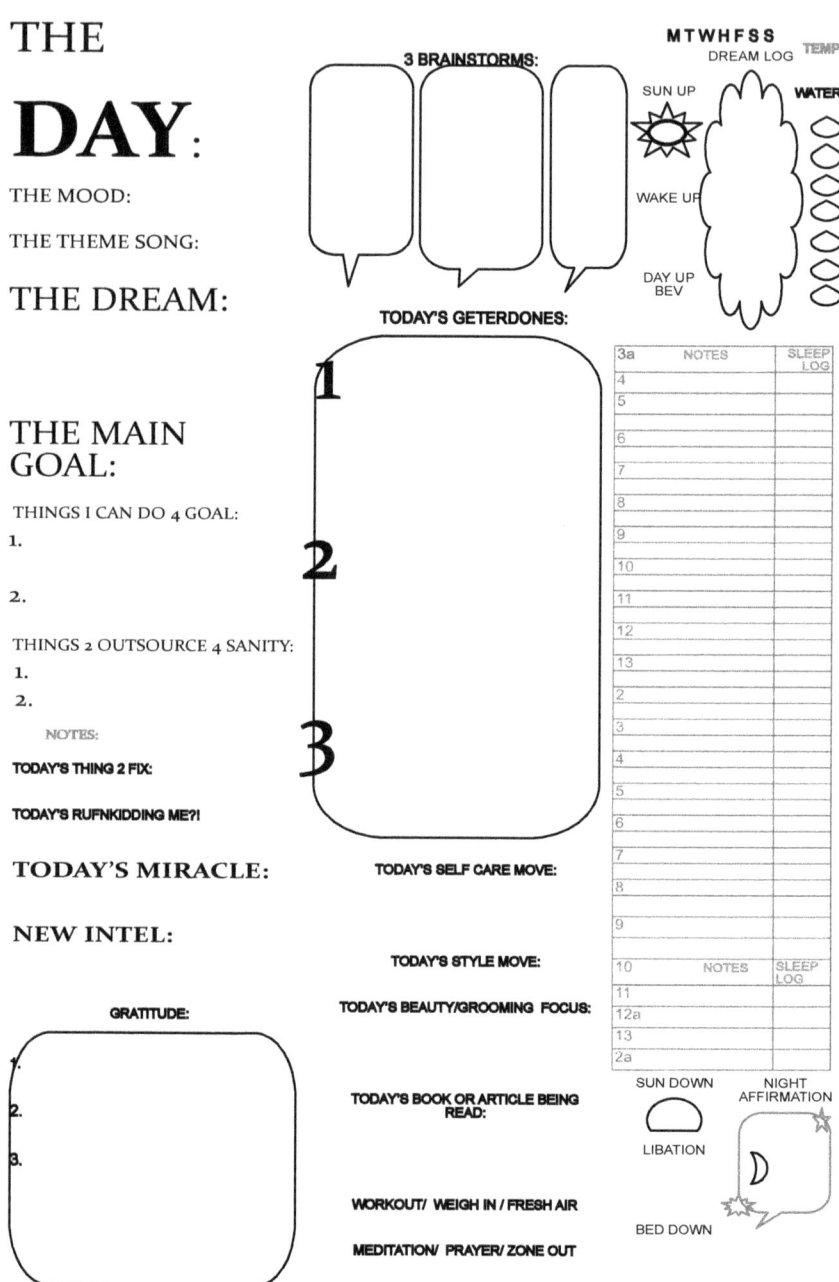

THE
pregaming:

THE recap:

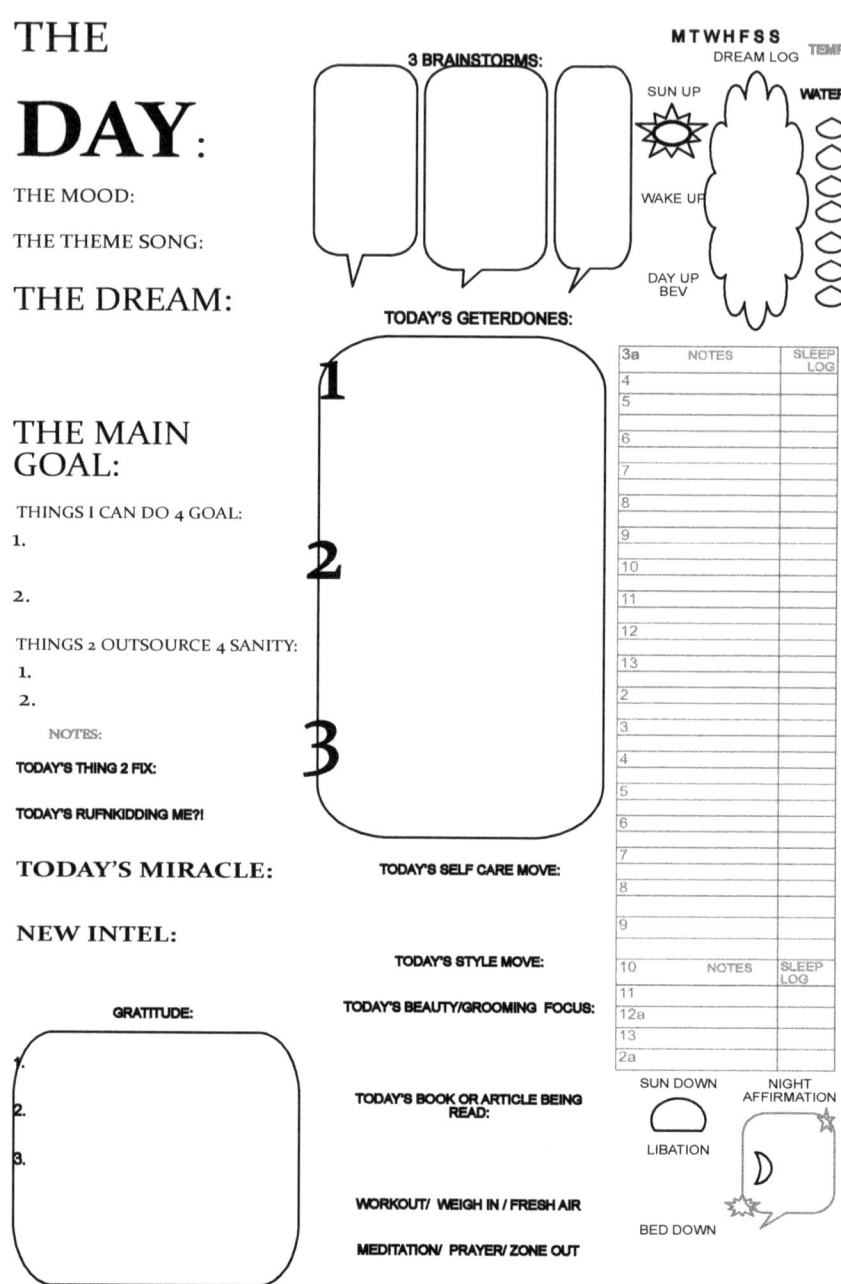

THE
pregaming:

THE recap:

THE DAY:

THE MOOD:

THE THEME SONG:

THE DREAM:

THE MAIN GOAL:

THINGS I CAN DO 4 GOAL:
1.
2.

THINGS 2 OUTSOURCE 4 SANITY:
1.
2.

NOTES:

TODAY'S THING 2 FIX:

TODAY'S RUFNKIDDING ME?!

TODAY'S MIRACLE:

NEW INTEL:

GRATITUDE:
1.
2.
3.

3 BRAINSTORMS:

TODAY'S GETERDONES:
1
2
3

TODAY'S SELF CARE MOVE:

TODAY'S STYLE MOVE:

TODAY'S BEAUTY/GROOMING FOCUS:

TODAY'S BOOK OR ARTICLE BEING READ:

WORKOUT/ WEIGH IN / FRESH AIR

MEDITATION/ PRAYER/ ZONE OUT

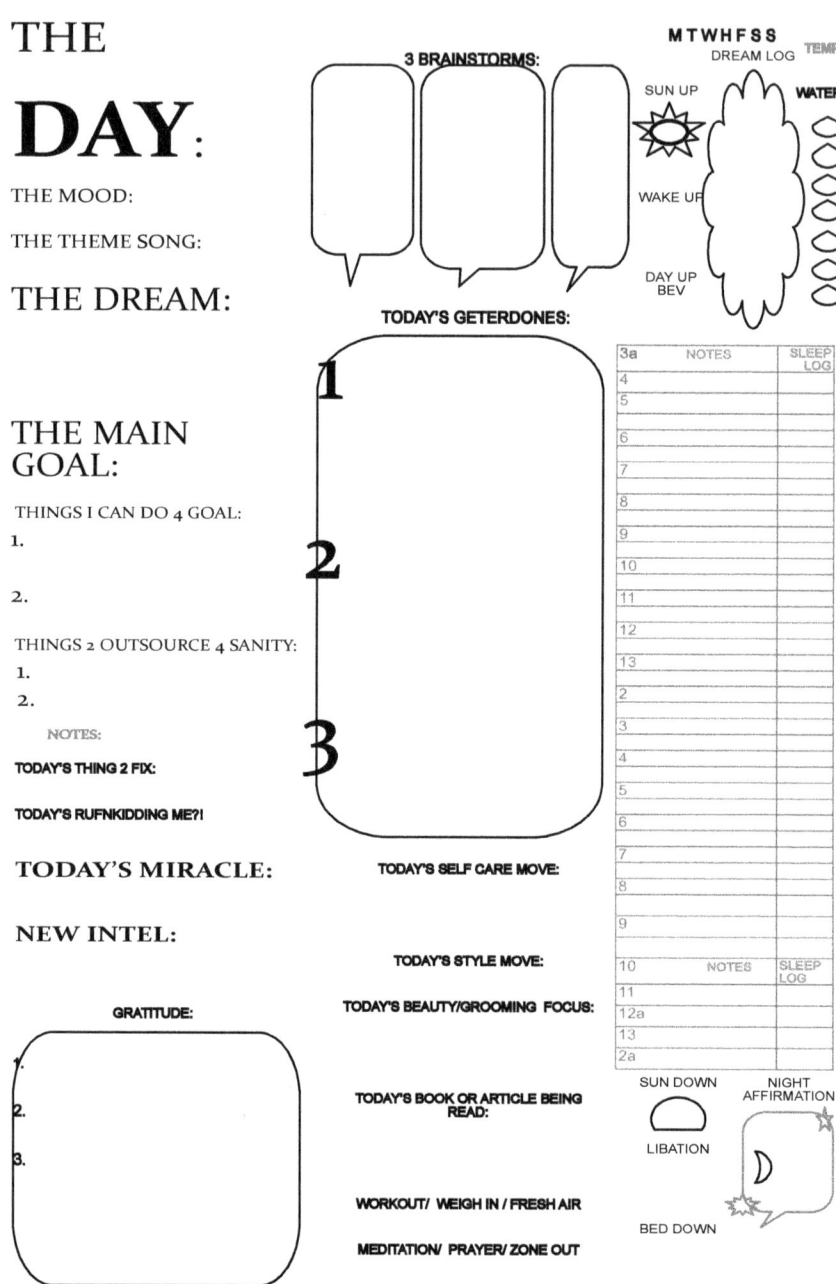

M T W H F S S
DREAM LOG   TEMP
SUN UP   WATER
WAKE UP
DAY UP BEV

	NOTES	SLEEP LOG
3a		
4		
5		
6		
7		
8		
9		
10		
11		
12		
13		
2		
3		
4		
5		
6		
7		
8		
9		
10	NOTES	SLEEP LOG
11		
12a		
13		
2a		

SUN DOWN   NIGHT AFFIRMATION
LIBATION
BED DOWN

THE
pregaming:

THE recap:

THE DAY:

THE MOOD:

THE THEME SONG:

THE DREAM:

THE MAIN GOAL:

THINGS I CAN DO 4 GOAL:
1.
2.

THINGS 2 OUTSOURCE 4 SANITY:
1.
2.

   NOTES:

TODAY'S THING 2 FIX:

TODAY'S RUFNKIDDING ME?!

TODAY'S MIRACLE:

NEW INTEL:

GRATITUDE:
1.
2.
3.

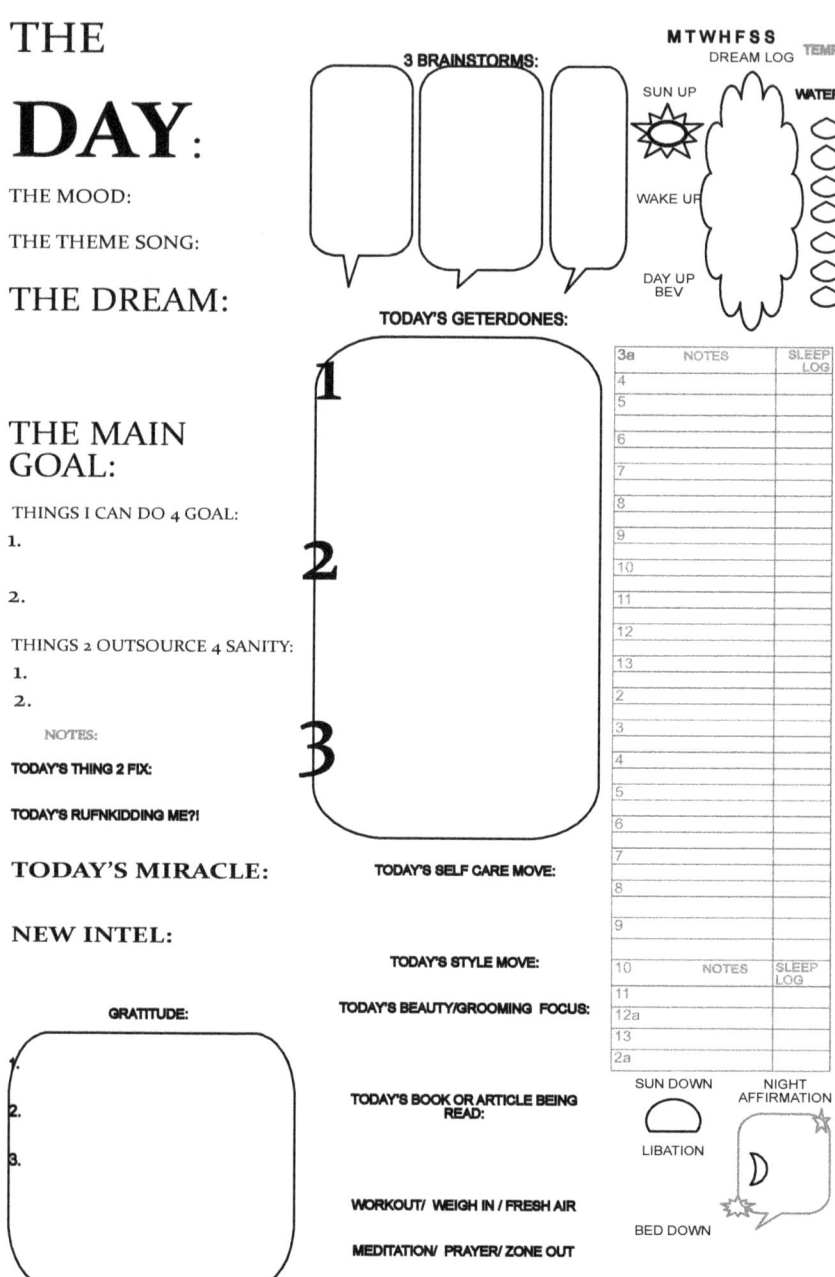

3 BRAINSTORMS:

TODAY'S GETERDONES:
1
2
3

TODAY'S SELF CARE MOVE:

TODAY'S STYLE MOVE:

TODAY'S BEAUTY/GROOMING FOCUS:

TODAY'S BOOK OR ARTICLE BEING READ:

WORKOUT/ WEIGH IN / FRESH AIR

MEDITATION/ PRAYER/ ZONE OUT

M T W H F S S
DREAM LOG   TEMP
SUN UP   WATER
WAKE UP
DAY UP BEV

3a	NOTES	SLEEP LOG
4		
5		
6		
7		
8		
9		
10		
11		
12		
13		
2		
3		
4		
5		
6		
7		
8		
9		
10	NOTES	SLEEP LOG
11		
12a		
13		
2a		

SUN DOWN   NIGHT AFFIRMATION

LIBATION

BED DOWN

THE pregaming:

THE recap:

THE DAY:

THE MOOD:

THE THEME SONG:

THE DREAM:

THE MAIN GOAL:

THINGS I CAN DO 4 GOAL:
1.

2.

THINGS 2 OUTSOURCE 4 SANITY:
1.
2.

NOTES:

TODAY'S THING 2 FIX:

TODAY'S RUFNKIDDING ME?!

TODAY'S MIRACLE:

NEW INTEL:

GRATITUDE:

1.

2.

3.

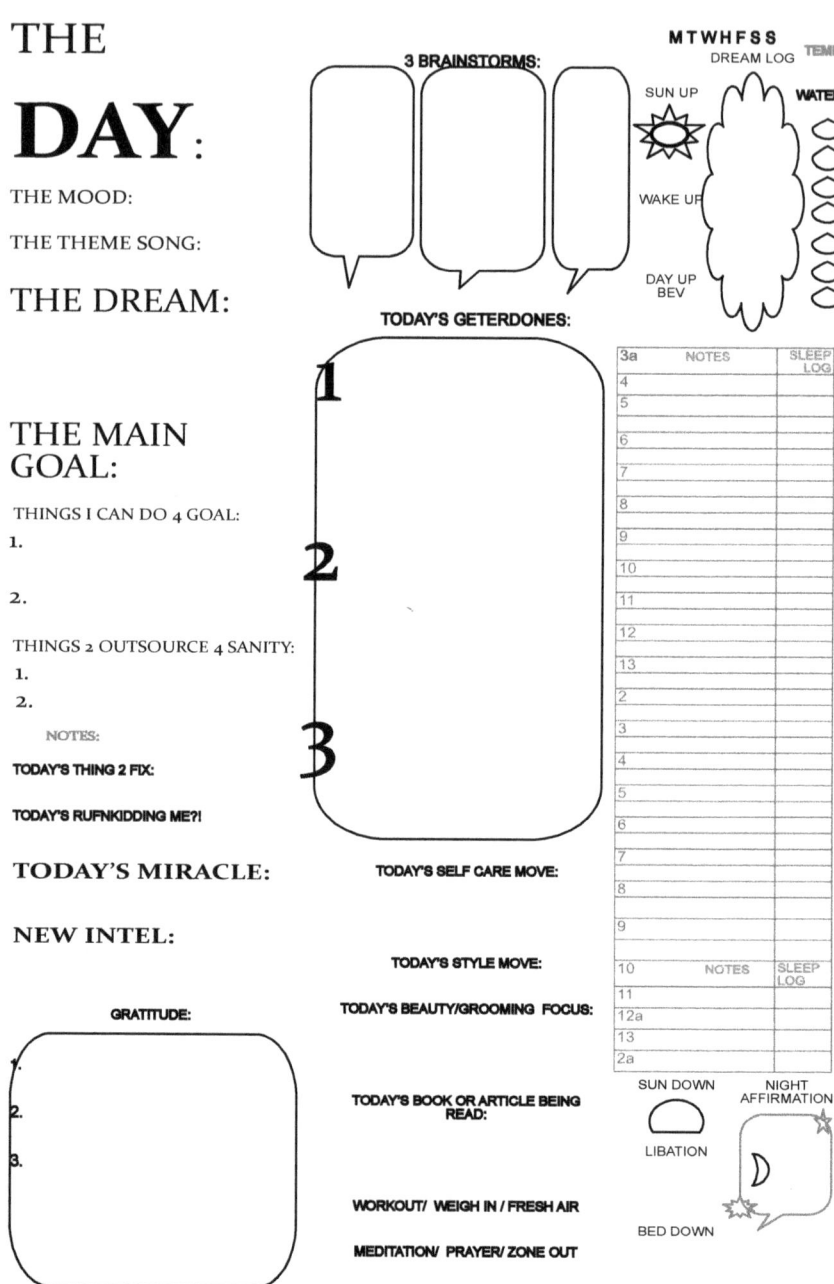

3 BRAINSTORMS:

TODAY'S GETERDONES:

1

2

3

TODAY'S SELF CARE MOVE:

TODAY'S STYLE MOVE:

TODAY'S BEAUTY/GROOMING FOCUS:

TODAY'S BOOK OR ARTICLE BEING READ:

WORKOUT/ WEIGH IN / FRESH AIR

MEDITATION/ PRAYER/ ZONE OUT

THE
pregaming:

THE recap:

THE
pregaming:

THE recap:

THE
DAY:

THE MOOD:

THE THEME SONG:

THE DREAM:

THE MAIN GOAL:

THINGS I CAN DO 4 GOAL:
1.

2.

THINGS 2 OUTSOURCE 4 SANITY:
1.
2.

NOTES:

TODAY'S THING 2 FIX:

TODAY'S RUFNKIDDING ME?!

TODAY'S MIRACLE:

NEW INTEL:

GRATITUDE:

1.

2.

3.

3 BRAINSTORMS:

TODAY'S GETERDONES:

1

2

3

TODAY'S SELF CARE MOVE:

TODAY'S STYLE MOVE:

TODAY'S BEAUTY/GROOMING FOCUS:

TODAY'S BOOK OR ARTICLE BEING READ:

WORKOUT/ WEIGH IN / FRESH AIR

MEDITATION/ PRAYER/ ZONE OUT

M T W H F S S
DREAM LOG   TEMP

SUN UP

WAKE UP

DAY UP BEV

WATER

	NOTES	SLEEP LOG
3a		
4		
5		
6		
7		
8		
9		
10		
11		
12		
13		
2		
3		
4		
5		
6		
7		
8		
9		
10	NOTES	SLEEP LOG
11		
12a		
13		
2a		

SUN DOWN

LIBATION

BED DOWN

NIGHT AFFIRMATION

THE
pregaming:

THE recap:

THE
pregaming:

THE recap:

THE DAY:

THE MOOD:

THE THEME SONG:

THE DREAM:

THE MAIN GOAL:

THINGS I CAN DO 4 GOAL:
1.
2.

THINGS 2 OUTSOURCE 4 SANITY:
1.
2.

NOTES:

TODAY'S THING 2 FIX:

TODAY'S RUFNKIDDING ME?!

TODAY'S MIRACLE:

NEW INTEL:

GRATITUDE:
1.
2.
3.

3 BRAINSTORMS:

TODAY'S GETERDONES:
1
2
3

TODAY'S SELF CARE MOVE:

TODAY'S STYLE MOVE:

TODAY'S BEAUTY/GROOMING FOCUS:

TODAY'S BOOK OR ARTICLE BEING READ:

WORKOUT/ WEIGH IN / FRESH AIR

MEDITATION/ PRAYER/ ZONE OUT

M T W H F S S
DREAM LOG — TEMP
SUN UP
WATER
WAKE UP
DAY UP BEV

3a	NOTES	SLEEP LOG
4		
5		
6		
7		
8		
9		
10		
11		
12		
13		
2		
3		
4		
5		
6		
7		
8		
9		
10	NOTES	SLEEP LOG
11		
12a		
13		
2a		

SUN DOWN
LIBATION
BED DOWN
NIGHT AFFIRMATION

THE
pregaming:

THE recap:

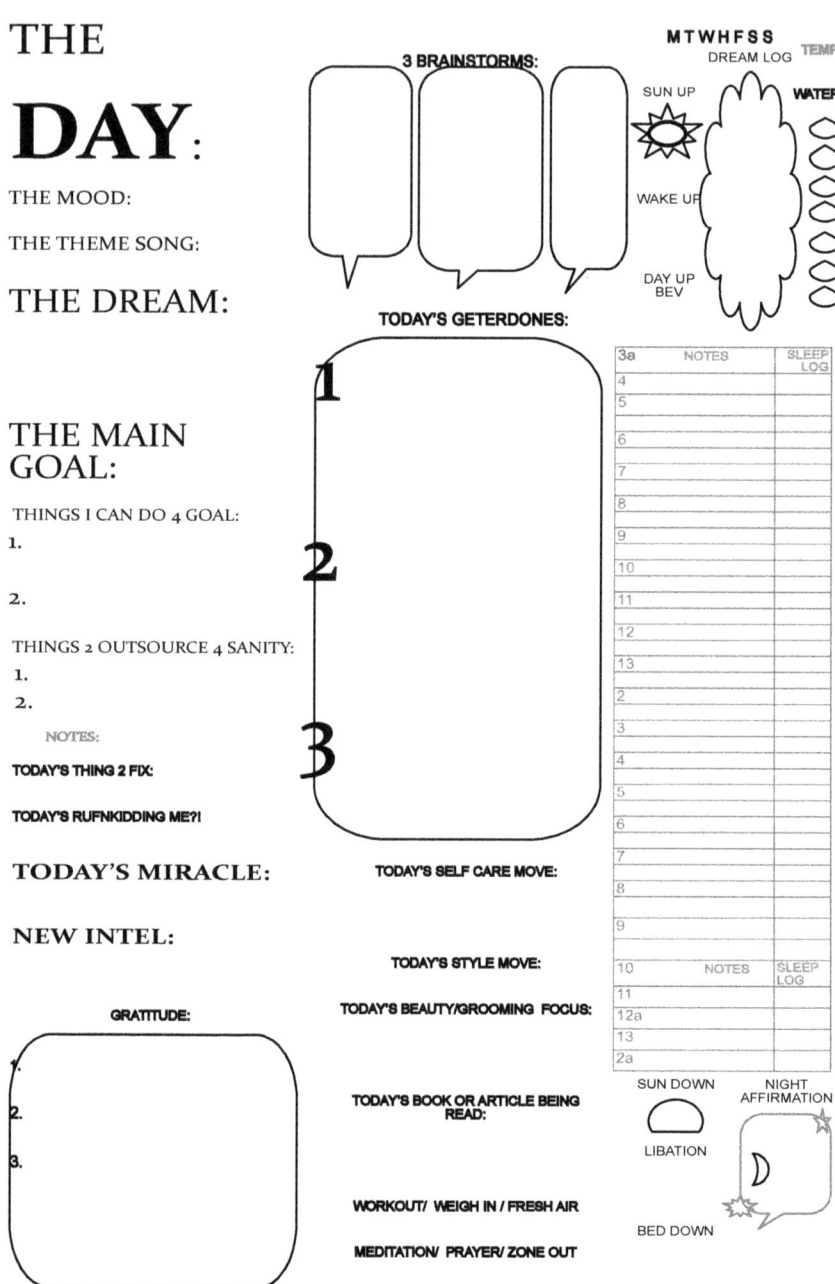

THE
pregaming:

THE recap:

THE
DAY:

THE MOOD:

THE THEME SONG:

THE DREAM:

THE MAIN GOAL:

THINGS I CAN DO 4 GOAL:
1.
2.

THINGS 2 OUTSOURCE 4 SANITY:
1.
2.

NOTES:

TODAY'S THING 2 FIX:

TODAY'S RUFNKIDDING ME?!

TODAY'S MIRACLE:

NEW INTEL:

GRATITUDE:
1.
2.
3.

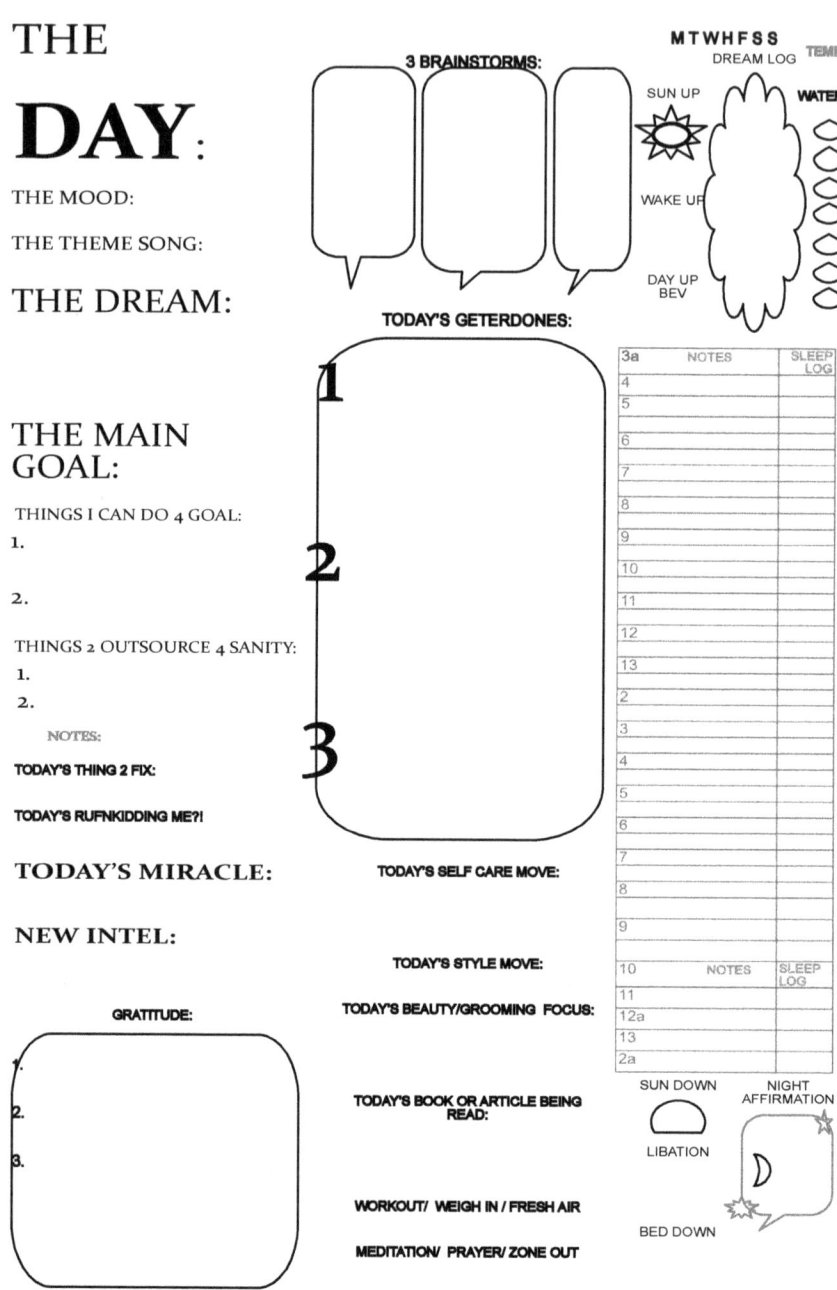

3 BRAINSTORMS:

TODAY'S GETERDONES:
1.
2.
3.

TODAY'S SELF CARE MOVE:

TODAY'S STYLE MOVE:

TODAY'S BEAUTY/GROOMING FOCUS:

TODAY'S BOOK OR ARTICLE BEING READ:

WORKOUT/ WEIGH IN / FRESH AIR

MEDITATION/ PRAYER/ ZONE OUT

M T W H F S S
DREAM LOG   TEMP
SUN UP   WATER
WAKE UP
DAY UP BEV

	NOTES	SLEEP LOG
3a		
4		
5		
6		
7		
8		
9		
10		
11		
12		
13		
2		
3		
4		
5		
6		
7		
8		
9		
10	NOTES	SLEEP LOG
11		
12a		
13		
2a		

SUN DOWN   NIGHT AFFIRMATION
LIBATION
BED DOWN

THE pregaming:

THE recap:

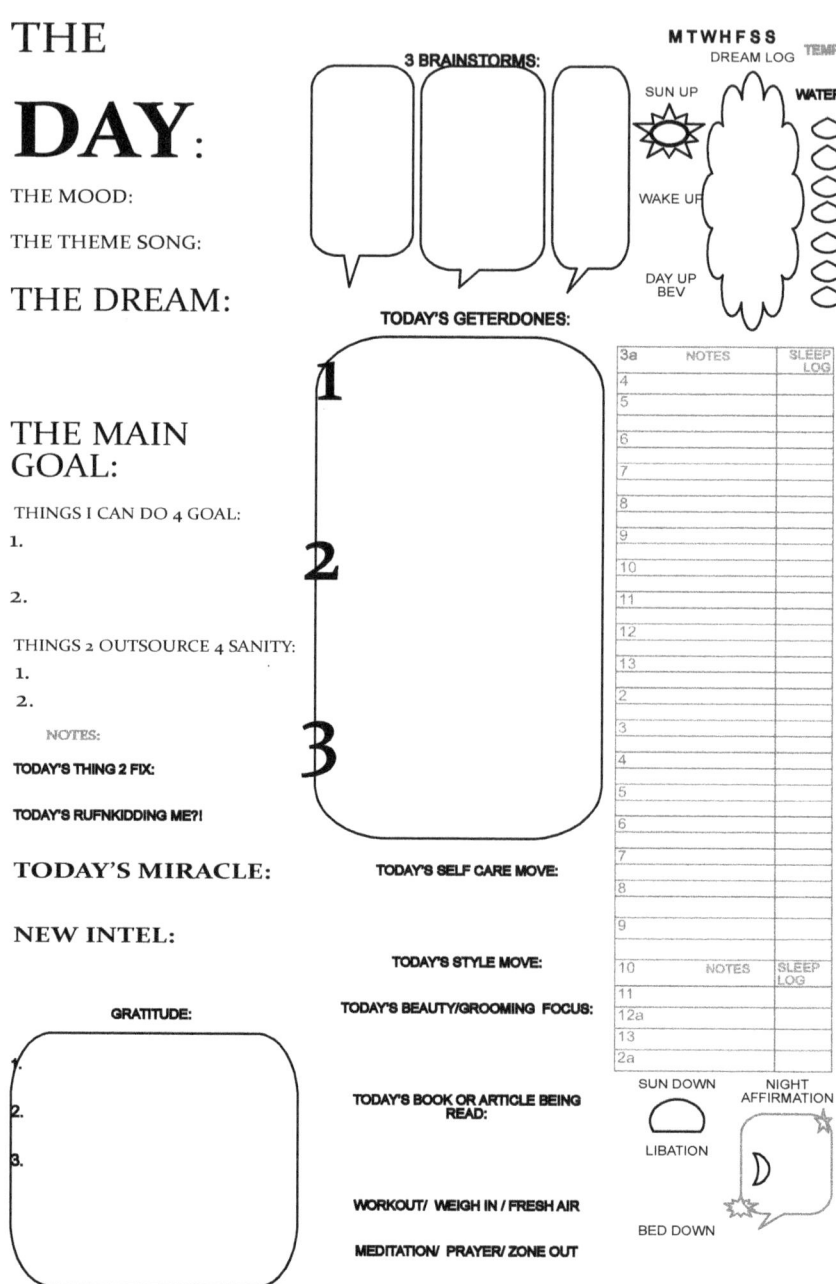

THE pregaming:

THE recap:

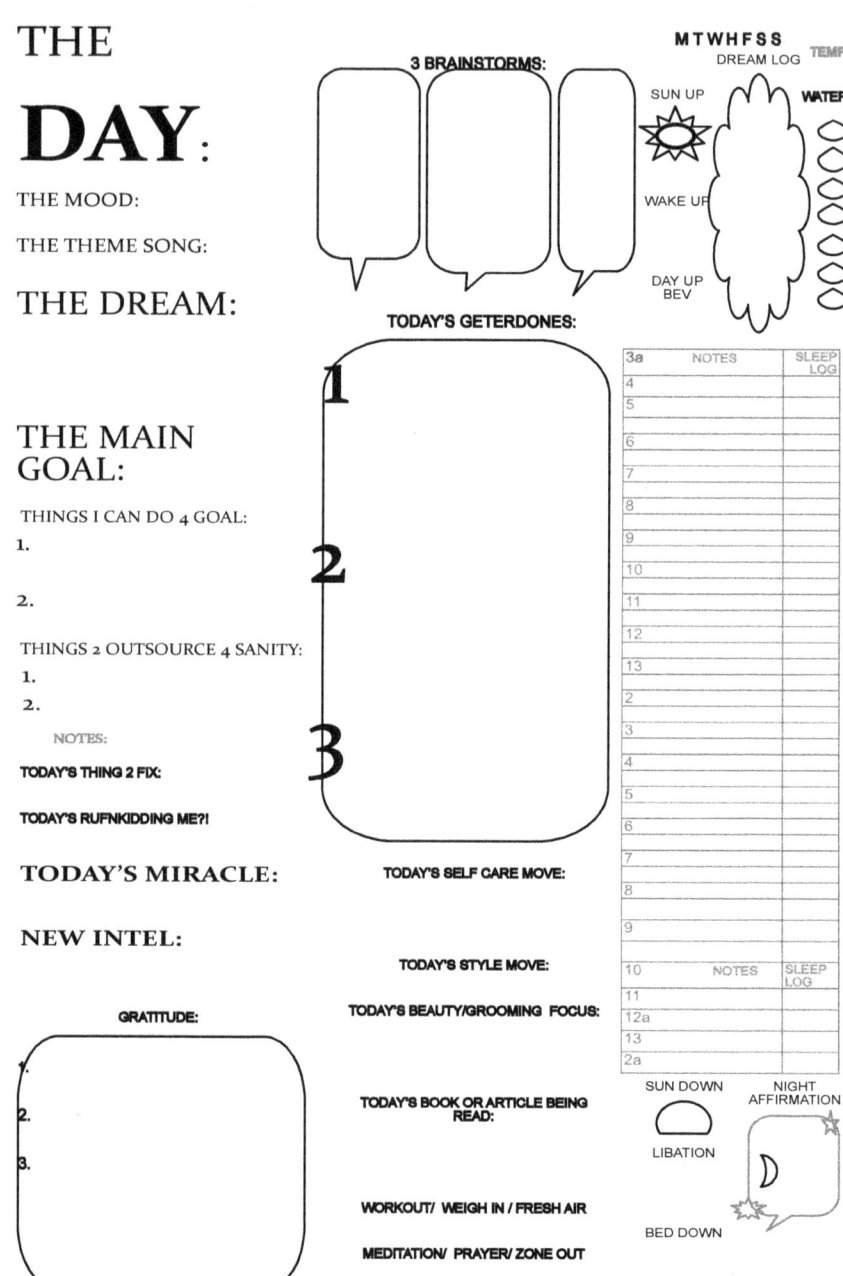

THE
pregaming:

THE recap:

THE
DAY:

THE MOOD:

THE THEME SONG:

THE DREAM:

THE MAIN GOAL:

THINGS I CAN DO 4 GOAL:
1.

2.

THINGS 2 OUTSOURCE 4 SANITY:
1.
2.
   NOTES:

TODAY'S THING 2 FIX:

TODAY'S RUFNKIDDING ME?!

TODAY'S MIRACLE:

NEW INTEL:

GRATITUDE:

1.

2.

3.

3 BRAINSTORMS:

TODAY'S GETERDONES:

1

2

3

TODAY'S SELF CARE MOVE:

TODAY'S STYLE MOVE:

TODAY'S BEAUTY/GROOMING FOCUS:

TODAY'S BOOK OR ARTICLE BEING READ:

WORKOUT/ WEIGH IN / FRESH AIR

MEDITATION/ PRAYER/ ZONE OUT

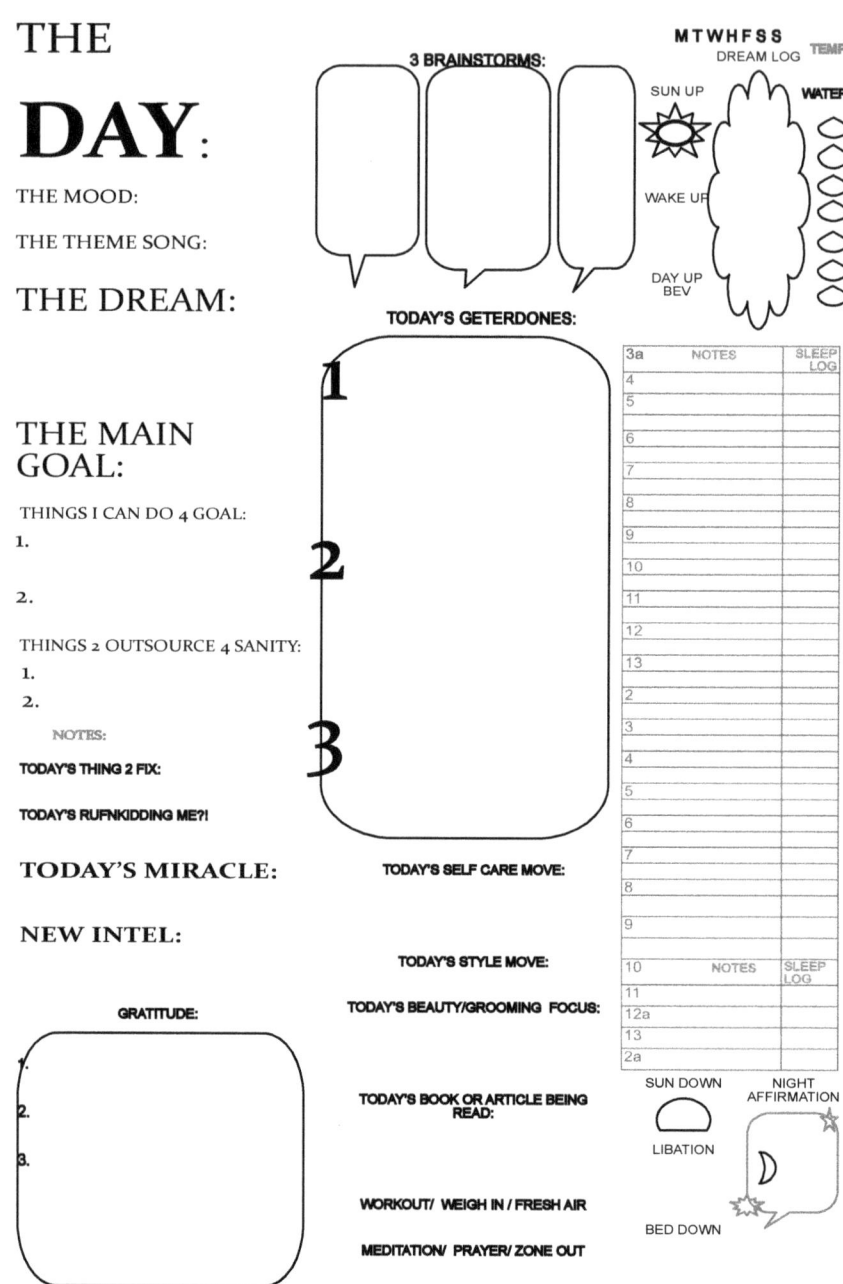

M T W H F S S
DREAM LOG   TEMP
SUN UP   WATER
WAKE UP
DAY UP BEV

3a	NOTES	SLEEP LOG
4		
5		
6		
7		
8		
9		
10		
11		
12		
13		
2		
3		
4		
5		
6		
7		
8		
9		
10	NOTES	SLEEP LOG
11		
12a		
13		
2a		

SUN DOWN   NIGHT AFFIRMATION
LIBATION
BED DOWN

THE
pregaming:

THE recap:

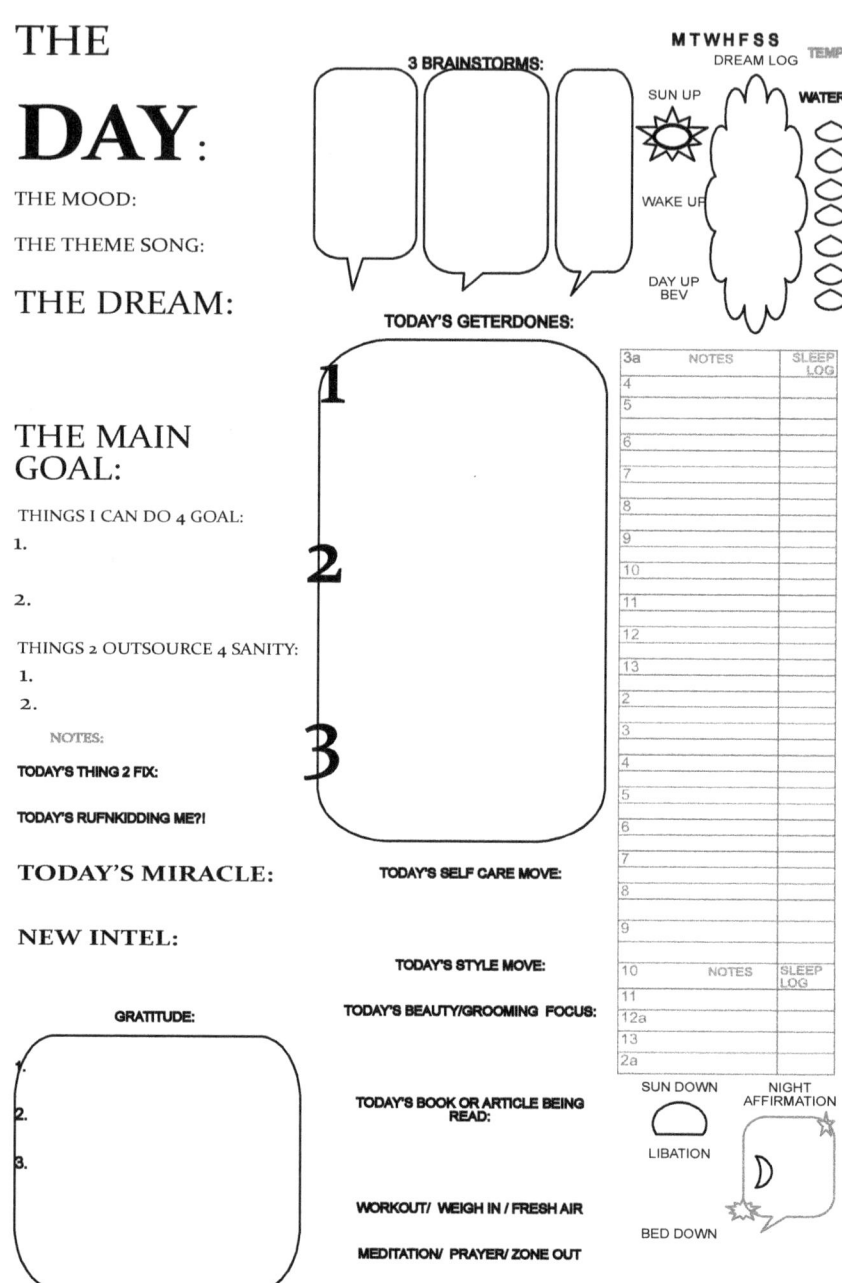

THE pregaming:

THE recap:

THE
DAY:

THE MOOD:

THE THEME SONG:

THE DREAM:

THE MAIN GOAL:

THINGS I CAN DO 4 GOAL:
1.

2.

THINGS 2 OUTSOURCE 4 SANITY:
1.
2.
   NOTES:

TODAY'S THING 2 FIX:

TODAY'S RUFNKIDDING ME?!

TODAY'S MIRACLE:

NEW INTEL:

GRATITUDE:

1.

2.

3.

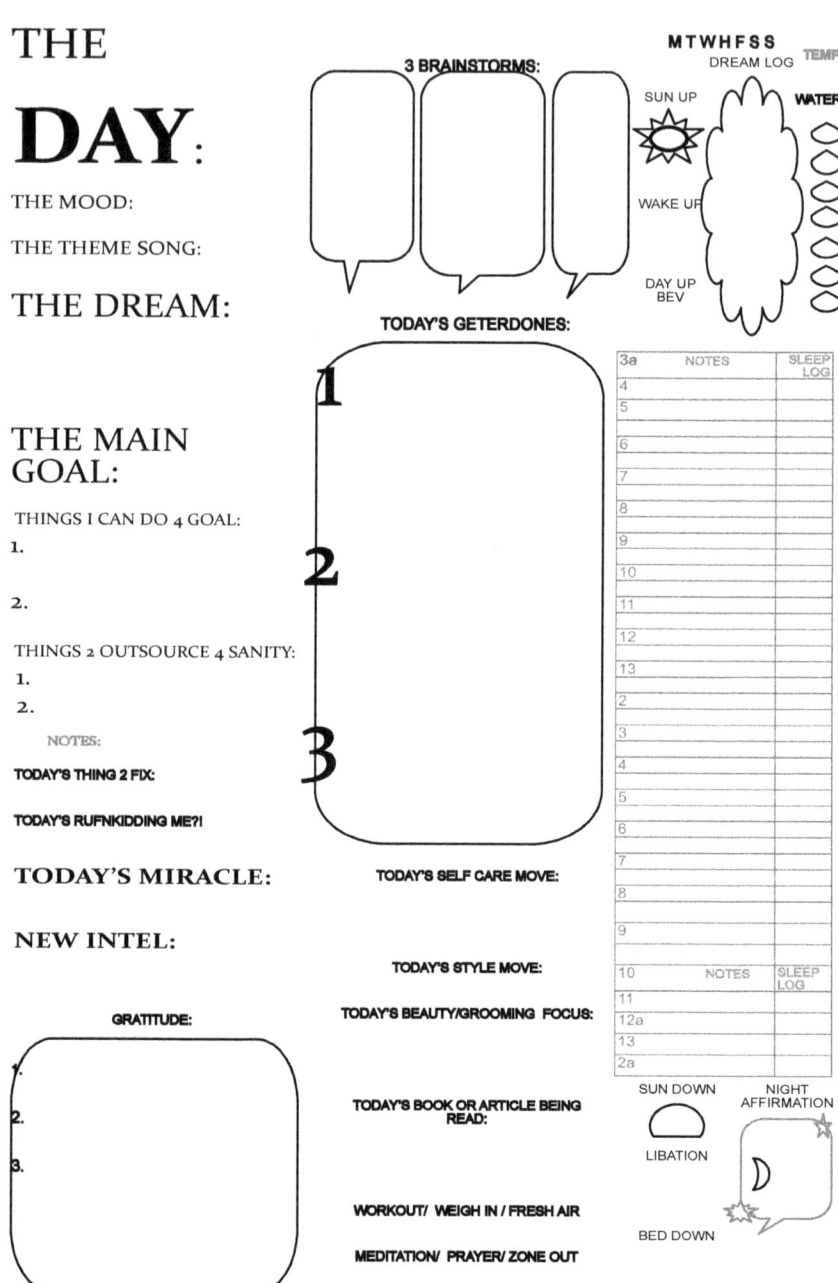

3 BRAINSTORMS:

TODAY'S GETERDONES:

1

2

3

TODAY'S SELF CARE MOVE:

TODAY'S STYLE MOVE:

TODAY'S BEAUTY/GROOMING FOCUS:

TODAY'S BOOK OR ARTICLE BEING READ:

WORKOUT/ WEIGH IN / FRESH AIR

MEDITATION/ PRAYER/ ZONE OUT

M T W H F S S
DREAM LOG   TEMP

SUN UP   WATER

WAKE UP

DAY UP BEV

	NOTES	SLEEP LOG
3a		
4		
5		
6		
7		
8		
9		
10		
11		
12		
13		
2		
3		
4		
5		
6		
7		
8		
9		
10	NOTES	SLEEP LOG
11		
12a		
13		
2a		

SUN DOWN   NIGHT AFFIRMATION

LIBATION

BED DOWN

THE
pregaming:

THE recap:

THE DAY:

THE MOOD:

THE THEME SONG:

THE DREAM:

THE MAIN GOAL:

THINGS I CAN DO 4 GOAL:
1.

2.

THINGS 2 OUTSOURCE 4 SANITY:
1.
2.

NOTES:

TODAY'S THING 2 FIX:

TODAY'S RUFNKIDDING ME?!

TODAY'S MIRACLE:

NEW INTEL:

GRATITUDE:
1.
2.
3.

3 BRAINSTORMS:

TODAY'S GETERDONES:
1
2
3

TODAY'S SELF CARE MOVE:

TODAY'S STYLE MOVE:

TODAY'S BEAUTY/GROOMING FOCUS:

TODAY'S BOOK OR ARTICLE BEING READ:

WORKOUT/ WEIGH IN / FRESH AIR

MEDITATION/ PRAYER/ ZONE OUT

M T W H F S S
DREAM LOG   TEMP
SUN UP   WATER
WAKE UP
DAY UP BEV

	NOTES	SLEEP LOG
3a		
4		
5		
6		
7		
8		
9		
10		
11		
12		
13		
2		
3		
4		
5		
6		
7		
8		
9		
10	NOTES	SLEEP LOG
11		
12a		
13		
2a		

SUN DOWN   NIGHT AFFIRMATION

LIBATION

BED DOWN

THE
pregaming:

THE recap:

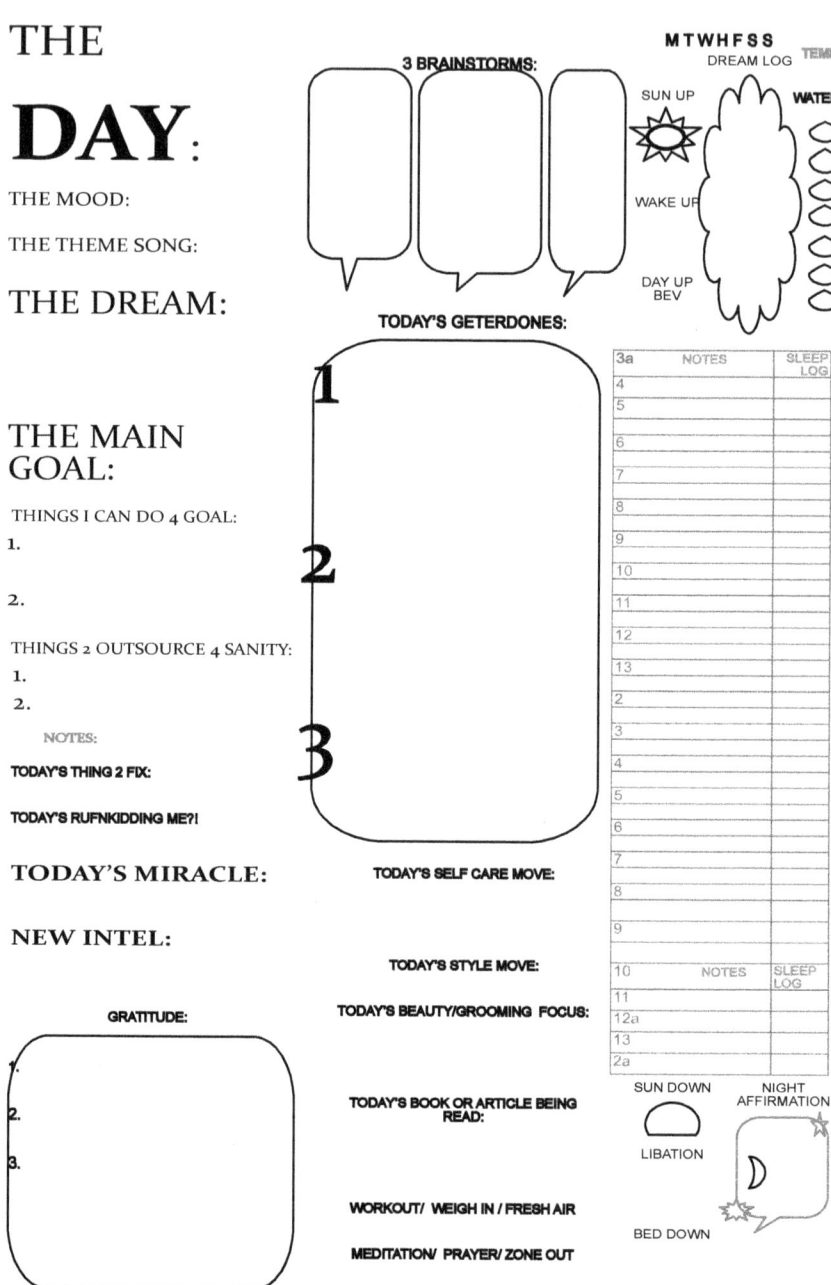

THE
pregaming:

THE recap:

THE
DAY:

THE MOOD:

THE THEME SONG:

THE DREAM:

THE MAIN GOAL:

THINGS I CAN DO 4 GOAL:
1.
2.

THINGS 2 OUTSOURCE 4 SANITY:
1.
2.

NOTES:

TODAY'S THING 2 FIX:

TODAY'S RUFNKIDDING ME?!

TODAY'S MIRACLE:

NEW INTEL:

GRATITUDE:
1.
2.
3.

3 BRAINSTORMS:

TODAY'S GETERDONES:
1
2
3

TODAY'S SELF CARE MOVE:

TODAY'S STYLE MOVE:

TODAY'S BEAUTY/GROOMING FOCUS:

TODAY'S BOOK OR ARTICLE BEING READ:

WORKOUT/ WEIGH IN / FRESH AIR

MEDITATION/ PRAYER/ ZONE OUT

THE
pregaming:

THE recap:

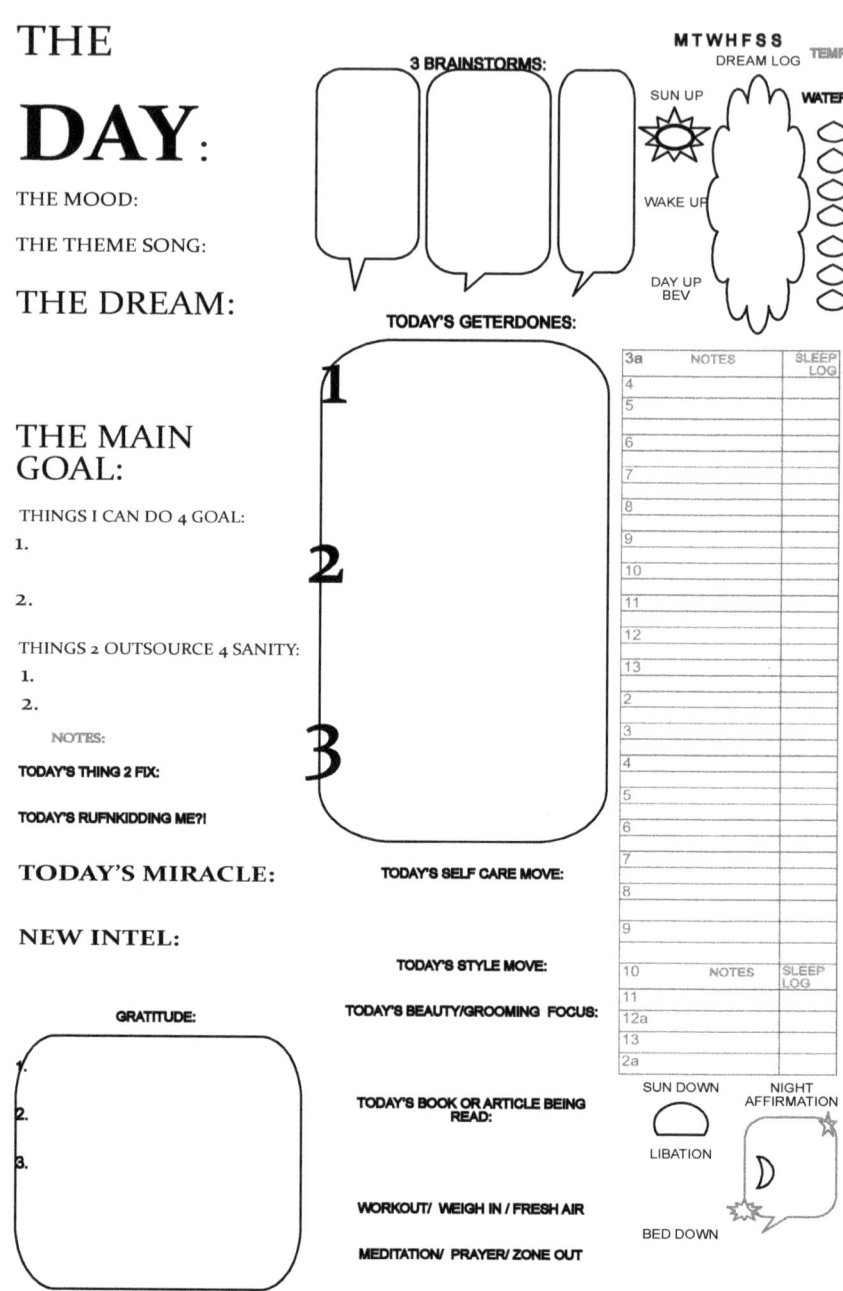

THE
pregaming:

THE recap:

THE DAY:

THE MOOD:

THE THEME SONG:

THE DREAM:

THE MAIN GOAL:

THINGS I CAN DO 4 GOAL:
1.
2.

THINGS 2 OUTSOURCE 4 SANITY:
1.
2.

NOTES:

TODAY'S THING 2 FIX:

TODAY'S RUFNKIDDING ME?!

TODAY'S MIRACLE:

NEW INTEL:

GRATITUDE:
1.
2.
3.

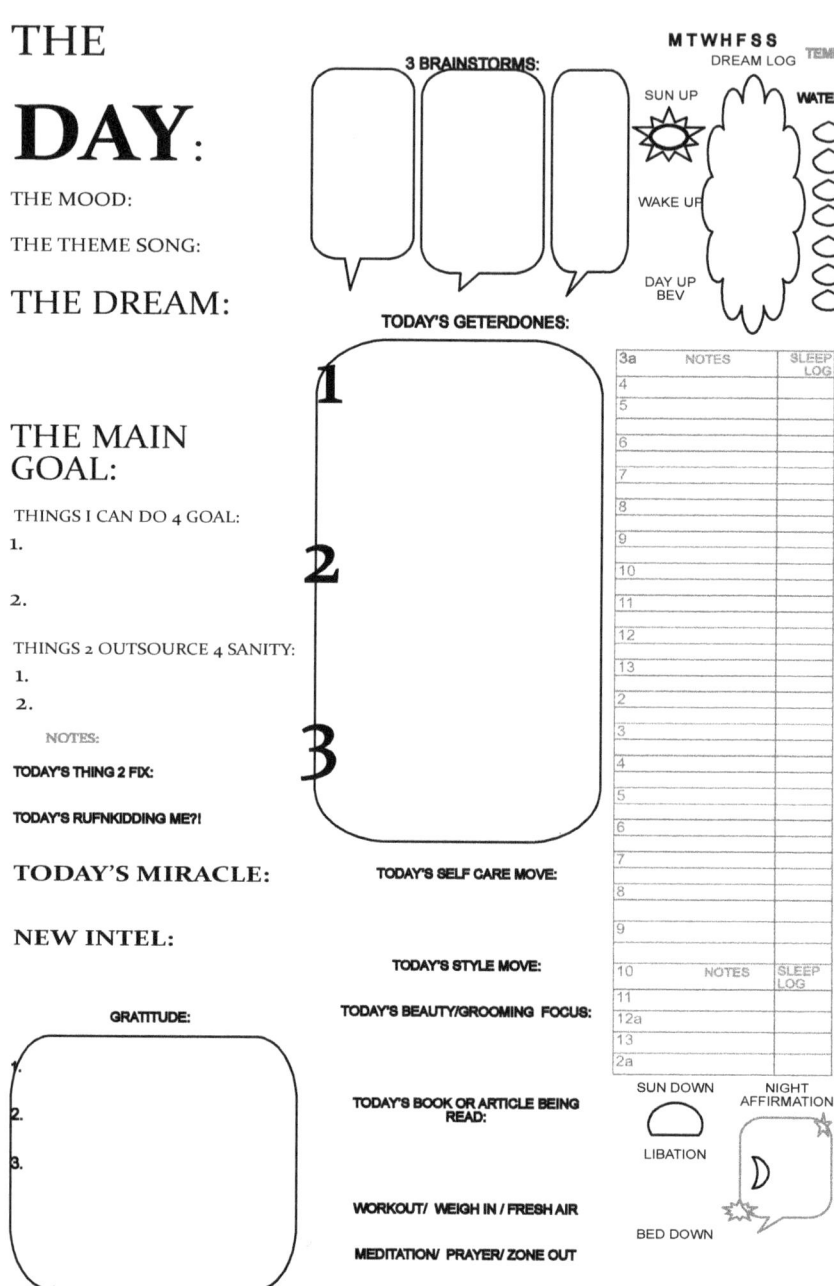

3 BRAINSTORMS:

TODAY'S GETERDONES:
1
2
3

TODAY'S SELF CARE MOVE:

TODAY'S STYLE MOVE:

TODAY'S BEAUTY/GROOMING FOCUS:

TODAY'S BOOK OR ARTICLE BEING READ:

WORKOUT/ WEIGH IN / FRESH AIR

MEDITATION/ PRAYER/ ZONE OUT

M T W H F S S
DREAM LOG   TEMP
SUN UP
WAKE UP
DAY UP BEV
WATER

NOTES | SLEEP LOG
3a
4
5
6
7
8
9
10
11
12
13
2
3
4
5
6
7
8
9
10 | NOTES | SLEEP LOG
11
12a
13
2a

SUN DOWN
LIBATION
BED DOWN
NIGHT AFFIRMATION

THE
pregaming:

THE recap:

THE pregaming:

THE recap:

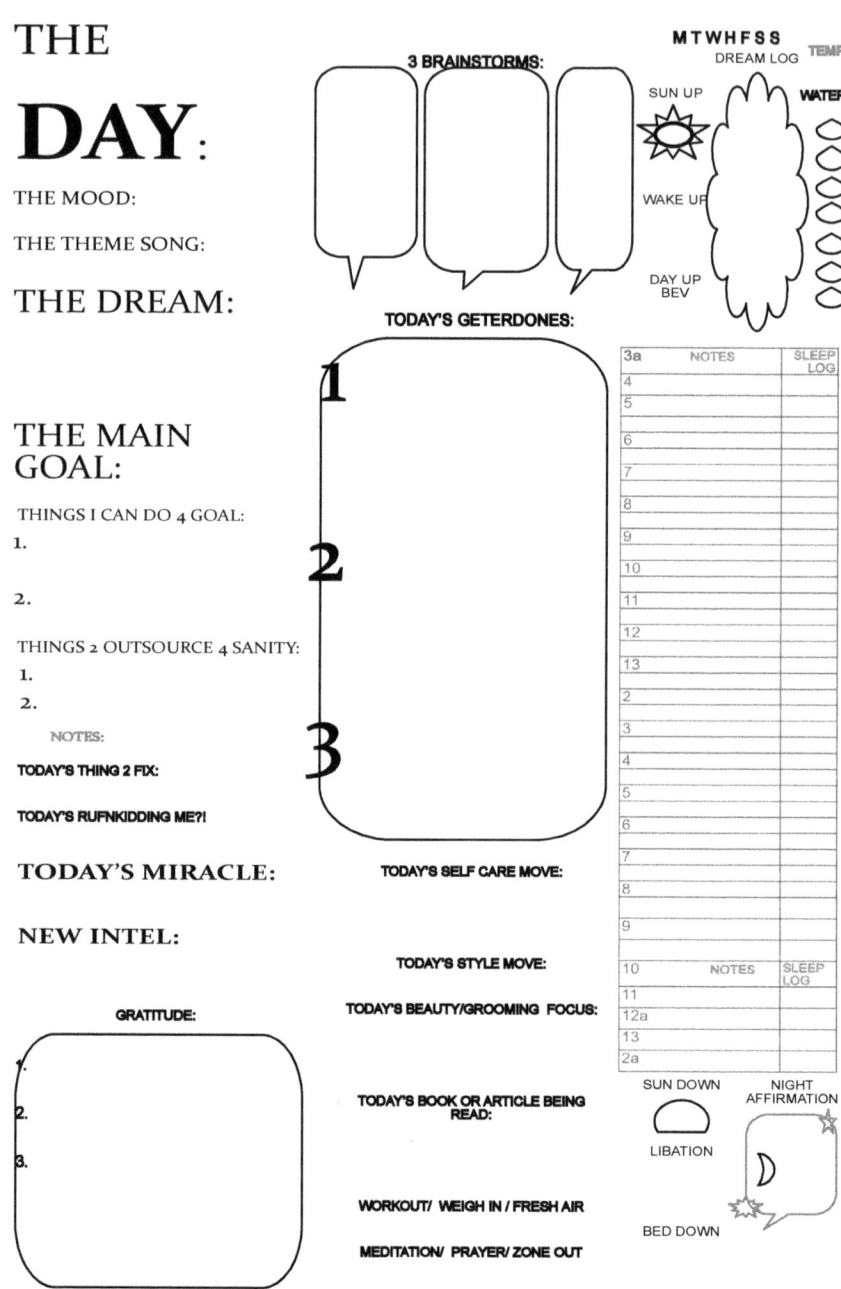

THE pregaming:

THE recap:

THE DAY:

THE MOOD:

THE THEME SONG:

THE DREAM:

THE MAIN GOAL:

THINGS I CAN DO 4 GOAL:
1.
2.

THINGS 2 OUTSOURCE 4 SANITY:
1.
2.
   NOTES:

TODAY'S THING 2 FIX:

TODAY'S RUFNKIDDING ME?!

TODAY'S MIRACLE:

NEW INTEL:

GRATITUDE:
1.
2.
3.

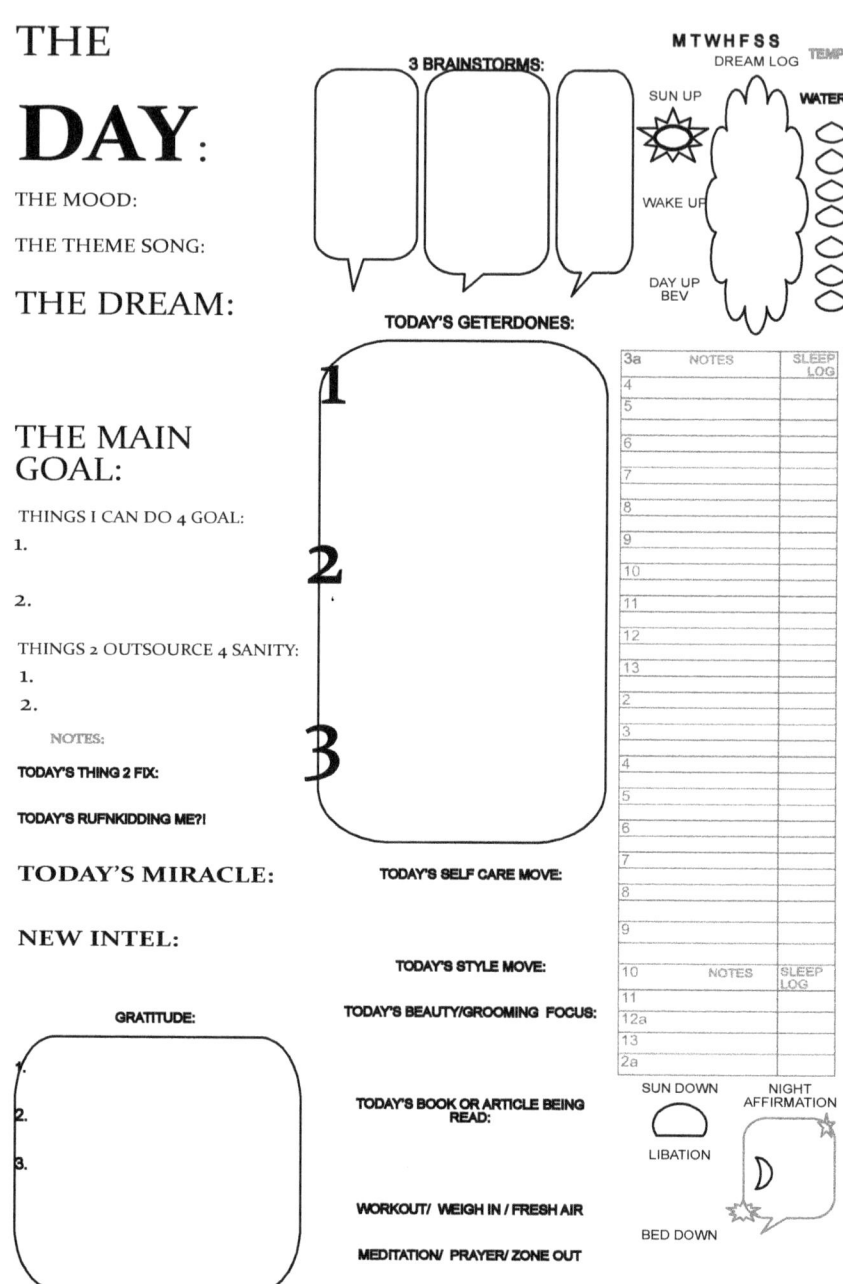

3 BRAINSTORMS:

TODAY'S GETERDONES:
1.
2.
3.

TODAY'S SELF CARE MOVE:

TODAY'S STYLE MOVE:

TODAY'S BEAUTY/GROOMING FOCUS:

TODAY'S BOOK OR ARTICLE BEING READ:

WORKOUT/ WEIGH IN / FRESH AIR

MEDITATION/ PRAYER/ ZONE OUT

M T W H F S S
DREAM LOG   TEMP
SUN UP   WATER
WAKE UP
DAY UP BEV

	NOTES	SLEEP LOG
3a		
4		
5		
6		
7		
8		
9		
10		
11		
12		
13		
2		
3		
4		
5		
6		
7		
8		
9		
10	NOTES	SLEEP LOG
11		
12a		
13		
2a		

SUN DOWN   NIGHT AFFIRMATION
LIBATION
BED DOWN

THE
pregaming:

THE recap:

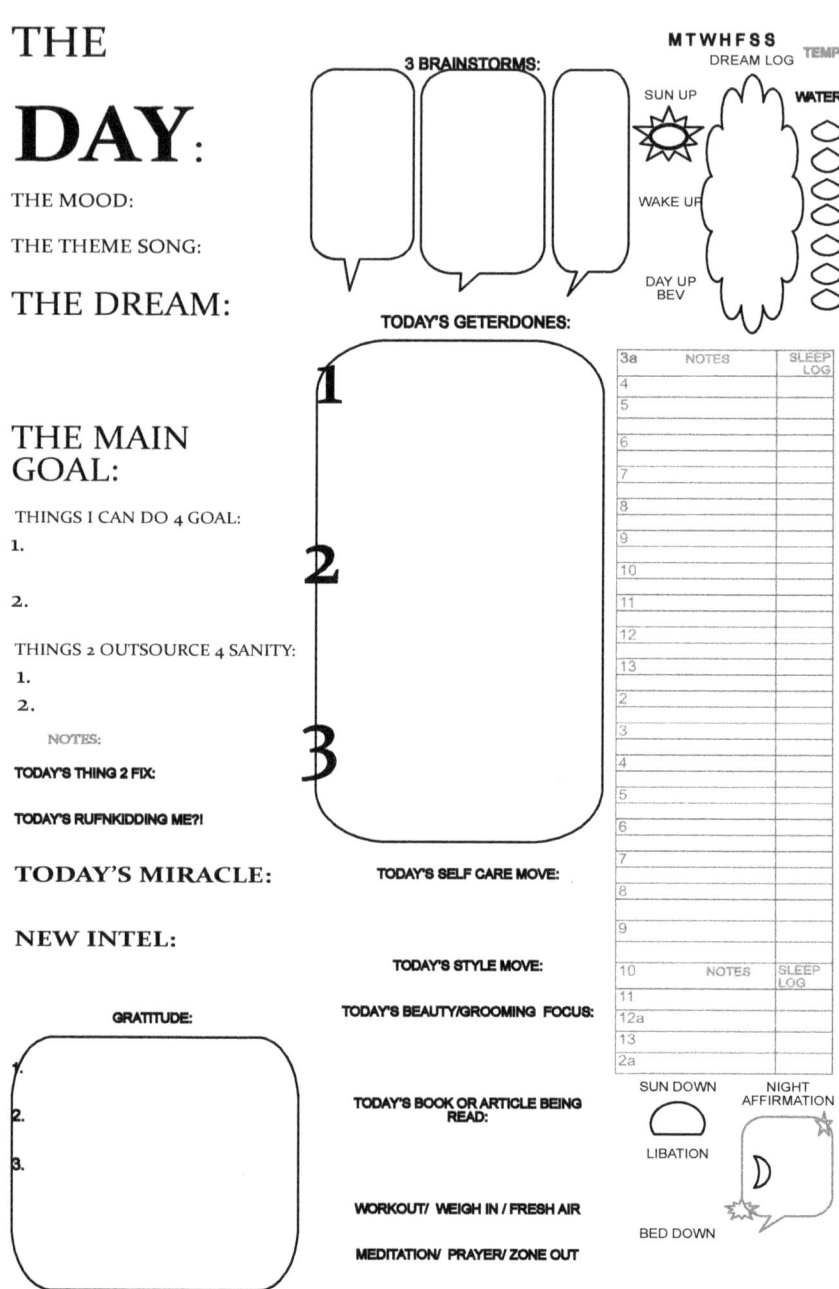

THE
pregaming:

THE recap:

THE
pregaming:

THE recap:

THE DAY:

THE MOOD:

THE THEME SONG:

THE DREAM:

THE MAIN GOAL:

THINGS I CAN DO 4 GOAL:
1.
2.

THINGS 2 OUTSOURCE 4 SANITY:
1.
2.

NOTES:

TODAY'S THING 2 FIX:

TODAY'S RUFNKIDDING ME?!

TODAY'S MIRACLE:

NEW INTEL:

GRATITUDE:
1.
2.
3.

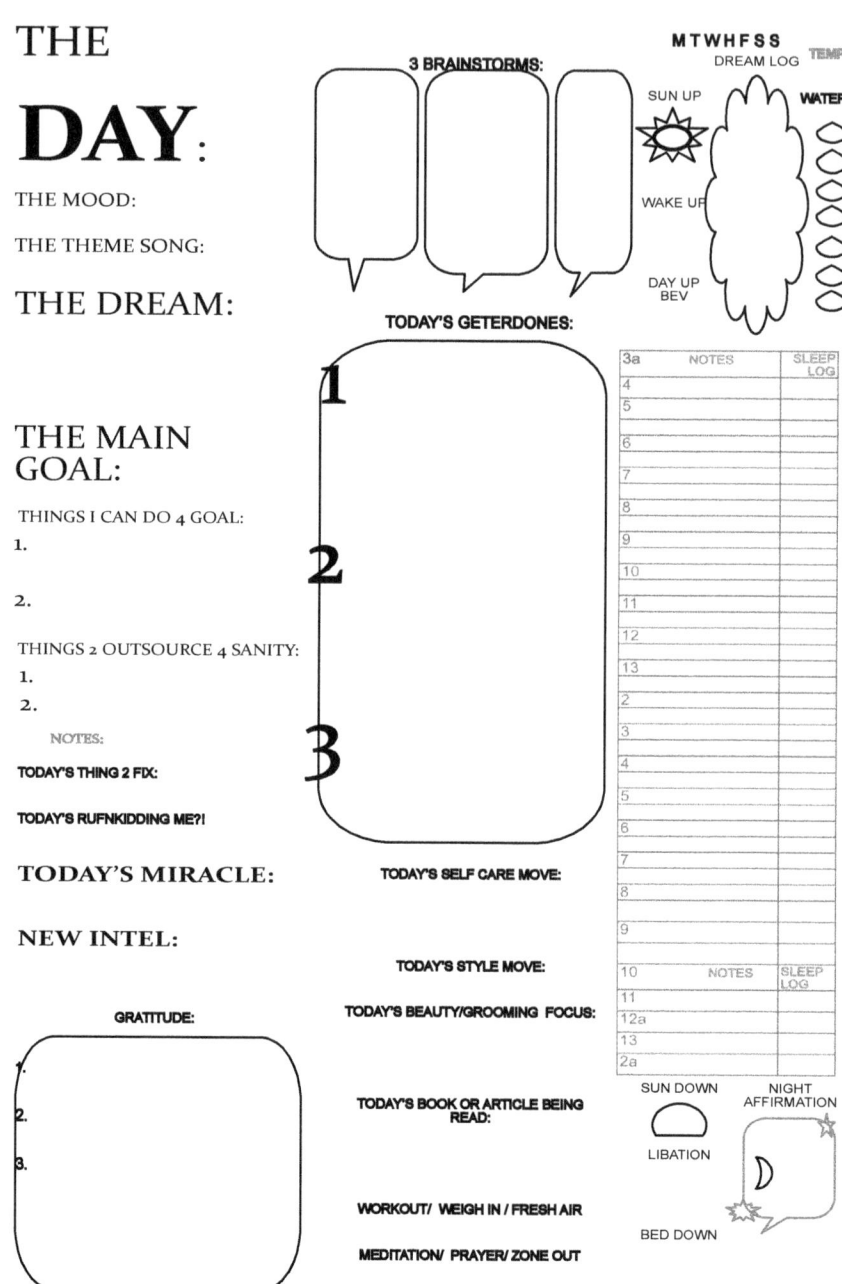

3 BRAINSTORMS:

TODAY'S GETERDONES:
1.
2.
3.

TODAY'S SELF CARE MOVE:

TODAY'S STYLE MOVE:

TODAY'S BEAUTY/GROOMING FOCUS:

TODAY'S BOOK OR ARTICLE BEING READ:

WORKOUT/ WEIGH IN / FRESH AIR

MEDITATION/ PRAYER/ ZONE OUT

M T W H F S S
DREAM LOG   TEMP

SUN UP   WATER

WAKE UP

DAY UP BEV

	NOTES	SLEEP LOG
3a		
4		
5		
6		
7		
8		
9		
10		
11		
12		
13		
2		
3		
4		
5		
6		
7		
8		
9		
10	NOTES	SLEEP LOG
11		
12a		
13		
2a		

SUN DOWN   NIGHT AFFIRMATION

LIBATION

BED DOWN

THE
pregaming:

THE recap:

THE
DAY:

THE MOOD:

THE THEME SONG:

THE DREAM:

THE MAIN GOAL:

THINGS I CAN DO 4 GOAL:
1.

2.

THINGS 2 OUTSOURCE 4 SANITY:
1.
2.

NOTES:

TODAY'S THING 2 FIX:

TODAY'S RUFNKIDDING ME?!

TODAY'S MIRACLE:

NEW INTEL:

GRATITUDE:

1.

2.

3.

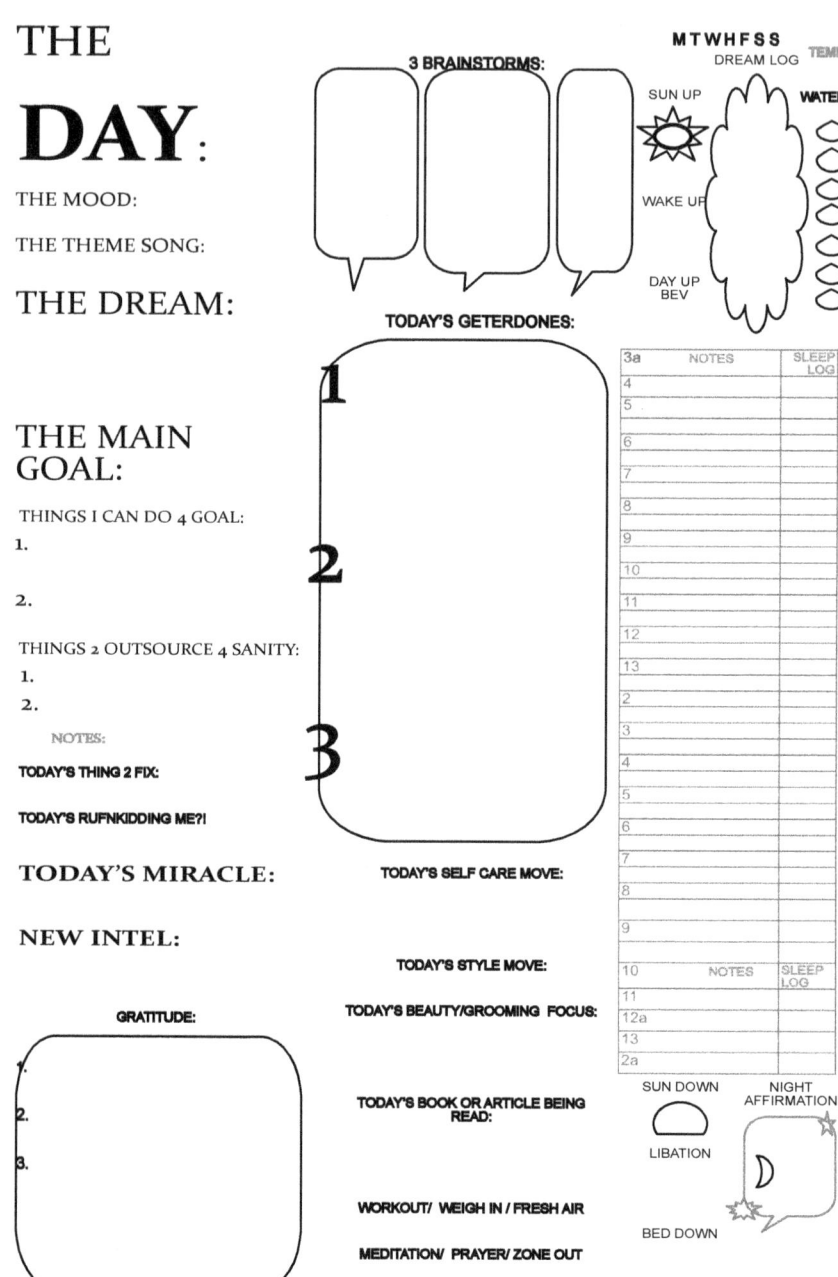

3 BRAINSTORMS:

TODAY'S GETERDONES:

TODAY'S SELF CARE MOVE:

TODAY'S STYLE MOVE:

TODAY'S BEAUTY/GROOMING FOCUS:

TODAY'S BOOK OR ARTICLE BEING READ:

WORKOUT/ WEIGH IN / FRESH AIR

MEDITATION/ PRAYER/ ZONE OUT

M T W H F S S
DREAM LOG   TEMP

SUN UP   WATER

WAKE UP

DAY UP BEV

	NOTES	SLEEP LOG
3a		
4		
5		
6		
7		
8		
9		
10		
11		
12		
13		
2		
3		
4		
5		
6		
7		
8		
9		
10	NOTES	SLEEP LOG
11		
12a		
13		
2a		

SUN DOWN   NIGHT AFFIRMATION

LIBATION

BED DOWN

THE pregaming:

THE recap:

THE
pregaming:

THE recap:

THE DAY:

THE MOOD:

THE THEME SONG:

THE DREAM:

THE MAIN GOAL:

THINGS I CAN DO 4 GOAL:
1.

2.

THINGS 2 OUTSOURCE 4 SANITY:
1.
2.

   NOTES:

TODAY'S THING 2 FIX:

TODAY'S RUFNKIDDING ME?!

TODAY'S MIRACLE:

NEW INTEL:

GRATITUDE:

1.

2.

3.

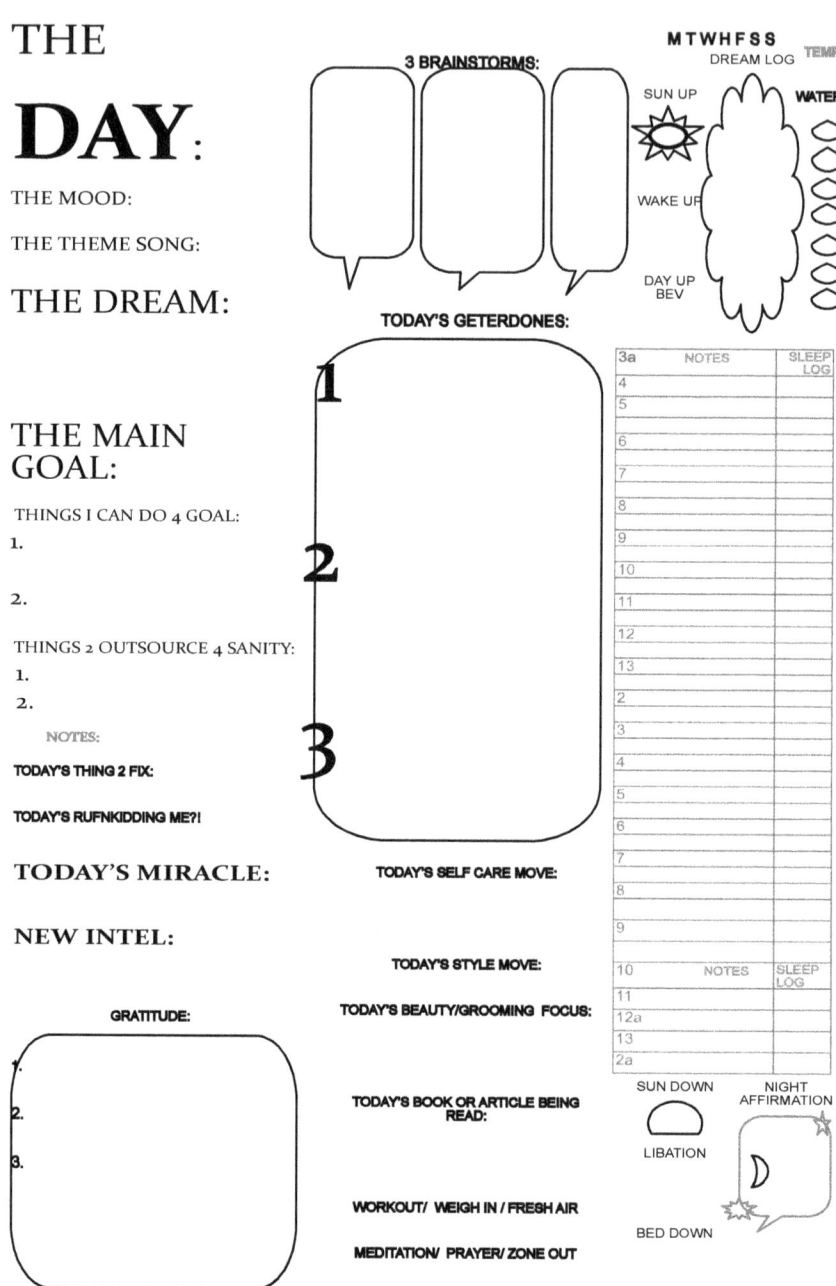

3 BRAINSTORMS:

TODAY'S GETERDONES:

1

2

3

TODAY'S SELF CARE MOVE:

TODAY'S STYLE MOVE:

TODAY'S BEAUTY/GROOMING FOCUS:

TODAY'S BOOK OR ARTICLE BEING READ:

WORKOUT/ WEIGH IN / FRESH AIR

MEDITATION/ PRAYER/ ZONE OUT

M T W H F S S
DREAM LOG   TEMP

SUN UP   WATER

WAKE UP

DAY UP BEV

3a	NOTES	SLEEP LOG
4		
5		
6		
7		
8		
9		
10		
11		
12		
13		
2		
3		
4		
5		
6		
7		
8		
9		
10	NOTES	SLEEP LOG
11		
12a		
13		
2a		

SUN DOWN   NIGHT AFFIRMATION

LIBATION

BED DOWN

THE pregaming:

THE recap:

THE
DAY:

THE MOOD:

THE THEME SONG:

THE DREAM:

THE MAIN GOAL:

THINGS I CAN DO 4 GOAL:
1.

2.

THINGS 2 OUTSOURCE 4 SANITY:
1.
2.

NOTES:

TODAY'S THING 2 FIX:

TODAY'S RUFNKIDDING ME?!

TODAY'S MIRACLE:

NEW INTEL:

GRATITUDE:
1.
2.
3.

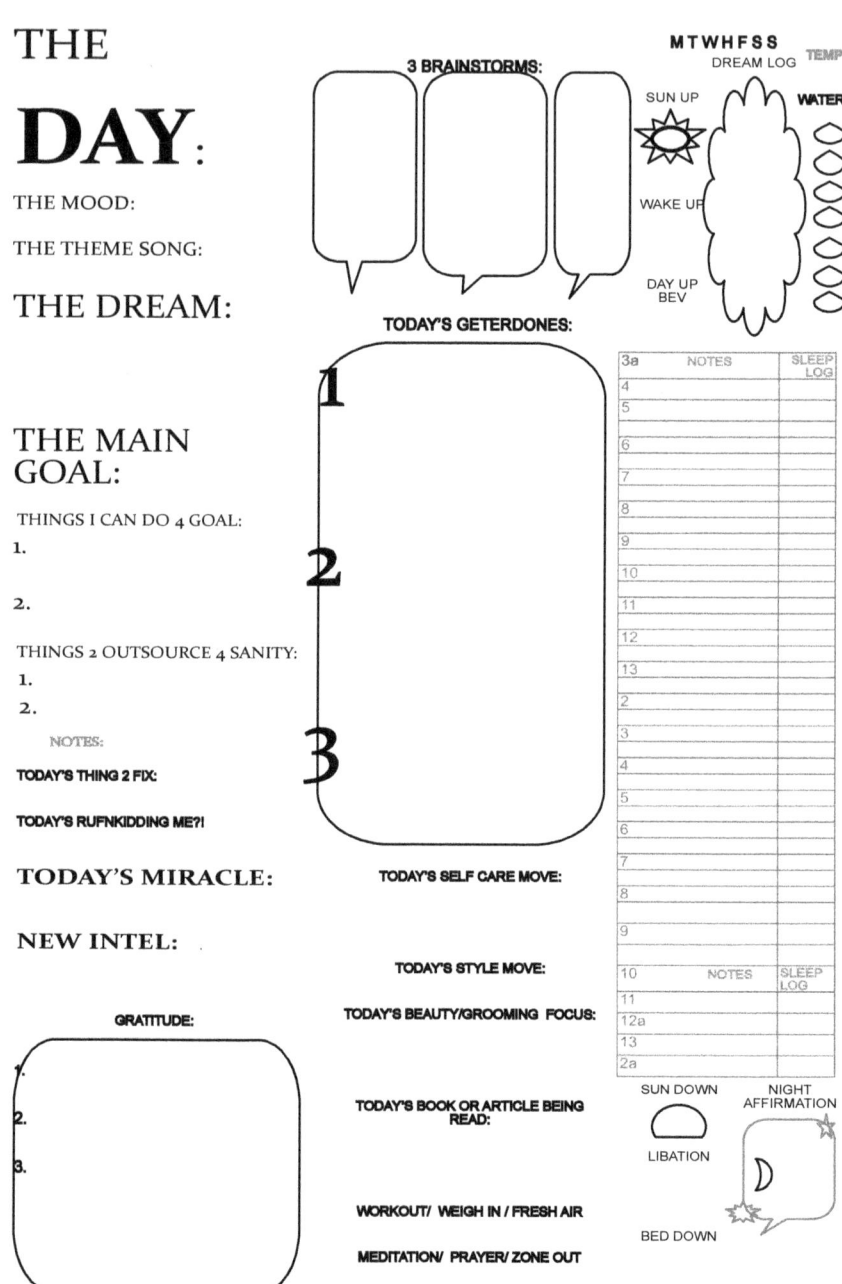

3 BRAINSTORMS:

TODAY'S GETERDONES:
1
2
3

TODAY'S SELF CARE MOVE:

TODAY'S STYLE MOVE:

TODAY'S BEAUTY/GROOMING FOCUS:

TODAY'S BOOK OR ARTICLE BEING READ:

WORKOUT/ WEIGH IN / FRESH AIR

MEDITATION/ PRAYER/ ZONE OUT

M T W H F S S
DREAM LOG   TEMP

SUN UP   WATER

WAKE UP

DAY UP BEV

	NOTES	SLEEP LOG
3a		
4		
5		
6		
7		
8		
9		
10		
11		
12		
13		
2		
3		
4		
5		
6		
7		
8		
9		
10	NOTES	SLEEP LOG
11		
12a		
13		
2a		

SUN DOWN   NIGHT AFFIRMATION

LIBATION

BED DOWN

THE
pregaming:

THE recap:

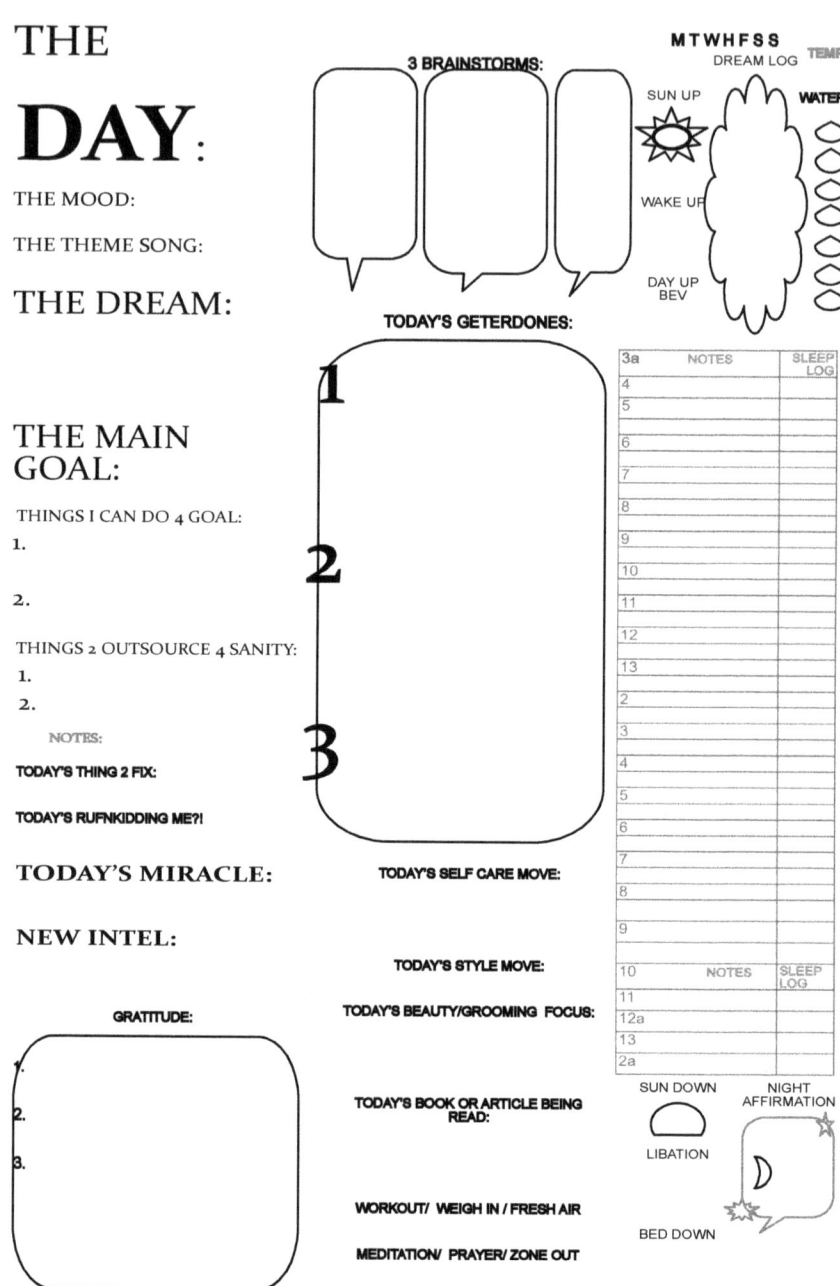

THE
pregaming:

THE recap:

THE DAY:

THE MOOD:

THE THEME SONG:

THE DREAM:

THE MAIN GOAL:

THINGS I CAN DO 4 GOAL:
1.
2.

THINGS 2 OUTSOURCE 4 SANITY:
1.
2.

NOTES:

TODAY'S THING 2 FIX:

TODAY'S RUFNKIDDING ME?!

TODAY'S MIRACLE:

NEW INTEL:

GRATITUDE:
1.
2.
3.

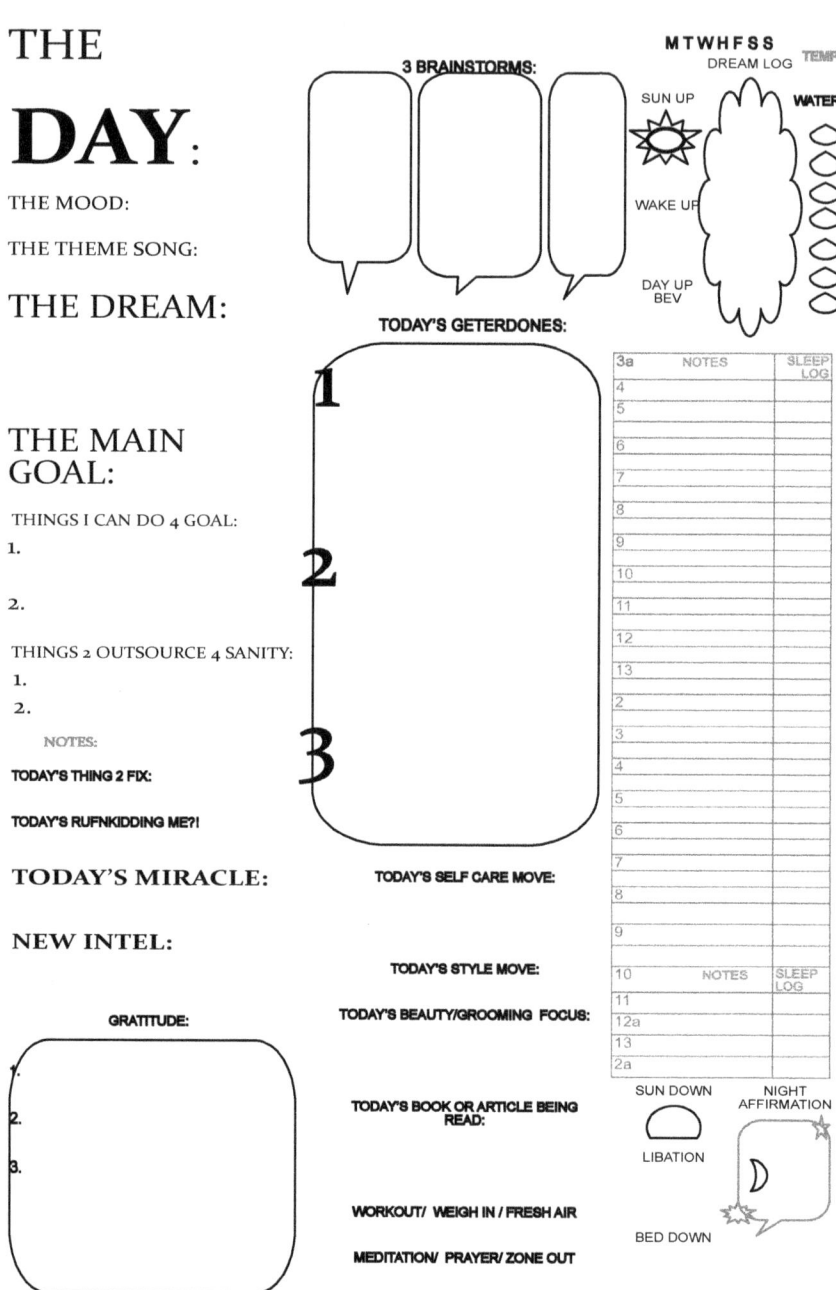

3 BRAINSTORMS:

TODAY'S GETERDONES:
1
2
3

TODAY'S SELF CARE MOVE:

TODAY'S STYLE MOVE:

TODAY'S BEAUTY/GROOMING FOCUS:

TODAY'S BOOK OR ARTICLE BEING READ:

WORKOUT/ WEIGH IN / FRESH AIR

MEDITATION/ PRAYER/ ZONE OUT

M T W H F S S
DREAM LOG   TEMP
SUN UP
WATER
WAKE UP
DAY UP BEV

3a	NOTES	SLEEP LOG
4		
5		
6		
7		
8		
9		
10		
11		
12		
13		
2		
3		
4		
5		
6		
7		
8		
9		
10	NOTES	SLEEP LOG
11		
12a		
13		
2a		

SUN DOWN
LIBATION
BED DOWN
NIGHT AFFIRMATION

THE
pregaming:

THE recap:

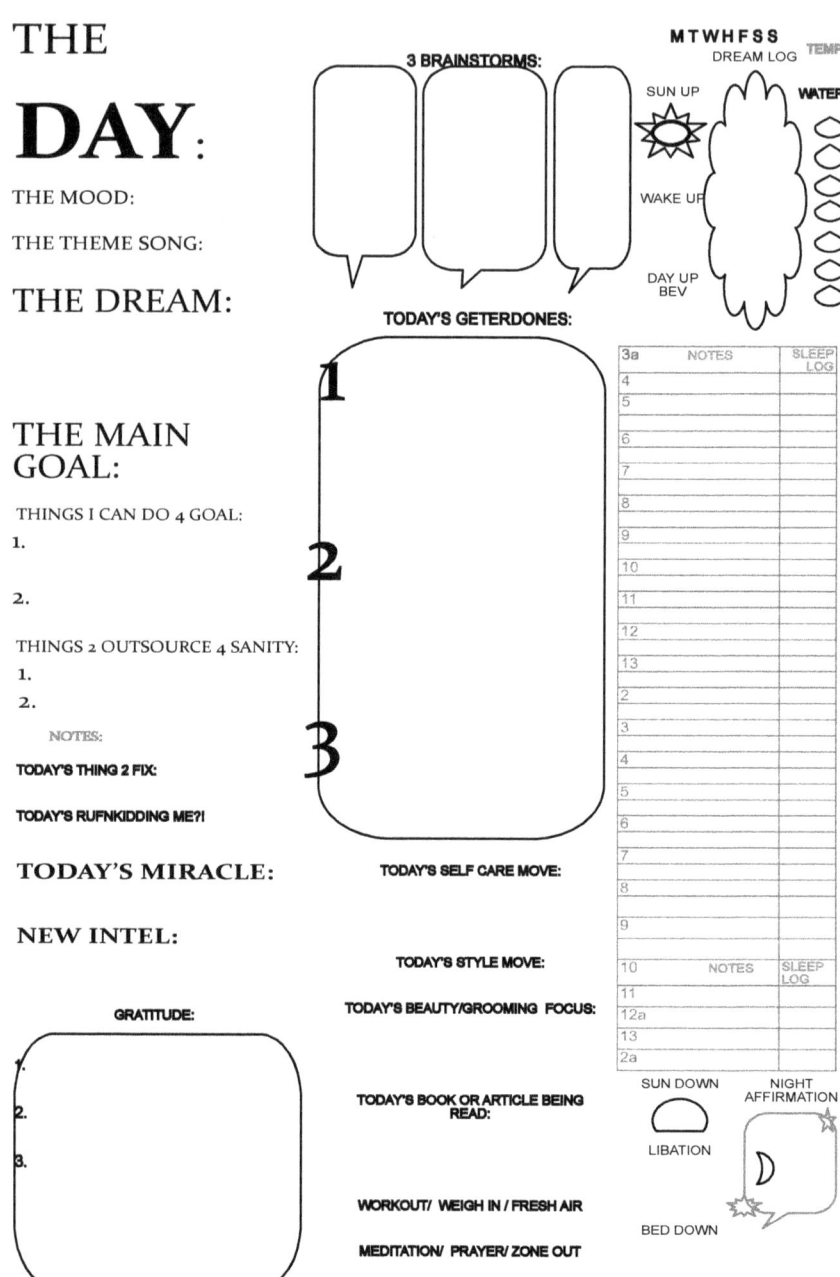

THE
pregaming:

THE recap:

THE pregaming:

THE recap:

THE DAY:

THE MOOD:

THE THEME SONG:

THE DREAM:

THE MAIN GOAL:

THINGS I CAN DO 4 GOAL:
1.
2.

THINGS 2 OUTSOURCE 4 SANITY:
1.
2.
   NOTES:

TODAY'S THING 2 FIX:

TODAY'S RUFNKIDDING ME?!

TODAY'S MIRACLE:

NEW INTEL:

GRATITUDE:
1.
2.
3.

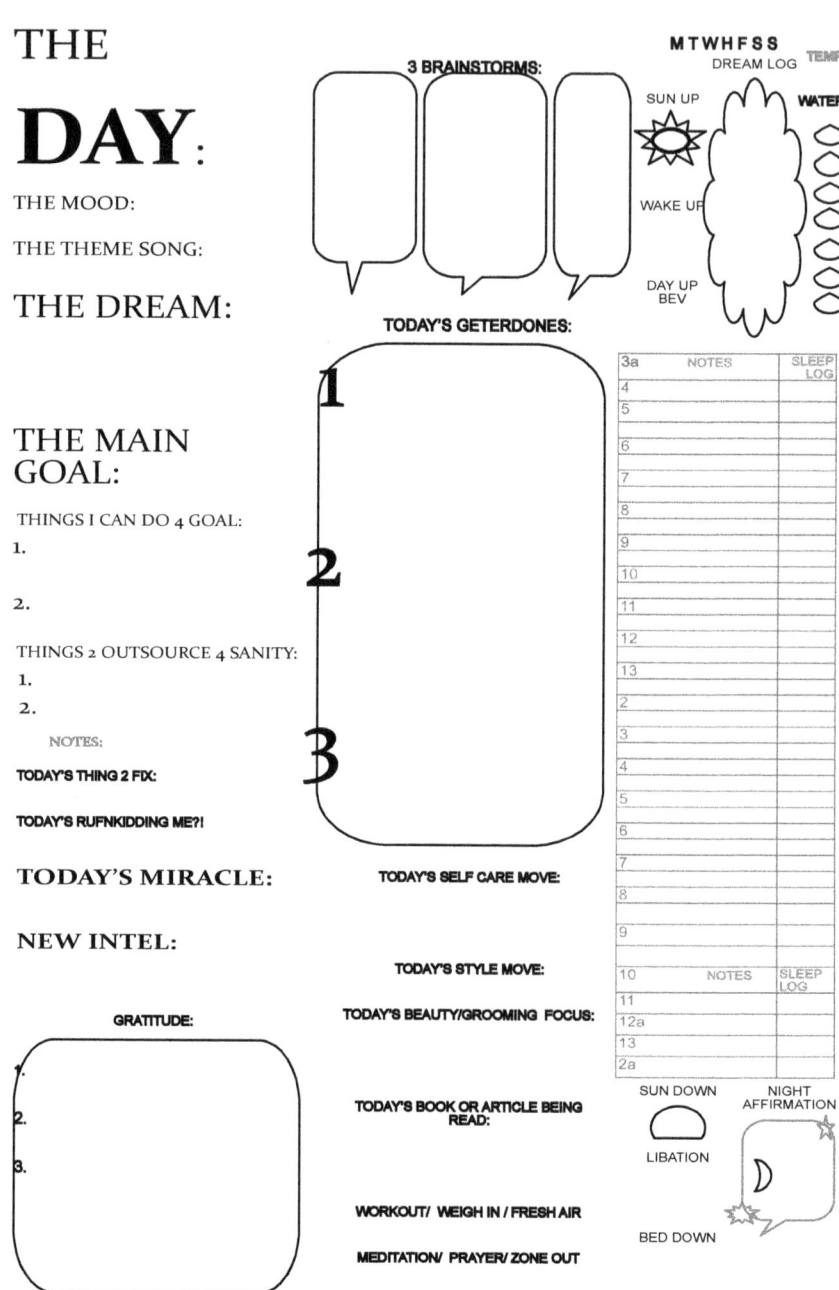

3 BRAINSTORMS:

TODAY'S GETERDONES:
1.
2.
3.

TODAY'S SELF CARE MOVE:

TODAY'S STYLE MOVE:

TODAY'S BEAUTY/GROOMING FOCUS:

TODAY'S BOOK OR ARTICLE BEING READ:

WORKOUT/ WEIGH IN / FRESH AIR

MEDITATION/ PRAYER/ ZONE OUT

M T W H F S S
DREAM LOG   TEMP

SUN UP   WATER

WAKE UP

DAY UP BEV

NOTES   SLEEP LOG
3a
4
5
6
7
8
9
10
11
12
13
2
3
4
5
6
7
8
9
10   NOTES   SLEEP LOG
11
12a
13
2a

SUN DOWN   NIGHT AFFIRMATION

LIBATION

BED DOWN

THE
pregaming:

THE recap:

THE DAY:

THE MOOD:

THE THEME SONG:

THE DREAM:

THE MAIN GOAL:

THINGS I CAN DO 4 GOAL:
1.

2.

THINGS 2 OUTSOURCE 4 SANITY:
1.
2.

NOTES:

TODAY'S THING 2 FIX:

TODAY'S RUFNKIDDING ME?!

TODAY'S MIRACLE:

NEW INTEL:

GRATITUDE:
1.
2.
3.

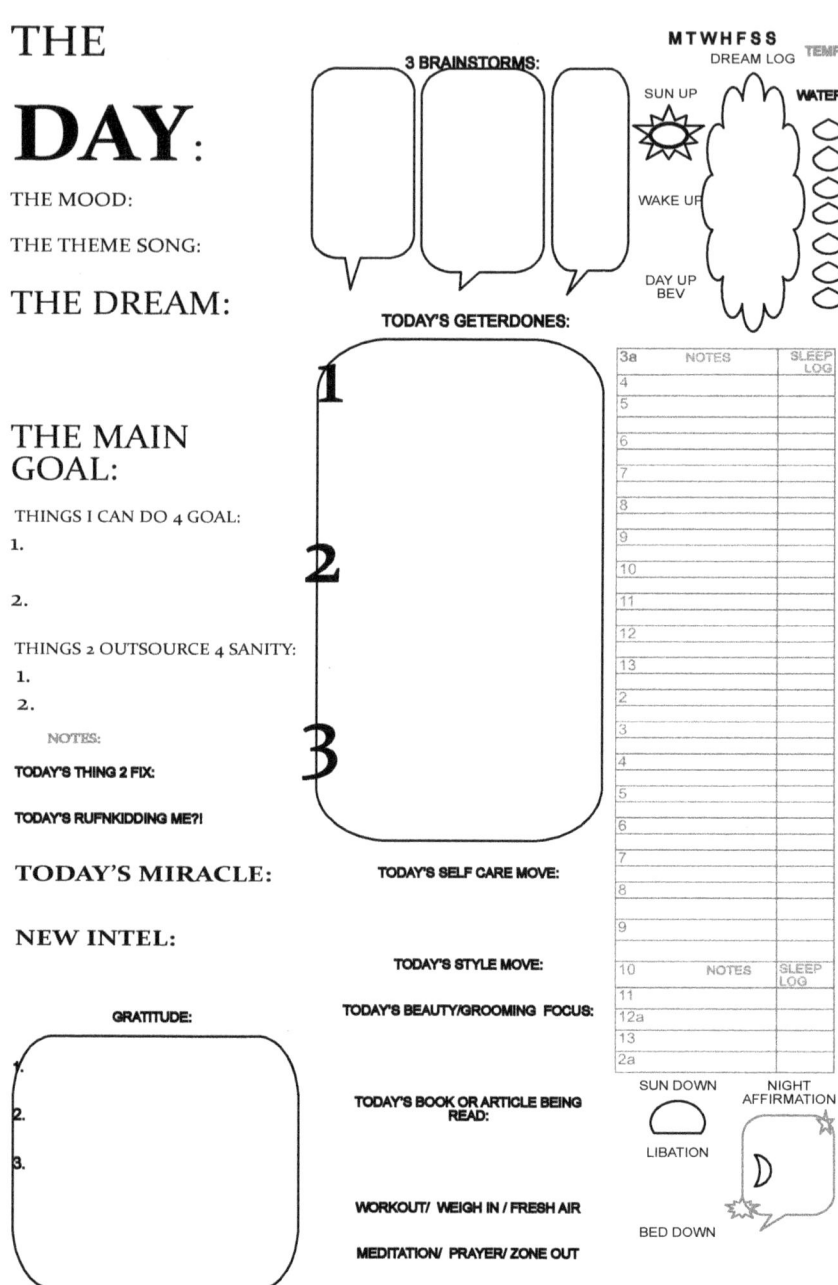

3 BRAINSTORMS:

TODAY'S GETERDONES:
1
2
3

TODAY'S SELF CARE MOVE:

TODAY'S STYLE MOVE:

TODAY'S BEAUTY/GROOMING FOCUS:

TODAY'S BOOK OR ARTICLE BEING READ:

WORKOUT/ WEIGH IN / FRESH AIR

MEDITATION/ PRAYER/ ZONE OUT

M T W H F S S
DREAM LOG   TEMP

SUN UP

WAKE UP

DAY UP BEV

WATER

3a NOTES   SLEEP LOG
4
5
6
7
8
9
10
11
12
13
2
3
4
5
6
7
8
9
10 NOTES   SLEEP LOG
11
12a
13
2a

SUN DOWN

LIBATION

BED DOWN

NIGHT AFFIRMATION

THE
pregaming:

THE recap:

THE DAY:

THE MOOD:

THE THEME SONG:

THE DREAM:

THE MAIN GOAL:

THINGS I CAN DO 4 GOAL:
1.

2.

THINGS 2 OUTSOURCE 4 SANITY:
1.
2.

   NOTES:

TODAY'S THING 2 FIX:

TODAY'S RUFNKIDDING ME?!

TODAY'S MIRACLE:

NEW INTEL:

GRATITUDE:
1.
2.
3.

3 BRAINSTORMS:

TODAY'S GETERDONES:

TODAY'S SELF CARE MOVE:

TODAY'S STYLE MOVE:

TODAY'S BEAUTY/GROOMING FOCUS:

TODAY'S BOOK OR ARTICLE BEING READ:

WORKOUT/ WEIGH IN / FRESH AIR

MEDITATION/ PRAYER/ ZONE OUT

M T W H F S S
DREAM LOG   TEMP
SUN UP   WATER
WAKE UP
DAY UP BEV

NOTES   SLEEP LOG

SUN DOWN   NIGHT AFFIRMATION
LIBATION
BED DOWN

THE
pregaming:

THE recap:

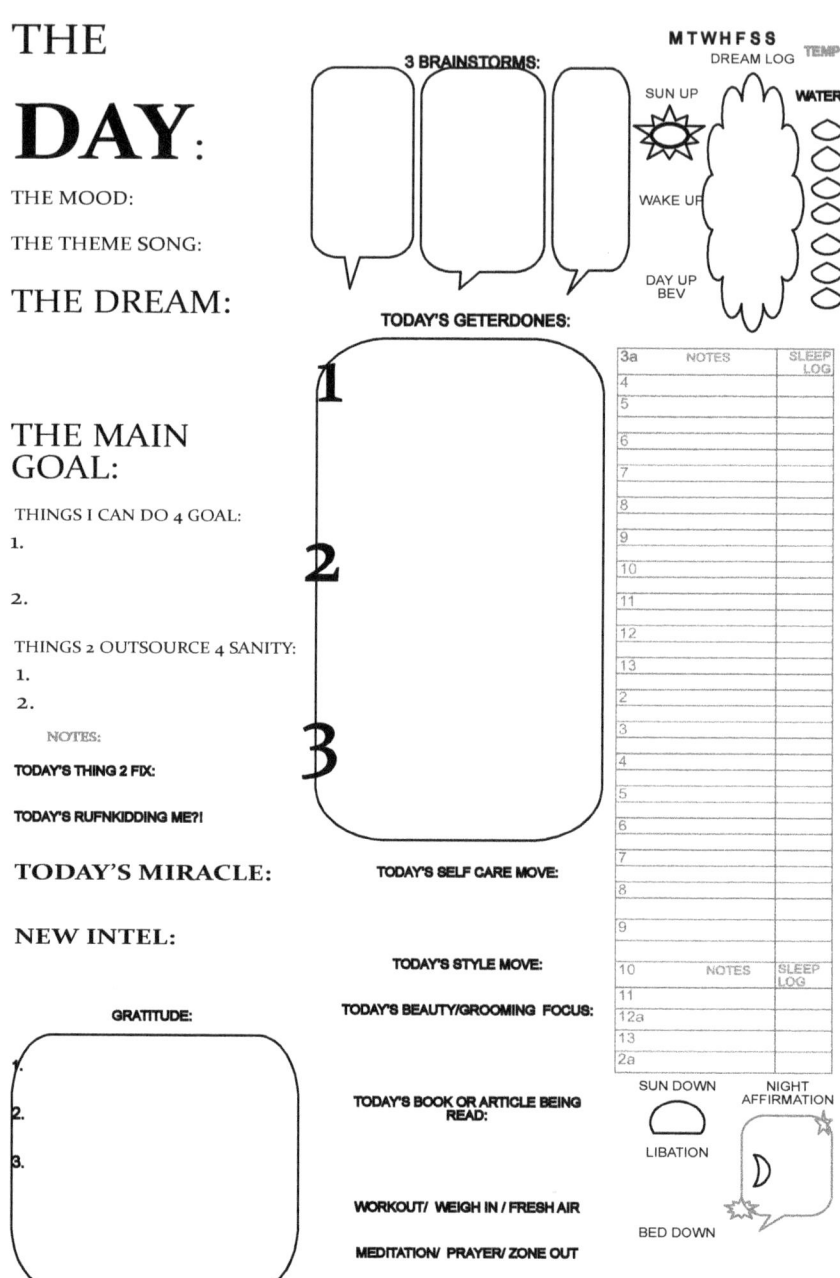

THE
pregaming:

THE recap:

THE
DAY:

THE MOOD:

THE THEME SONG:

THE DREAM:

THE MAIN GOAL:

THINGS I CAN DO 4 GOAL:
1.
2.

THINGS 2 OUTSOURCE 4 SANITY:
1.
2.

NOTES:

TODAY'S THING 2 FIX:

TODAY'S RUFNKIDDING ME?!

TODAY'S MIRACLE:

NEW INTEL:

GRATITUDE:
1.
2.
3.

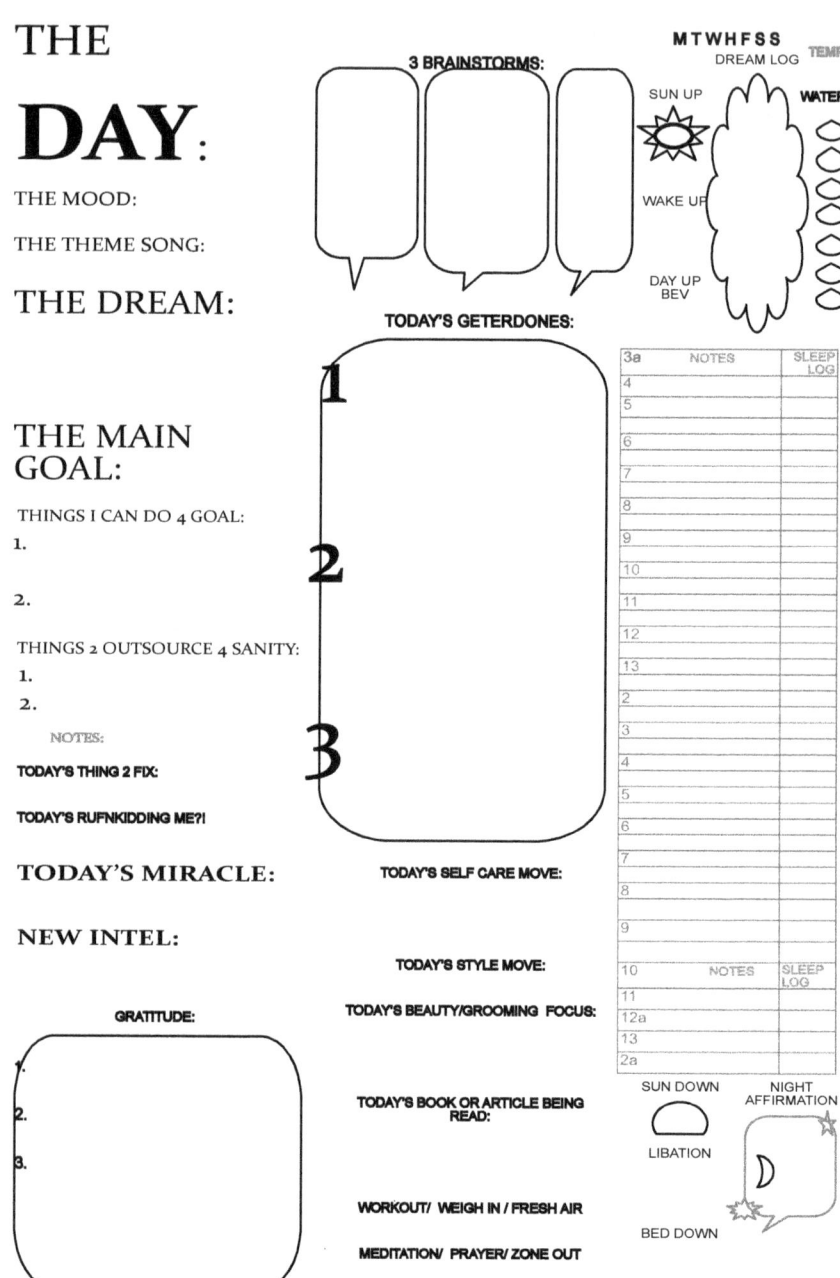

3 BRAINSTORMS:

TODAY'S GETERDONES:
1
2
3

TODAY'S SELF CARE MOVE:

TODAY'S STYLE MOVE:

TODAY'S BEAUTY/GROOMING FOCUS:

TODAY'S BOOK OR ARTICLE BEING READ:

WORKOUT/ WEIGH IN / FRESH AIR

MEDITATION/ PRAYER/ ZONE OUT

M T W H F S S
DREAM LOG   TEMP

SUN UP   WATER

WAKE UP

DAY UP BEV

	NOTES	SLEEP LOG
3a		
4		
5		
6		
7		
8		
9		
10		
11		
12		
13		
2		
3		
4		
5		
6		
7		
8		
9		
10	NOTES	SLEEP LOG
11		
12a		
13		
2a		

SUN DOWN

LIBATION

BED DOWN

NIGHT AFFIRMATION

THE
pregaming:

THE recap:

THE
pregaming:

THE recap:

THE pregaming:

THE recap:

THE
DAY:

THE MOOD:

THE THEME SONG:

THE DREAM:

THE MAIN GOAL:

THINGS I CAN DO 4 GOAL:
1.
2.

THINGS 2 OUTSOURCE 4 SANITY:
1.
2.

NOTES:

TODAY'S THING 2 FIX:

TODAY'S RUFNKIDDING ME?!

TODAY'S MIRACLE:

NEW INTEL:

GRATITUDE:
1.
2.
3.

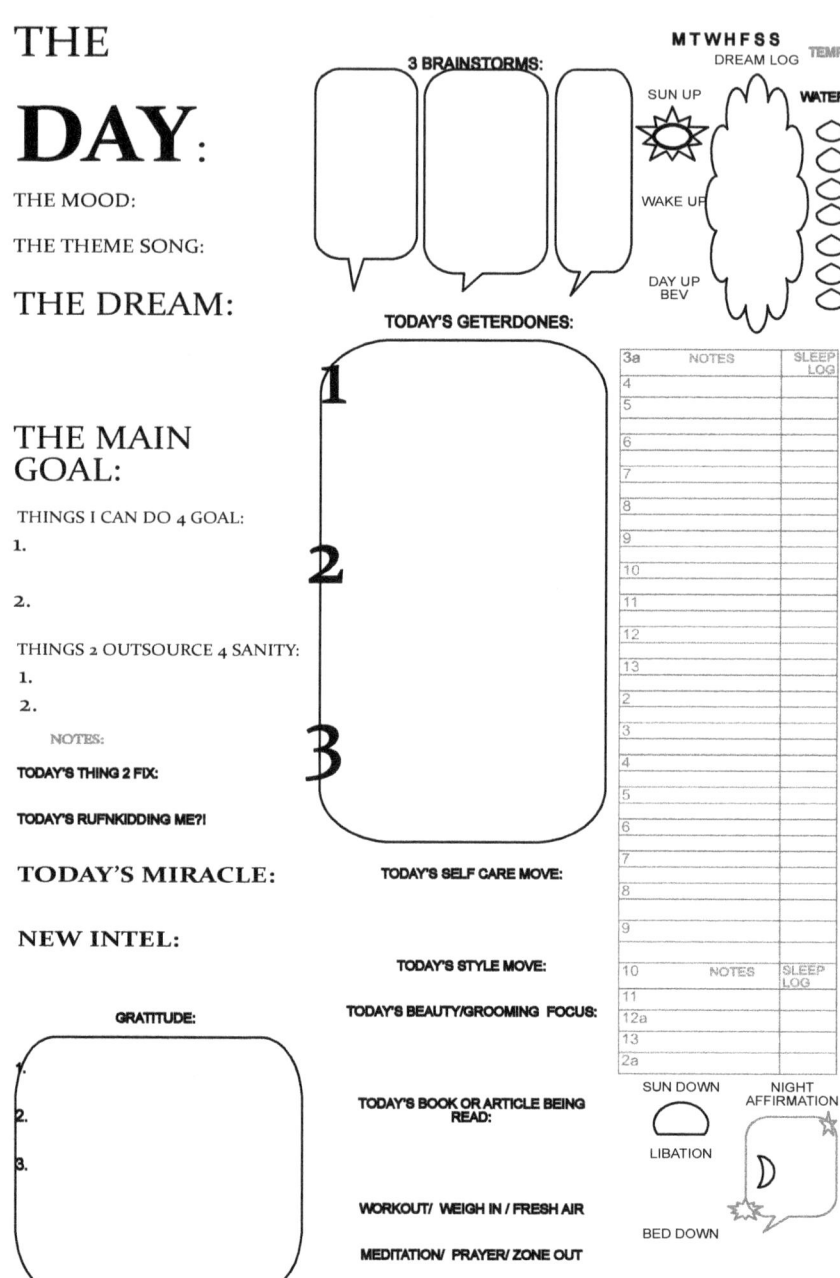

3 BRAINSTORMS:

TODAY'S GETERDONES:
1
2
3

TODAY'S SELF CARE MOVE:

TODAY'S STYLE MOVE:

TODAY'S BEAUTY/GROOMING FOCUS:

TODAY'S BOOK OR ARTICLE BEING READ:

WORKOUT/ WEIGH IN / FRESH AIR

MEDITATION/ PRAYER/ ZONE OUT

M T W H F S S
DREAM LOG   TEMP

SUN UP   WATER

WAKE UP

DAY UP BEV

	NOTES	SLEEP LOG
3a		
4		
5		
6		
7		
8		
9		
10		
11		
12		
13		
2		
3		
4		
5		
6		
7		
8		
9		

	NOTES	SLEEP LOG
10		
11		
12a		
13		
2a		

SUN DOWN

LIBATION

BED DOWN

NIGHT AFFIRMATION

THE
pregaming:

THE recap:

THE
DAY:

THE MOOD:

THE THEME SONG:

THE DREAM:

THE MAIN GOAL:

THINGS I CAN DO 4 GOAL:
1.

2.

THINGS 2 OUTSOURCE 4 SANITY:
1.
2.
   NOTES:

TODAY'S THING 2 FIX:

TODAY'S RUFNKIDDING ME?!

TODAY'S MIRACLE:

NEW INTEL:

GRATITUDE:

1.

2.

3.

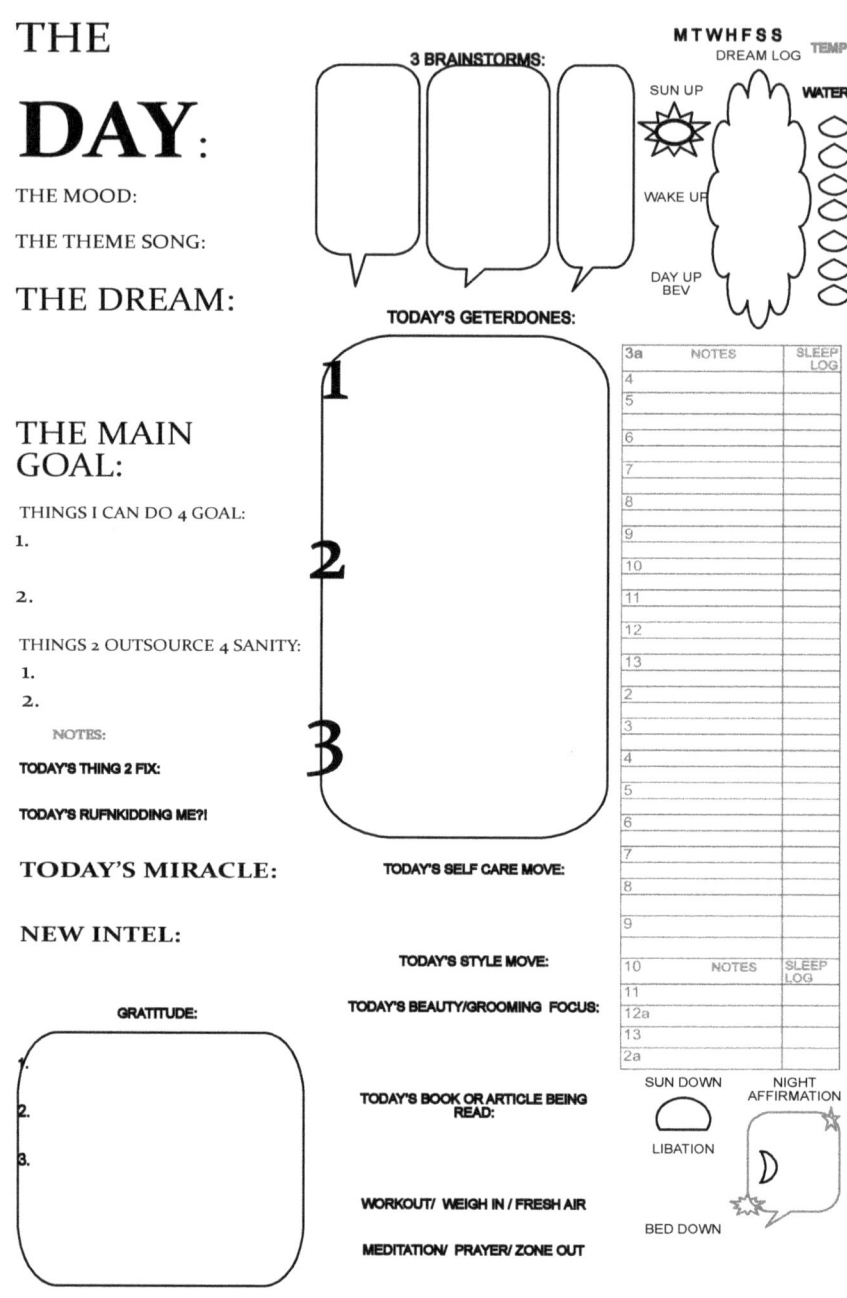

3 BRAINSTORMS:

TODAY'S GETERDONES:
1
2
3

TODAY'S SELF CARE MOVE:

TODAY'S STYLE MOVE:

TODAY'S BEAUTY/GROOMING FOCUS:

TODAY'S BOOK OR ARTICLE BEING READ:

WORKOUT/ WEIGH IN / FRESH AIR

MEDITATION/ PRAYER/ ZONE OUT

THE
pregaming:

THE recap:

THE
DAY:

THE MOOD:

THE THEME SONG:

THE DREAM:

THE MAIN GOAL:

THINGS I CAN DO 4 GOAL:
1.

2.

THINGS 2 OUTSOURCE 4 SANITY:
1.
2.
   NOTES:

TODAY'S THING 2 FIX:

TODAY'S RUFNKIDDING ME?!

TODAY'S MIRACLE:

NEW INTEL:

GRATITUDE:

1.

2.

3.

3 BRAINSTORMS:

TODAY'S GETERDONES:

1

2

3

TODAY'S SELF CARE MOVE:

TODAY'S STYLE MOVE:

TODAY'S BEAUTY/GROOMING FOCUS:

TODAY'S BOOK OR ARTICLE BEING READ:

WORKOUT/ WEIGH IN / FRESH AIR

MEDITATION/ PRAYER/ ZONE OUT

M T W H F S S
DREAM LOG   TEMP

SUN UP   WATER

WAKE UP

DAY UP BEV

	NOTES	SLEEP LOG
3a		
4		
5		
6		
7		
8		
9		
10		
11		
12		
13		
2		
3		
4		
5		
6		
7		
8		
9		
10	NOTES	SLEEP LOG
11		
12a		
13		
2a		

SUN DOWN   NIGHT AFFIRMATION

LIBATION

BED DOWN

THE
pregaming:

THE recap:

NOTES

Bonus-Bonus...

Try your hand at 7 days of a Lil HARDCORE.

THE DAY:

THE MOOD:

THE THEME SONG:

THE DREAM:

THE MAIN GOAL:

THINGS I CAN DO 4 GOAL:
1.
2.
3.

THINGS 2 OUTSOURCE 4 SANITY:
1.
2.

NOTES:

TODAY'S SELF CARE MOVE:

TODAY'S STYLE MOVE:

TODAY'S BEAUTY/GROOMING FOCUS:

TODAY'S BOOK OR ARTICLE BEING READ:

WORKOUT/ WEIGH IN / FRESH AIR

MEDITATION/ PRAYER/ ZONE OUT

GRATITUDE:
1.
2.
3.

FIVE BRAINSTORMS:

TODAY'S GETERDONES:
1.
2.
3.
4.

NEW INTEL:

TODAY'S THING 2 FIX:

TODAY'S RUFNKIDDING ME?!

TODAY'S MIRACLE:

M T W H F S S TEMP

DREAM LOG

SUN UP

WAKE UP

DAY UP BEV

DAY UP MOVES

	NOTES	SLEEP LOG
3a		
4		
5		
6		
7		
8		
9		
10		
11		
12		
13		
2		
3		
4		
5		
6		
7		
8		
9		
10	NOTES	SLEEP LOG
11		
12a		
13		
2a		

SUN DOWN

LIBATION

BED DOWN

NIGHT AFFIRMATION

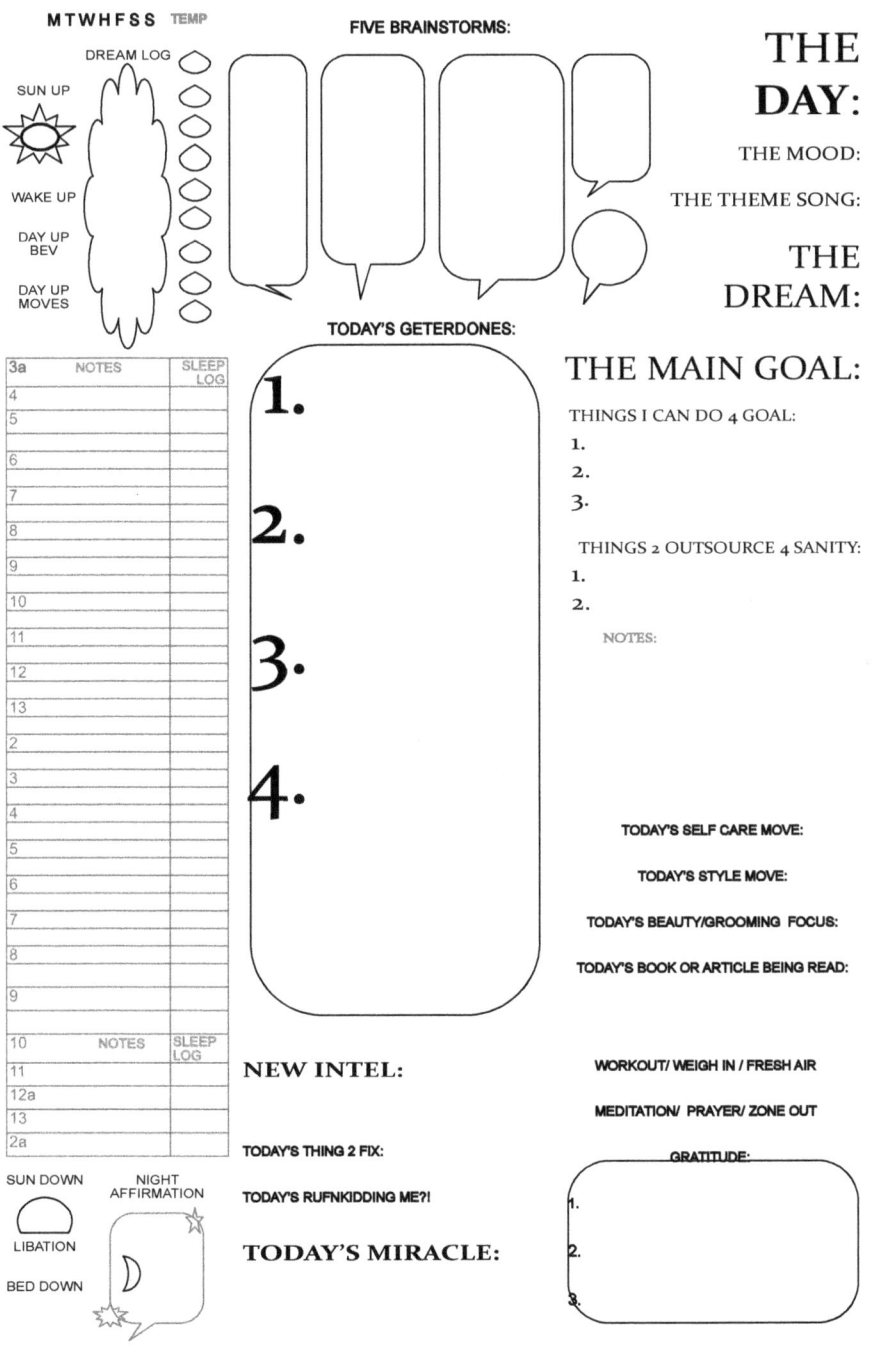

THE DAY:

THE MOOD:

THE THEME SONG:

THE DREAM:

THE MAIN GOAL:

THINGS I CAN DO 4 GOAL:
1.
2.
3.

THINGS 2 OUTSOURCE 4 SANITY:
1.
2.

NOTES:

TODAY'S SELF CARE MOVE:

TODAY'S STYLE MOVE:

TODAY'S BEAUTY/GROOMING FOCUS:

TODAY'S BOOK OR ARTICLE BEING READ:

WORKOUT/ WEIGH IN / FRESH AIR

MEDITATION/ PRAYER/ ZONE OUT

GRATITUDE:
1.
2.
3.

FIVE BRAINSTORMS:

TODAY'S GETERDONES:
1.
2.
3.
4.

NEW INTEL:

TODAY'S THING 2 FIX:

TODAY'S RUFNKIDDING ME?!

TODAY'S MIRACLE:

M T W H F S S TEMP

DREAM LOG

SUN UP

WAKE UP

DAY UP BEV

DAY UP MOVES

	NOTES	SLEEP LOG
3a		
4		
5		
6		
7		
8		
9		
10		
11		
12		
13		
2		
3		
4		
5		
6		
7		
8		
9		
10	NOTES	SLEEP LOG
11		
12a		
13		
2a		

SUN DOWN

LIBATION

BED DOWN

NIGHT AFFIRMATION

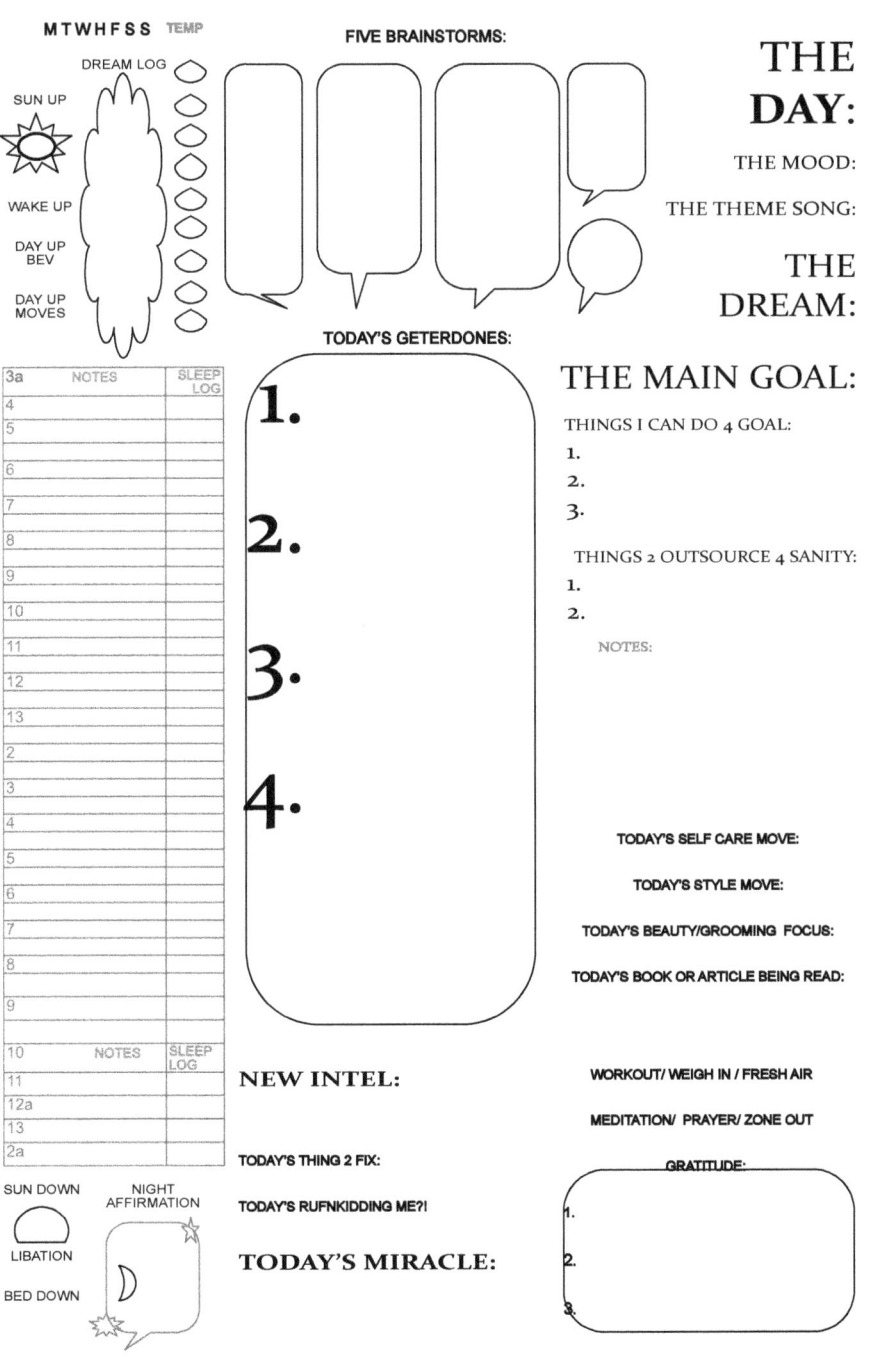

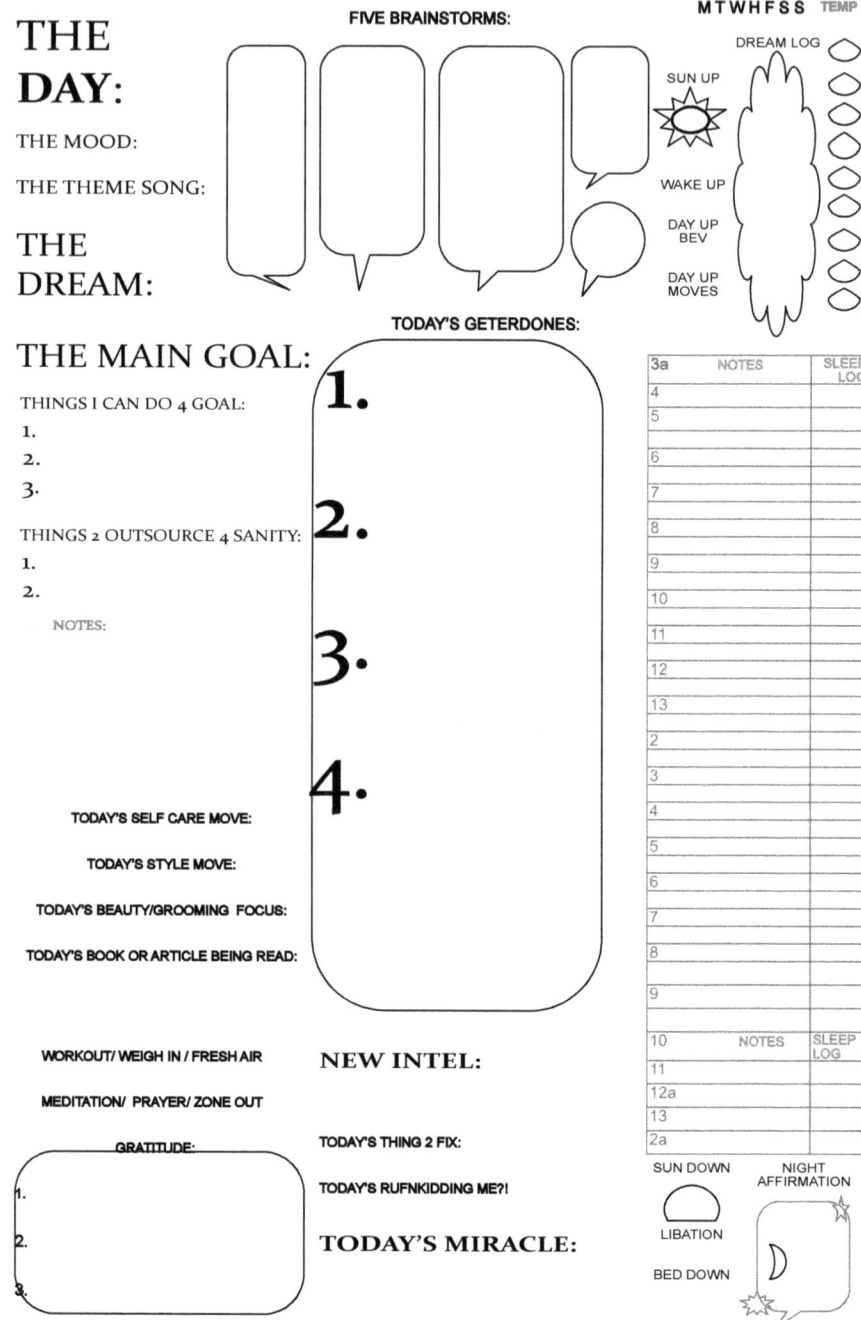

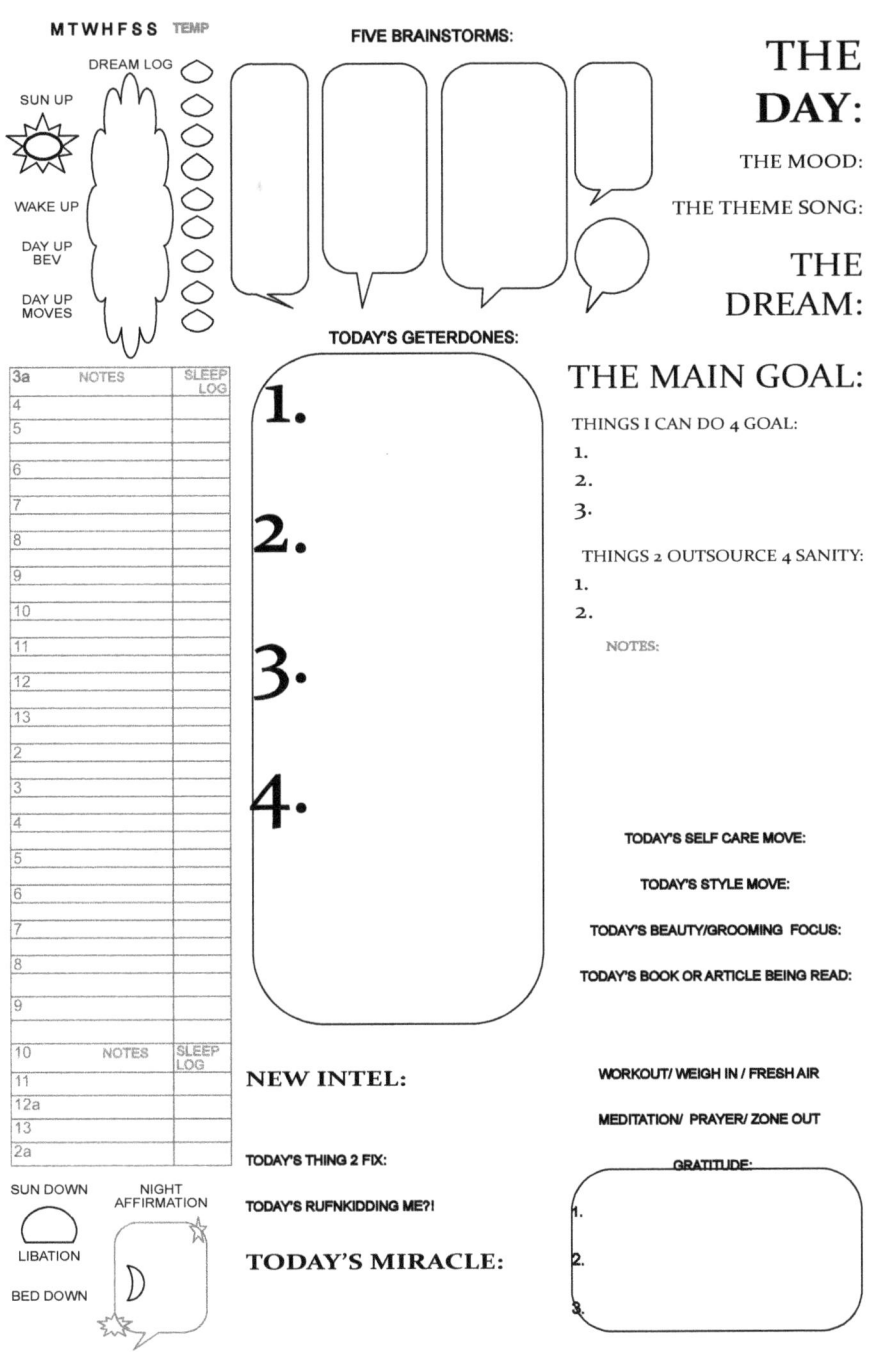

NOTES

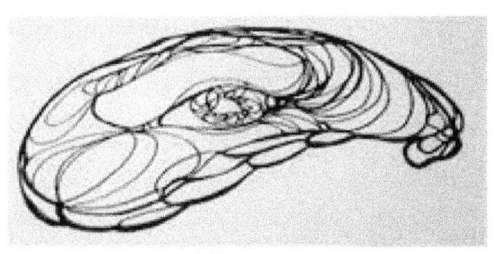

angel brynner.

KOKOPELLIMA PRESS

www.ingramcontent.com/pod-product-compliance
Lightning Source LLC
Chambersburg PA
CBHW050858240426
43673CB00009B/276